LARGE FAMILY
Logistics

Other Books from Vision Forum

The Adventure of Missionary Heroism

Be Fruitful and Multiply

The Bible Lessons of John Quincy Adams for His Son

The Birkenhead Drill

The Boy's Guide to the Historical Adventures of G.A. Henty

Christian Modesty and the Public Undressing of America

Coming In on a Wing and a Prayer

Destination: Moon

The Elsie Dinsmore Series

The Family

Family Man, Family Leader

How God Wants Us to Worship Him

John Calvin: Man of the Millennium

The Letters and Lessons of Teddy Roosevelt for His Sons

The Life and Campaigns of Stonewall Jackson

The Little Boy Down the Road

Little Faith

Missionary Patriarch

Mother

The New-England Primer

Of Plymouth Plantation

The Original Blue Back Speller

Poems for Patriarchs

The Princess Adelina

Reformation & Revival: The Story of the English Puritans

The R.M. Ballantyne Christian Adventure Library

Safely Home

Sergeant York and the Great War

So Much More

The Sinking of the Titanic

Ten P's in a Pod

Thoughts for Young Men

Verses of Virtue

The Art and Science of Managing the Large Family

by Kim Brenneman

THE VISION FORUM, INC.
SAN ANTONIO, TEXAS

First Printing: October 2010
Eighth Printing: October 2012
Copyright © 2010, 2012 The Vision Forum, Inc.
All Rights Reserved

"Where there is no vision, the people perish." (Proverbs 29:18)

The Vision Forum, Inc.
4719 Blanco Rd., San Antonio, Texas 78212
www.visionforum.com

ISBN-10 1-934554-49-9
ISBN-13 978-1-934554-49-4

Cover Design and Typography by Justin Turley

Printed in the United States of America

Dedicated to my daughters and all the future generations of mothers raising their children to the glory of God.

"Home is Where Each Lives for the Other and All Live for Christ."
—From a plaque hanging on the wall of my childhood home

Table of Contents

Part Two

Foreword

It's easy to think that, because of the nineteen children God has blessed Jim Bob and me with, I have it all figured out when it comes to managing a busy household. But I am learning and growing, just like every mother out there is.

I came from a large family with a mother who was a real organizer. As the youngest of seven children, I didn't realize how much I took for granted concerning household management until I was married, and God began to give us children. I very quickly recognized that I was not a natural-born organizer, as some moms are.

Growing up as a girl, the scissors were always in the scissors drawer. The hair brush was always where it was supposed to be, and we all knew where it went. But as a young mother, my home was not this way at all. It was not running smoothly. And as more children came, I realized it was urgent that I get my act together, or I would risk going under. I wanted to go beyond survival and really be able to conquer this thing called organization.

If this wonderful book by Kim Brenneman had been available then, I would have snatched it up and slept with it under my pillow. It would have been my manual to keep me moving in the grand adventure of large family logistics.

I didn't have Kim's book, yet God was gracious to lead me by trial and error to embrace many of the principles she explains so well in this resource.

The first was setting a schedule for our daily activities. We had to fit a lot in a day, and things needed to run smoothly. Second, we had to get rid of the clutter and conquer the two big monsters moms face: the kitchen and laundry room.

Third, we saw the importance of embracing the "buddy system" which involved organizing our routines so that the older children could help the younger children throughout the day—working on chores, school projects, and music lessons together as teams. This really revolutionized how much we were able to accomplish and served to knit our children's hearts closer to one another.

Kim develops all three of these points in depth in this book.

Yet even with these changes in our family, I struggled sometimes in figuring it all out. I think my biggest challenge was learning to delegate and realizing that I didn't need to do it all—and couldn't do it all—this was simply impossible. And when I tried to carry the whole load, my children had a grumpy Mommy, and this was a real problem. I desperately wanted to be a joyful mother to my children. That was my heart's desire before God.

To reach this goal, I had to learn to delegate responsibilities. In time, God began to show me practical ways to get my family involved so it wasn't one person carrying all the weight. To be effective, I had to write it out. There were stickers all over our cabinets, in our drawers, and on our walls to show "this is where this belongs." Or "this is how you clean the bathroom"—there are seven steps to follow. You just go down the list, and it's done.

By God's grace, I have learned over time to minimize inefficiencies and become proficient in my role as wife and mother.

Reading Kim's book recently was a big boost for me as a mother, and if you're anything like me when you find a goldmine like this, your copy will be highlighted and dog-eared, with the margins full of notes for later reference. Every mom is going to have her favorite chapters and pages she goes back to again and again.

The theological foundation is the best place to start. Practical advice helps best when it is undergirded by biblical truth. In Part I of this book, Kim lays out the vision for the "wise woman" of God, the wife and mother who seeks to build up her house through her work and do her husband and children well through all that she does.

Key to this is being biblically grounded. Kim encourages moms to stay in the Word and not let the tyranny of the urgent rob them of the joy of their high calling. She encourages busy mothers to maintain a positive attitude amidst interruptions, to actively cultivate self-discipline day-to-day, and to set a cheerful tone in how they guide the affairs of the home. She also discusses the family dynamic and the need for moms to embrace both careful planning and flexibility as part of their job description.

Part II is chock-full of practical ideas for moms, from bedroom and bathroom management to meal planning, from dealing with the laundry monster to managing large family outings.

Every mom can benefit from this book. Whether you have one child or fifteen, you should strive to have a loving and Christ-centered home that will strengthen everybody to do those mundane tasks of life and know that you can do them with joy and bring all the glory and honor to the Lord. But the more children you have, the more dynamics and logistics become.a challenge to manage. That's when careful planning becomes critically important.

What Kim Brenneman does is separate all the different needs of the house and of the family day and helps moms effectively sort and prioritize them. From your time with the Lord to your self-discipline, from your exercise routine to managing babies, from taking care of home office responsibilities to shopping days—Kim helps you think through all the parts of a mom's day and organize them creatively so that you can stay focused on the most important thing—the relationship to your husband and your children's hearts.

From one mom to another, I highly recommend this book to you.

Michelle Duggar

2 Cor. 12:9

October 2012

Preface: Why I Wrote This Book

Many years ago, I was the mother of one small baby boy in a little rental house. My husband and I were committed to having me stay at home to raise our little boy. I remember being embarrassed because of the dust, laundry piled up, and dirty dishes, and I scrambled to make something for supper just minutes before my hard-working husband came home.

Why couldn't I handle the basics? My shortcomings as a homemaker frustrated me. I had read enough to know that I had it easy compared to women in the past. I didn't have to go outside and pump water like my grandmother did. I didn't have to kill a chicken and dress it to make supper. I had a gas stove, a refrigerator, a freezer, a crockpot, a washer and dryer. I was rich compared to women throughout the ages, and I knew it. What was wrong with me?

Thankfully, I didn't have far to go for help as my mom, mother-in-law, and grandmother lived close-by. Across the road, I had another grandmother-type homekeeper and mother of six who was willing to help me. I consulted with these Titus 2 women. I traded coping strategies with the moms in my weekly Bible study while our babies and toddlers played under our feet. I searched out books and learned the art and science of managing a family one step at a time, one day at a time, one season at a time, one baby at a time, and I'm still learning and growing in my skills as a wife and mother. It has been a process that I am still not finished with. I'm not done bringing up my children or learning all the techniques for keeping the home.

Back in that little rental home, struggling with one baby, I desired to master the basics—dusting, laundry, dishes—so that I could move on to more creative expressions as a homemaker. In high school, I had taken a class called "Early American Homemaking." We learned all the arts that our foremothers practiced amidst the tremendous amount of work that they did.

I knew that homekeeping was a dynamic life. My grandmother, mother, mother-in-law, and elderly neighbor were wonderful gardeners, and they put up lots of food for the rest of the year. They created healthy and wholesome food from the garden, in their kitchens. To this day, I cannot make fried chicken like my mom. My grandmother sewed beautiful quilts from scraps left over from the clothing she sewed for herself. My elderly neighbor was a master at flower gardening, drying, and making arrangements. She could tell me the names of every plant that popped up in my yard those springs that I lived near her. I could see that the opportunities for creativity in the home know no bounds!

I longed to master the simple, care for my baby, and explore the creative, and I worked towards that goal. It didn't magically happen—I had to learn it bit by bit.

This book has grown out of this years-long experience. It began as a journal I wrote to my daughters recording all of the things I had learned and was in the process of learning as a mother. My goal in writing to them was to prepare them for the life of motherhood and home management. I did not want to see them struggle with what, how, and when to do the next thing in managing their homes, as I had done. I wanted to record for them how I worked to overcome those issues.

My problems in effective home management are directly related to the inexperience of my upbringing. I grew up in a Christian home with wonderful parents, but for thirteen years I left my home each day at 7:20 in the morning and came home at 4:00 in the afternoon. During my high school years, there were many seasons where I came home simply to sleep and then leave again. My parents did require me to do chores in our home and on the farm. We cleaned the house every single Saturday. I made supper when I was home and my mom was working.

What I did not experience was the daily, hour-by-hour work that a home and children require. I knew how to do housekeeping tasks, but I struggled with when to do what, and how to do my work with the distractions of a baby. I struggled with the self-discipline of doing tasks in a regular manner. In school I had become a master at procrastination and got away with it. That doesn't transfer well to house chores. I learned as I struggled. Sometimes it felt like two steps forward and one step back. A lot of lessons were painful. Each baby that came along added more challenges to be overcome.

There are many things I have learned the hard way over the years that I wanted to pass on to my daughters—so I wrote.

As the years of writing this book have progressed, I learned two more things. One is that my daughters are now learning all the things that I learned as a young mom, because they are home, working alongside me. Thankfully, they probably are not going to need this book!

Second, I found that there are many young moms who are in the same position that I was—unprepared for keeping the home with lots of children. While women historically were equipped to be the caretakers of thriving, busy households when they reached maturity, most of today's women are ill-equipped for such responsibility. This change has happened in the wake of feminism, which teaches young women that they can have a career and be a mom. Guidance counselors in the schools encourage those who enjoy children to be teachers or day care providers. Childbearing is an experience to have after practicing with a dog or a cat for a few years. I read recently that in some circles children are an economic status symbol along with all the accoutrements to buy for them.

When the Internet came along, I met many fellow casualties of feminism. I realized that I was not the only woman who desired to be a faithful homemaker who was crying out to God, "How do I do this?" That realization caused me to begin sharing my ideas through blog writing, articles, and, eventually, completing this book for those moms who were a step behind me in the journey of motherhood and homekeeping. I am motivated to take the time to write now because the answer I often heard to my own question of "How?" was, "I don't know, I just did it." There's truth in that answer—there are so many things that we need to just do—but I wanted specifics. The specifics pass into the deep recesses of our minds because often they are small tips, tricks, or ingrained habits that require little thought. My goal is to write those things down for those who are struggling with "How?"

My hope and prayer for the women who read this book is that you will be encouraged in your life as a homekeeper and mother, that you will learn methods and systems that will help you in your endeavors— and that you will be able to love God and enjoy Him more abundantly in your life as homekeeper.

How to Use This Book

This book is designed in such a way that you can flip it open to a particular topic and read for inspiration or start at the beginning and methodically implement each skill as it is presented. Part One is philosophical and gives encouragement for our lives as homekeepers, wives, and mothers. It includes undergirding foundations and overarching methods that will help you implement Part Two, which is the nitty-gritty particulars of how to keep the home.

If you are in dire straits, then you will want to go to the two appendixes and start with a detailed strategy on how to bail out of a big mess. Don't stop there, though; come back to the beginning and nail down the details of homekeeping and attitude management.

Part One

CHAPTER 1
The Wise Woman

The wisest of women builds her house, but folly with her own hands tears it down.
—Proverbs 14:1

If you have picked up this book on "Large Family Logistics", there's a good likelihood that you are looking for practical advice on how to be a better homemaker amidst the hurly burly of responsibilities that come with your role. As a wife and mother, I've been in your shoes—looking for ideas from whatever helpful sources I could find on how to be more effective in guiding the affairs of the home.

But before we can delve into all the details, we must have our fundamental priorities straight. We must start with the right foundation, or our efforts will fall short. Our goal should not be to merely gain knowledge on a host of issues related to keeping a home, though knowledge is a good thing, but to be wise so that we will know how to order our priorities correctly—to have a firm grasp of what we as women should aspire to attain.

To be wise, we must seek what God says, for we will not find wisdom apart from Him, as the writer of Proverbs explains: "There is no wisdom nor understanding nor counsel against the LORD" (Proverbs 21:30, KJV). Thankfully, God has not left us in the dark but has imparted His wisdom to us in His inscripturated Word which serves as a "lamp to [our] feet, and a light to [our] path" (Psalms 119:105). God's Word has been given to equip us for all we put our hands to do:

All Scripture is breathed out by God and profitable for teaching, for reproof, for correction, and for training in righteousness, that the man of God may be competent, equipped for every good work. —2 Timothy 3:16

Wisdom for "every good work" includes what a wife and mother needs to fulfill her role. The Bible provides a clear picture of what a wise woman looks like, so we're not left to wonder or flounder aimlessly. And there's no more powerful illustration of this found in Scripture than the woman described in Proverbs 31:10-31. This passage provides us with a clear model of the characteristics that make up a faithful homekeeper. She's called the "Excellent Wife" (Proverbs 31:10).

Reading this passage will likely cause you to squirm. It certainly causes me to every time I read it. There is always something convicting I find. The accomplished woman pictured here sounds like the impossible dream, but hers is an example worth pursuing.

With this in mind, I want to lay out some of the key qualities of the Proverbs 31 woman as we begin our discussion on "Large Family Logistics", qualities that serve as the foundation for managing a household God's way. Our look at this passage will not be exhaustive—I encourage you to carefully study Proverbs 31 in detail on your own—but what I will briefly outline here are critical establishing points that will serve as the springboard for the rest of this book.

The Heart of Her Husband Trusts in Her

10 An excellent wife who can find? She is far more precious than jewels.

In this acrostic Hebrew poem, King Lemuel's mother explains to him that an excellent wife is a rare find, far more precious than jewels. Some translations use the word "ruby", where jewels is used here, which was the most valuable jewel of its time.

You don't find a ruby in any old place. It's not an ordinary rock found along the road somewhere. It's not even a pretty rock you would find in a mountain river bed. You have to know where to go, and you have to know that the source is valid. You don't want a fake.

A jewel such as a ruby is an extraordinary rock that goes through quite a process to become what it is—both from its discovery to its careful refinement when it shines with striking beauty.

An excellent wife represents such a rarity, and, in this passage, it's her husband first and foremost who recognizes her great value. She is a trustworthy treasure who he implicitly depends on for his positive welfare.

11 The heart of her husband trusts in her, and he will have no lack of gain.

In the Hebrew, "no lack of gain" literally translates to "prey, plunder, and spoil". The Excellent Wife is prudent and careful in the management of the home and its expenses. She increases her husband's prosperity. She is so proficient that her husband is at peace and able to focus on his own workload. A wise woman takes care of those things in her charge which not only glorifies her heavenly Father, but also blesses her husband.

The Excellent Wife demonstrates reliability to her husband. This is the first specific quality we learn about her, and it should become a central priority for us as wives. Trust is something earned, not demanded, and each of us should seek to gain the trust of our husband by consistently striving to advance his interests, rather than acting unwisely so as to undermine his confidence in us. While we will never gain perfection, we must strive to be consistent day-in and day-out in how we help to manage our husband's affairs.

12 She does him good, and not harm, all the days of her life.

Jesus "went about doing good" (Acts 10:38). With Jesus as our example, a wife should try to understand her husband so that she can learn how to best do him good. She should study him and learn his likes, dislikes, gifts, faults, so that she can understand how to be an effective complement to him.

Hear your husband's dreams and help him to reach his goals. Listen to his suggestions, and be attentive to his needs when planning your day and organizing your long-term domestic goals, whether you are shopping, taking care of the children, or pursuing a remodeling project. Make sure that your priorities reflect his.

Our men work so hard for us. They are sweating and striving against thorns and thistles. We should seek to become a jewel and a crown for our husband and to make our home a castle and fill it with comfort for him. Earlier in Proverbs, we read this powerful corollary thought:

> *An excellent wife is the crown of her husband, but she who brings shame is like rottenness in his bones. —Proverbs 12:4*

While being our husband's "crown" conveys a noble and stately image, the thought of being "rottenness in his bones" is a horrible word picture that we should take very seriously! When I don't take calcium and magnesium, the bones in my hand hurt and become weak. "Rottenness in his bones" must be extremely painful and debilitating. To think that we as wives can do that to our husbands should sober us. I would much rather aim at being my husband's crown than cause rottenness through my folly.

Becoming a crown to our husbands is not something that comes automatically. It takes diligent focus and effort. Titus 2, for example, indicates that younger women need to be taught to "love their husbands" (Titus 2:4). That is a strange concept in our culture which equates love with romance and lust. Biblically speaking, love is a choice and commitment. It is seeing your husband as God sees him and loving him as God loves you. It is a deeper and richer love than worldly love. I would encourage you to learn more of God's love and how we are to love, as He does.

Titus 2 also states that we as wives are to learn to be "submissive to [our] own husbands" (Titus 2:5). In Ephesians 5:22-24, we read further: "Wives, submit to your own husbands, as to the Lord. For the husband is the head of the wife even as Christ is the head of the church, his body, and is himself its Savior. Now as the church submits to Christ, so also wives should submit in everything to their husbands."

This directive does not mean that we are to be a doormat as wives. Yet we are to willingly support our husbands in their decisions, and we are to demonstrate our support through agreeing and submitting, as long as we are not being asked to sin (Ephesians 5).

Seek to understand your husband's goals and choices. Discuss them respectfully, calmly, and kindly. Love is working at knowing each other and recognizing that we're not the same. Men are so different from women—God made it that way. For one thing, most men aren't as verbal as women, and this can be a hard thing sometimes. Yet rather than respond negatively to who your husband is, recognize his uniqueness and learn to communicate with him accordingly. Discover what makes him the man he is. Know him well, and learn to love who he is.

Christ calls everyone to serve each other (Mark 9:35). Serving your husband is not about manipulating him to get what you want. We were created to help our husbands. We were fit specifically for him, as Genesis 2:18 explains, "Then the Lord God said, 'It is not good that the man should be alone; I will make him a helper fit for him.'"

Try to anticipate your husband's needs and meet them before he outwardly expresses them. Plan to help him every day by asking him in the morning, "What can I do for you today?"

A dose of real humility is also in order. It's important to recognize that you are a sinner and that you married a sinner. That's the ugly truth. All those in Christ are sinners, saved by grace. We must therefore be willing to both repent and forgive, as we have been forgiven. Be sorry for your sins against God and your husband and forgive your husband for his sins. Don't blame him for everything, for oftentimes we are part of the problem when things go wrong. And sometimes we are much more than "part of it"—we are squarely at fault for problems in the home. It's thus important that we own up to our shortcomings and approach our husbands in humility.

> *Do nothing from rivalry or conceit, but in humility count others more significant than yourselves. Let each of you look not only to his own interests, but also to the interests of others. Have this mind among yourselves, which is yours in Christ Jesus. —Philippians 2:3-5*

23 Her husband is known in the gates when he sits among the elders of the land.

In ancient times, the gates were the public meeting place where business, counsel, and judgment occurred. The elders were those in authority. The husband of the Proverbs 31 woman was able to pursue his own business and be active in the public life because she was skillful and diligent with the management of the home. He didn't have to concern himself with food or clothing because she was taking care of that. His wife was making prudent deals. The financial undertakings she is overseeing are going well. If her husband had been trying to do his job and her work at home, he wouldn't be "known" and successful as he was. Put simply, he was known and respected because of the excellent wife that he had. Thanks to her faithful service in the domestic sphere, she brought him glory (1 Corinthians 11:7) in the public arena, where he helped to govern the affairs of the land.

Her husband's response to her diligent labors was to give her public praise:

28b her husband also [blesses her], and he praises her:

29 "Many women have done excellently, but you surpass them all."

The husband of the Excellent Wife calls her blessed (translated also as happy). The Excellent Wife is happy, skilled, wise, and she has pleasant relationships with her children (verse 28) and husband.

The husband's praise and appreciation is a reward to her. He thinks she's the best!

She Looks Well to the Way of Her Household

The Excellent Wife looks well to the way of her household. Exploring the details of this will form the crux of our discussion in this book as I will seek to demonstrate how, in our time, to effectively manage a large family household. While living today is far different than it was when Proverbs 31 was penned, the principles are the same.

13 She seeks wool and flax, and works with willing hands.

The Excellent Wife works with willing hands for her husband and family. Several years ago, my great-aunt Edna went to be with Jesus. I remember her grape vines, her gardens, her canning kitchen, big meals at her home, and her delicious pies. At her funeral, one of her granddaughters shared a beautiful vignette called "Grandma's Hands". Even I, who was only a great niece, was brought to tears because I remembered Aunt Edna's hands. I remember what my grandmother's hands looked like kneading bread dough, peeling apples, and quilting. I can also picture my mother's hands washing dishes, holding storybooks, and putting on band aids. Willing working hands are a beautiful and blessed thing to behold!

The Excellent Wife takes care of the clothing needs for her family. She seeks just the right apparel for them.

Women have a unique need and longing to do things for their loved ones. It's an innate drive that manifests itself in a variety of ways. 1 Samuel 2:19 gives us a prime example of this in describing Hannah's efforts to make clothing for her son Samuel, "And his mother used to make for him a little robe and take it to him each year when she went up with her husband to offer the yearly sacrifice."

If I were Hannah, I would have been working on that little robe every day and praying every minute of that work-time for my little boy. While we don't have to make our clothing from scratch now, I know from experience and in talking to others how rewarding it is to sew clothes, create things, or buy just the right item for members of our family.

As women, we should embrace opportunities to meet our family's clothing needs, working willingly with our hands.

14 She is like the ships of the merchant; she brings her food from afar.

As in ancient times, there are foods that I can't grow or get locally. Sea salt, coconut oil, bananas, lettuce in winter—these things aren't available in Iowa. That's the short list.

The Excellent Wife anticipates this reality and pursues the acquisition of supplemental food from beyond her immediate region. She considers health, flavor, and the food variety that will make her ministry in meal-making the best it can be, and she takes steps to get the items her menu-planning requires—including food from afar.

The point here is this: We shouldn't be lazy about our menus. We need to plan ahead and look to wherever is necessary to feed our family well within the budget constraints that we have.

15 She rises while it is yet night and provides food for her household and portions for her maidens.

The Excellent Wife is up very early. If you're a mom, you know what that's about. Babies and hungry little children expect to be fed, and we must be ready for this. The Excellent Wife is organized and has breakfast prepared for her family and maidens.

Beyond the necessity of food for the body, Scripture emphasizes the importance of spiritual food as well:

Oh, taste and see that the Lord is good! —Psalm 34:8

How sweet are your words to my taste, sweeter than honey to my mouth! —Psalm 119:103

Jesus said to them, "My food is to do the will of him who sent me and to accomplish his work." —John 4:34

Even as you give physical food to your children, you should read the Scriptures and pray with them with just as much effort.

18b Her lamp does not go out at night.

There are two reasons for using a lamp at night. One is for fellowship, and the other is work. Remember that these people didn't have electricity. Generally speaking, they did their work during the sunny hours, and they slept at night. Think of the Amish. This verse is similar to Proverbs 13:9 which refers to a lit house as a prosperous house. They could afford the oil to have a light at night.

The passage doesn't indicate whether the Excellent Wife used the oil for work or fellowship, but in either case, her industriousness is clearly shown: for either she had managed her household well enough to afford oil lamps for evening fellowship, or she is engaging in important work after hours rather than being idle and indolent.

19 She puts her hands to the distaff, and her hands hold the spindle.

The distaff and spindle are tools used to spin fiber into thread. While I have never seen the spindle and distaff in use outside of pictures, the task of working with these tools involves the coordination of both hands diligently working together. This image emphasizes yet again that the Excellent Wife actively and adeptly works with her hands for the good of her family.

Among the articles she makes are bed coverings and clothing, as we read a few verses down in the passage:

22 She makes bed coverings for herself; her clothing is fine linen and purple.

The Hebrew word for "fine linen" could also be "silk." Fine linen came from Egypt, was very thin, and was worn by those with status and wealth. It was difficult to dye. Silk was even more valuable, coming from Asian countries to the east. It was fine and held vivid colors. Purple was valued highly.

The Excellent Wife was not clad in rags. She cared about her clothing and took active steps to make apparel for her family that reflected her regal character as well as her husband's position as an elder in the community. Even as she did with food, she sought fabric from afar to aid her in dressing her family well and bringing honor to her husband.

When Christians dress slovenly, they are a poor witness for Christ. This doesn't mean that families should spend beyond their means on clothing—"to keep up with the Joneses", so to speak. Far from it. But providing tasteful and appropriate clothing is one important area of focus a wife should have in managing her household.

God cares about details, and so should we. Think about the intricate details He gave for the construction of the Tabernacle and later for the Temple. He cared about the color of the thread used to embroider the Tabernacle, among many other specifics.

This being said, it is important that wives not swing to the other extreme and become consumed by looks and clothing, as the Apostle Peter counseled: "Do not let your adorning be external—the braiding of hair and the putting on of gold jewelry, or the clothing you wear—but let your adorning be the hidden person of the heart with the imperishable beauty of a gentle and quiet spirit, which in God's sight is very precious." (1 Peter 3:3-4)

Our temporal clothing is important, but our spiritual dress commands a higher priority: "Clothe yourselves, all of you, with humility toward one another" (1 Peter 5:5). Elsewhere, in Ephesians 6, we are directed to put on the full armor of God.

Our efforts to provide clothing for our family should be kept in accord and not transcend our most important kingdom pursuits. Jesus' words on this are clear: "But seek first the kingdom of God and his righteousness, and all these things [food, clothing, etc.] will be added to you" (Matthew 6:28-33).

We can infer two things from these various passages. First, God cares about the details of our outer clothing and will help us provide it for our family; but, more importantly, He desires for us to be spiritually dressed with His character. It's this priority structure that we should seek to emulate.

27 She looks well to the ways of her household

The Excellent Wife looks well to the ways of her household. We've discussed several examples of this so far, but an obvious but important point should not be lost in our discussion: that she diligently tends to her household, not her neighbor's. She's not a nosy busybody, in other words.

Scripture has strong words to say about busybodies—putting them in the same category as thieves, murderers, and evil doers (1 Peter 4:15). In Titus 2, Paul's concern is that the lifestyle of the Christians demonstrates the gospel and tells the older women to instruct the younger women in several things including to be working at home. When we look back over Proverbs 31, we can see that there is not time in the day for her to do all that she does and be a busybody. Being a busybody would be folly.

27b and does not eat the bread of idleness.

"Idleness" is also translated "sluggishness" and "laziness." "Eat the bread" gives the idea of "feeding on". When I feed my sugar cravings, I only want more sugar. When I grow accustomed to going to sleep at a certain time or waking up at a certain time, it is hard to move from those times. Newton's Law of

Motion states that a body will persist in its state of rest or of uniform motion in a straight line unless it is compelled to change that state by forces impressed on it. The Excellent Wife does not feed idleness but exerts a force that jars her from any course of idleness that might otherwise develop. 2 Peter 1 has some things to say concerning the exercise of diligence:

> [M]ake every effort to supplement your faith with virtue, and virtue with knowledge, and knowledge with self-control, and self-control with steadfastness, and steadfastness with godliness, and godliness with brotherly affection, and brotherly affection with love. For if these qualities are yours and are increasing, they keep you from being ineffective or unfruitful in the knowledge of our Lord Jesus Christ. —2 Peter 1:5-8

The second part of this book in particular addresses organizing our days so that we can work with self-control and steadfastness. When we accomplish these things, then there is time in the day for being more industrious and for engagement in ministry.

She Is Industrious and Engaged

16a She considers a field and buys it;

The Excellent Wife is not just a doer; she's a thinker. She's considering a business transaction—she's creating a business plan and a cash flow analysis. She's successful and she reinvests.

In our house, we have a couple of sayings concerning purchases. "Big cows make little cows" meaning, if your purchase is not going to grow the business—is it truly necessary?

Think before you buy.

16b with the fruit of her hands she plants a vineyard.

A vineyard requires extreme diligence and patience—planting, trellising, pruning, and then waiting years for a significant harvest. The illustration of a vineyard is suggestive of a pattern of long-term planning and careful diligence on the part of the Excellent Wife. She is someone who plans, reinvests, exercises diligence in tending to her business affairs, and is patient in her business endeavors.

20 She opens her hand to the poor and reaches out her hands to the needy.

The excellent wife is generous. Another word for "hand" in the Hebrew is "power." She exerts her influence to help the poor. "Poor" translated can also mean "weak, afflicted, wretched, humble, lowly." We can look inside our own homes and see that our children fall into this description being weak, but this connotation doesn't capture the thrust of the verse. In the second stanza, we see that she isn't simply opening her hand, she reaches out. She is involved with the needy. She's reaching towards them.

Needy translates also as subject to oppression and abuse, needing help, deliverance from trouble, especially as delivered by God, and is a general reference to the lowest class. Put simply, the Excellent Wife is deeply involved with ministering to those in dire straits.

24 She makes linen garments and sells them; she delivers sashes to the merchant.

Not only is she making things for her own home, she is selling linen garments and sashes. She has an industry going on here. Are you wondering how she gets all of these things done in the day? Don't overlook the part in verse 15 where she was up early getting portions for her maidens. We might not have flesh-and-blood maidens, but we do have mechanical maidens via our clothes washer, crockpots, etc. If the Lord blesses your investments, perhaps you will be able to add maidens or workers in your metaphorical vineyard.

We can't effectively branch out into these kind of pursuits if we can't manage the more essential needs of our homes first. Home management, investments, and ministering outside the home all have to dovetail. It requires hard work and organization—things this book seeks to address in further chapters.

She Laughs at the Time to Come

21 She is not afraid of snow for her household, for all her household are clothed in scarlet.

The Excellent Wife is prepared and unafraid. Everyone in her household, which would include her servants, is ready for a time of hardship. According to Nelson's Illustrated Encyclopedia of Bible Facts, snow may fall a couple of times in the rainy season of Jerusalem melting quickly, but "a very heavy snowfall occurs once in 15 years." The implication here is that the Proverbs 31 woman is prepared far in advance of inclement weather that only occurs rarely; she's not a procrastinator.

We also learn that "she is not afraid." "Fear not" is a theme found throughout the Bible. "...the word of the Lord came to Abram in a vision: "fear not, Abram, I am your shield..."(Genesis 15:1). Later in Genesis, God hears Hagar and her son crying in the wilderness, "Fear not, for God has heard..." And again in Genesis God speaks to Isaac saying, "Fear not, for I am with you..." Throughout the Bible, God says over and over to His people, "Fear not."

Consider the bravery of some of the Bible's most notable women. Rahab hid the spies and trusted that they would save her when Jericho fell. Jael drove a tent stake through the temple of General Sisera as he lay sleeping. Not only was she brave, she was strong! Ruth courageously left her homeland for a strange country; full of more courage, she approached Boaz in the night as her redeemer. Esther risked death with her uninvited approach to the king in his court. Then she was courageous in exposing the king's favorite advisor. Abigail, in 1 Samuel 25, courageously went against the will of her capricious husband Nabal and brought gifts to David, fell down on her face before him and his army who were on the warpath against Nabal, and pleaded for mercy. Mary, mother of Jesus, was given mind-boggling and challenging news by an angel who prefaced it with: "Do not be afraid". Her courageous response; "let it be to me according to your word." From Genesis to Revelation, we are told "fear not" again and again:

> *"Fear not, I am the first and the last, and the living one. I died, and behold I am alive forevermore, and I have the keys of Death and Hades." —Revelation 1:17-18*

Several sins uniquely prevalent among women are directly related to fear. We worry, we fret, we stew about things, and those things lead to other sins when we try to take things into our own hands. We expend energy on things we can't do anything about when we should be putting that effort into prayerfully preparing for the future.

If you lie down, you will not be afraid; When you lie down, your sleep will be sweet. Do not be afraid of sudden terror or of the ruin of the wicked, when it comes, for the Lord will be your confidence and will keep your foot from being caught. —Proverbs 3:24-26

25b and she laughs at the time to come.

The excellent wife is more than confident of the future; she laughs at it. She rejoices in it. She knows that, each year, she is growing in wisdom, strength, and graciousness, ready to take on more difficult challenges with joyful contentment in Christ.

One of the goals of this book is not only to help you learn to be prepared in your home management skills, but also to help you adjust your attitude so that you will be able to lean on God for courage as you face the future—and laugh at the time to come.

She is Clothed with Strength and Dignity

17a She dresses herself with strength

The Hebrew says that The Excellent Wife girds her loins with strength. Gird means "to dress". The loin muscles are the back muscles that hold us up. These muscles are connected with muscles that encircle our torso. If these muscles are strong, then we have strength to do so much more. Eerdsman's *Handbook to the Bible* says that girding up the loins meant tucking the tunic into the girdle around the waist in order to work or run. With either interpretation, the bottom line is that the Excellent Wife was fit, strong, and able.

17b and makes her arms strong.

This lady doesn't just have strong arms, she makes her arms strong through exercise. Those willing working hands can do so much more attached to strong arms and a strong back. Physical strength translates to ability, and it is important to cultivate this in order to be God's best for our husband, children, and home. I knew a coach whose mantra was "physically strong—mentally strong". When we force ourselves to move our bodies, we are strengthening our mental muscles also.

25 Strength and dignity are her clothing,

The Hebrew word for strength is "might, strength: material or physical; personal or social or political". Dignity is translated "splendor, majesty, honor, glory". These terms indicate the positive words for power.

The woman described here is a confident lady. She knows who she is. She sees herself in God's eyes, not the eyes of the world. Psalm 139:14 says this about knowing who you are in the Lord:

I praise you, for I am fearfully and wonderfully made. Wonderful are your works; My soul knows it very well.

In 1 Samuel 2, Hannah acknowledged where her strength came from as she prayed:

My heart exults in the Lord; My strength is exalted in the Lord. My mouth derides my enemies, Because I rejoice in your salvation.

It's this realization—that God made us and keeps us safely in His hands—that gives us as wives the spiritual strength to rejoice and to overcome difficulties; to not only have physical stamina, but to demonstrate spiritual fortitude as well.

She Speaks with Wisdom and Kindness

26a She opens her mouth with wisdom,

The Excellent Wife is wise, and she dispenses her wisdom to others. She shares the insights she has learned for those around her to benefit from.

And where does she find this wisdom to impart? She looks to Christ "[i]n whom are hidden all the treasures of wisdom and knowledge" (Colossians 2:3, see 1 Corinthians 1:18-30 also). She searches God's Word, believing that "the Lord gives wisdom; from His mouth come knowledge and understanding; He stores up sound wisdom for the upright" (Proverbs 2:6-7).

King Solomon declared that "Wisdom is the principal thing; Therefore get wisdom. And in all your getting, get understanding" (Proverbs 4:7, KJV). Yet wisdom doesn't come automatically. It takes time and diligence to obtain. Solomon's own life testifies to this fact, as, when he was a young man, he acknowledged his need for wisdom in governing the Israelites, and God gave it to him when he asked (I Kings 3:4-13). In Luke 2:52, Scripture tells us that Jesus grew in wisdom and stature.

The point is this: We don't arrive on the scene as wise pillars of the faith, as women who know all there is to know about being a faithful wife and mother. Gaining wisdom is a process, and it starts by recognizing our need for it and then asking God to grant it to us, even as Solomon did. As Christians, we are given this comforting promise:

> If any of you lacks wisdom, let him ask God, who gives generously to all without reproach, and it will be given him. —James 1:5

To be a wise women, we need to be women of the Word, and I firmly believe that the book of Proverbs, in particular, should be read daily. It's full of so much practical wisdom, and by studying it, it will get in your heart and come out of your mouth. For us to be wellsprings of wisdom, like the Proverbs 31 Woman, we need to fill up our reservoir with the living water found in Christ (John 4:10-14).

26b and the teaching of kindness is on her tongue.

When we look back through the blueprint of The Excellent Wife, we see that in all of her actions she shows kindness and good will toward others. Here in this verse we see that this kindness is not only demonstrated in her actions, but it is on her tongue, and she is teaching kindness to others. 1 Corinthians 13, The Love Chapter, lists kindness as a component of love. Webster's 1828 Dictionary defines it as:

> Good will; benevolence; that temper or disposition which delights in contributing to the happiness of others, which is exercised cheerfully in gratifying their wishes, supplying their wants or alleviating their distresses; benignity of nature. Kindness ever accompanies love.

Some versions translate the word teachings as "law": "The law of kindness is on her tongue." It is a rule for her tongue that guides the words that she speaks. Our tongue should thus be governed by kindness.

Proverbs 25:11 notes that "A word fitly spoken is like apples of gold in a setting of silver." It is both beautiful and treasured. In view of this truth, it is difficult to underestimate the value of the encouragement we bring when we speak kind words to our family.

My counsel to you is this: Be Christ to your family and others. Praise them for the good things they do. Bless them with uplifting words. Show His love through the kindness of your tongue.

Her Children and Husband Praise Her

28 Her children rise up and call her blessed; her husband also, and he praises her:

29 "Many women have done excellently, but you surpass them all."

The result of the Excellent Wife's efforts to bless her family through careful management of the home and kind encouragement is that she is in turned blessed with words of praise by her husband and children. What a powerful picture of reciprocal love and esteem we see evidenced here!

This use of "blessed" in Hebrew can also be translated "to pronounce happy". Have you ever been around children whose mother is not a happy person? Have you heard the saying, "If Mama ain't happy, nobody's happy"? How true this is. A wife and mother's mood definitely affects the mood of those around her—for better or for worse.

While there are exceptions, a happy mom generally makes for happy children and a happy husband. Proverbs 17:22 says, "A joyful heart is good medicine, but a crushed spirit dries up the bones." We must not take this truth for granted. As wives and mothers, we must realize the impact that our example has on the culture and pulse of our home. If we are cheerful, even when challenges arise, we can help buoy the spirits of our fellow family members. Come what may, it is important that we keep our focus on Jesus, learn to love Him more, seek His ways, and spread His joy to others.

A word of counsel: Don't be a grumbler—you can be happy while you work! This is an imperative we'll explore more later in the book, but it's one that I would urge you to begin mastering now.

The Success Secret of the Wise Woman

30 Charm is deceitful, and beauty is vain, but a woman who fears the Lord is to be praised.

So what is the secret of the wise woman's success? What makes her stand out as an exemplary model to others? What is the root of her character that causes her to be worthy of such high acclaim?

She fears the Lord, and as a result, she finds wisdom. "The fear of the LORD is the beginning of wisdom" (Proverbs 9:10), King Solomon explained. This may seem counter-intuitive, but this is what the Scriptures teach. Elsewhere in Proverbs, Solomon notes, "The fear of the Lord is the beginning of knowledge" (Proverbs 1:7a). Put simply, wisdom and knowledge are founded in the fear of God.

Not only does God grant wisdom and knowledge to those who fear Him, but He pronounces other blessings as well—His abundant goodness, good pleasure, and compassion—so that His children lack nothing.

> *Oh, how abundant is your goodness, which you have stored up for those who fear you and worked for those who take refuge in you, in the sight of the children of mankind! —Psalm 31:19*

> *His delight is not in the strength of the horse, nor his pleasure in the legs of a man, but the Lord takes pleasure in those who fear him, in those who hope in his steadfast love. —Psalm 147:10-11*

> *As a father shows compassion to his children, so the Lord shows compassion to those who fear him. —Psalm 103:13*

> *Oh, fear the Lord, you his saints, for those who fear him have no lack! —Psalm 34:9*

The Wise Woman's fear of God is not a scary "horror" type of a fear. It is awe in the Creator God. He is the one and only God who is so good and perfect that He cannot look upon sin. He loved us so much that He willingly gave up His son to die a horrific death on a cross to pay the penalties for all of our sins so that we could go to be with Him forever. His intrinsic holiness and selfless sacrifice on our behalf should fill our hearts with humble reverence toward Him:

> *Therefore let us be grateful for receiving a kingdom that cannot be shaken, and thus let us offer to God acceptable worship, with reverence and awe, for our God is a consuming fire. —Hebrew 12:28-29*

The secret success of the wise woman lies in her fear of God. "The secret counsel of the Lord is for those who fear him, and he makes known to them his covenant" (Psalm 25:14). For us to become wise, we must follow in her steps.

> *Teach me your way, O Lord, that I may walk in your truth; unite my heart to fear your name. —Psalm 86:11*

The Wise Woman is a Blessed Woman

31 Give her of the fruit of her hands, and let her works praise her in the gates.

Being a Wise Woman is God's plan for us—isn't that encouraging? And the path to wisdom is laid out in His Word. It comes when we fear God and learn to know Him more fully. It comes when we see our work as wives and mothers as He sees it—not as drudgery, but as a high and noble calling that bears eternal fruit. Whenever we embrace this vision and put it into action, our labors are appreciated, blessed, and rewarded. What we've invested comes back to us in greater measure:

> *Give and it will be given to you. Good measure, pressed down, shaken together, running over, will be put into your lap. —Luke 6:38*

Look back at The Excellent Wife, and see that she is making home and family life beautiful. Eight of twenty-one verses in the passage pertain to "housework". This is an important focus that she maintains. But her efforts go beyond this. Two verses relate to a home business. One is related to physical and/or spiritual strength. One is related to ministry. Two have to do with her attitude and character. Three are directly related to her husband's confidence in her and the blessing he receives from her faithful labors.

When we look at our work, we need to see it for what it is: serving the Lord, our husbands, our children, and all those who visit our home. Caring for others is an awesome responsibility. There is beauty in the necessary mechanics, and we need not look at them as something to just endure so that we can move on to the next thing. By all means, make your work efficient, but while you do what you have to do, learn to embrace it as work done unto the Lord that will impact generations for eternity!

> *Whatever you do, work heartily, as for the Lord and not for men, knowing that from the Lord you will receive the inheritance as your reward. You are serving the Lord Christ.*
> *—Colossians 3:23-24*

The Wise Woman studies God's Word regularly and applies what she learns. I would thus encourage you to read this book of practical counsel and encouragement with your Bible in the other hand as you seek wisdom on how to better manage the large family logistics in your home.

Build a firm foundation on the Holy Scriptures. Become a Wise Woman. Become an Excellent Wife that shines as a precious jewel to your husband and family.

CHAPTER 2
Goals

Yet, if at any stage of life you feel you're "flying by the seat of your pants," taking each day as it comes without having anticipated it, planned for it, shaped it, and prayed over it, then take time off and get back to poring over your goals. Then you will control your days, instead of letting them control you. —Anne Ortlund

Setting clearly-defined goals is an important part of faithful stewardship. Careful planning helps us as wives and mothers to identify what our key goals are for our families and to make the most of our opportunities. It helps us to know what to deliberately aim for, rather than haphazardly reacting to our circumstances.

When we prepare our way and seek to reach specific goals, we will move towards victorious living. Our effectiveness in our personal lives and our family's life will substantially increase. This is especially true when we take the time to establish long-term goals. A vision for the future keeps us moving forward rather than getting bogged down in the here and now. Without a vision, chaos ensues:

Where there is no vision, the people perish: but he that keepeth the law, happy is he. —Proverbs 29:18, KJV

Foundational Goals

In the previous chapter, we outlined key qualities of the Proverbs 31 woman that provide us clear categories of goals to strive toward as wives and mothers. Before moving forward with advice on making "goal lists", however, I would like to offer a couple of additional guideposts we must understand and embrace or else we will get off course as we seek to chart out specific goals for our family.

As Christians, our ultimate goal must be to love God with all our heart, soul, and mind (the Sh'ma, Deuteronomy 6), and to love our neighbor as ourselves (Mark 12:29-31). All that we set our hands to do should flow from these two core commitments.

If we love God, we will desire to "keep [his] commandments" (John 14:15)—to understand what He would have us to do and then do it.

God's prescription for married women is found in Scripture, and to properly understand our role, we must go back to the first marriage that He established in the Garden of Eden. God Himself declares His reason for creating Eve and giving her to Adam for his wife in Genesis 2:18:

> *Then the Lord God said, "It is not good that the man should be alone; I will make him a helper fit for him."*

God makes it clear in establishing marriage that the goal of a wife is to help her husband succeed in his goals; to complete his mission; to help fulfill him in the dominion work God has called him to pursue (Genesis 1:28). A wife should thus seek to make her husband's goals, not her own, the focus of her labors. The Apostle Paul affirms this point in his first letter to the Corinthians: "Neither was the man created for the woman; but the woman for the man" (I Corinthians 11:9, KJV).

Our goal should be to complement and complete our husband in our efforts as his wife with the home as our primary base of activity:

> *...train the young women to love their husbands and children, to be self-controlled, pure, working at home, kind, and submissive to their own husbands, that the word of God may not be reviled. —Titus 2:14-15*

Even as we seek to help our husband fulfill his dominion goals, we should seek the blessing of children as a couple (Genesis 1:28) and raise those He gives to us as "godly offspring" (Malachi 2:15).

All of our goals should be guided by these principles first and complemented with the rest of Scripture.

Make Goals with Your Husband

For a wife to further her husband's goals, she must understand what his goals are. It's important for you to discover what your husband's priorities are for your family and home. Find out what his vision for the Christian home life is. Talk together about such things as child training, family worship, the aesthetics of the home, playtime, friendships to nurture, mealtimes, ministry, and more, and then set goals accordingly.

Goals made with your husband will be more realistic and aid both of you to better reach those goals, because the two of you will be on the same page. Making goals together is important for unity and cohesiveness. Dad and Mom should be moving in the same direction as a family; otherwise, you will create confusion for your kids and your family as a whole.

In outlining goals with your husband, it is important to understand where he prefers to give you broad parameters to run with and where he prefers to be more particular about the smaller details. Every husband is different in this regard.

There are certain areas where you need to be a problem solver, while other areas he will want to dictate his goals to you down to the small specifics. For example, your husband may give you a budget to buy food and clothing, and it will be your job to figure out the best way to meet this budget, including where to shop, when to buy (in light of sales), etc. In contrast, he may direct your family to meet for family worship in the morning at a specific time and come ready to answer specific questions.

As you help to manage the home as second-in-command, it is important for you to get to know your husband's preferences in goal-setting: to understand where he prefers to delegate more broadly, and where he is more particular about the details. By tuning in closely to your husband's pulse on this, you will be more faithful and effective as you organize and carry out your responsibilities as his help-meet.

Goal areas to plan for include Personal, Family, Spiritual, Home, Community Outreach, Educational, Physical, Recreational, and Financial. You and your husband might think of more areas, you might want to break it up into smaller areas, or you might want to group areas together. Do not get bogged down in too many details if this is all new to you. It is easier to make changes in one area at a time. Success breeds success, so build upon the areas in which your family makes positive progress.

Our goals reflect our vision of the future, and as Christians our goals must be aligned with Scripture. Don't make your goal to be like another family, beautiful as that family may be. Study the Scriptures and create your family vision in accordance with it.

Make long-term goals, short-term goals, and immediate goals. Where you will be in three months is determined by what you do today. Make your actions today count towards the future. The immediate daily and weekly goals will be the stepping stones to the short-term goals. The short-term goals are the steps taken to reach the long-term goals.

Write Your Goals Down

I have found that in whatever I'm trying to change about my life, writing it out is very fruitful. Rather than just having a goal in my head, it gives further commitment to a thought. In writing goals down, I am able to prioritize them more effectively and to evaluate my progress in reaching or falling short of them. I've written prayers, goal sheets, and resolutions, in addition to my daily list of things to do, and formalizing these in writing has been essential in getting my act together as a mom.

As you strategize with your husband on your family's priorities, don't just talk about your goals; write them down. Organize them, prioritize them, and begin to take action. Then regularly compare your progress against what you have committed to in writing, and make adjustments to your list of goals as necessary.

A Plan for Victory: One Step at a Time

Put your goals a step beyond writing them down and closer to actually getting them done by breaking them down into specific steps. Sometimes we need small steps, even baby steps. With this in mind, I'm going to walk you through how to set a specific goal and the steps to take to reach that goal.

EXAMPLE ONE: AN EXERCISE PLAN

You probably have made some sort of New Year's resolutions. For ease, I'll use the classic "I'm going to exercise more this year." This is a pretty big and broad goal, so let's break it down a bit.

First, examine why you have this as a goal and write down the whys:

- The body is the temple of the Holy Spirit and I need to care for the temple.

- The Excellent Wife worked at having a strong back and strong arms.

- I need to be a good steward of God's gifts and that includes this body He gave me.

- I need to be physically fit to take care of my children and grandchildren.

- I want to enjoy my senior years with good health and that means taking care of my body now.

With your goals, you need to be more specific about the end and choose a goal that will prove your results both now and in the future. With the "exercise more" goal, pick the end point, such as "run the local 5k in September." Now plan backwards. You have 8 months to be able to run the 5k. Then, establish monthly goals, planning backwards:

8. 5k

7. Run most of 5k, walk the rest

6. Run half of 5k, walk half—run, walk, run

5. Run 1/4 of 5k, walk 3/4—run, walk, run

4. Run, walk, run 5k as able

3. Run, walk, run 4k as able

2. Run, walk, run 3k as able

1. Run, walk, run 2k as able; research better methods of walking and running stretches and form

I find it helpful to have some sort of tangible reward for meeting each monthly goal. Some "rewards" for meeting a specific goals in your quest to run the 5k might include a new T-shirt you wear for running, a subscription to a running magazine, or weights to wear while running. Of course, there are real physical rewards of increased energy, strength, and the ability to do more than sit on the old duff that you will benefit from along the way as you persevere!

Here are more pertinent questions to consider as you plan backwards for the 5k. You know that the summer months are hot, so what time of day will you run: morning or evening? Who will watch the children when you engage in this exercise? How will this affect your schedule? How about your wake time? Will you need to go to sleep earlier?

Write out a new schedule that includes your running time and shower. Then, write on the calendar at the end of each month the reward you will give yourself for meeting the goal.

Now you are at the starting point. Get some good running shoes and look through your closet for running clothes. Consult the new schedule and set out your running things, and then go do it!

EXAMPLE TWO: A HOSPITALITY CALENDAR

Let's plan backwards again with a new goal: to open your home and show more active hospitality as a family.

First examine the why:

- There are biblical commands for it.

- We have a need to be social.

- We enjoy getting together with friends and family.

- Having people over is motivating to get some extra work done around the house and yard.

Why aren't we more hospitable? One reason is that we tend to be lazy and unfocused in this area. By setting goals and putting planning exercises in place, we can learn to be more self-disciplined and effective in the hospitality that you portray.

If our end goal is to be able and willing to have people over any time, to welcome drop-in guests, and to spontaneously invite others over after church, how do we get there? Let's plan backwards again.

Let's say that next holiday season you want your home to be an Open House—not just for one evening, but the whole month. That's eleven months away. What do we need to work on to be more hospitable? A hospitable attitude, a presentable house, appetizing food and drink.

Food and drink are easy because fruit and cheese are beautiful when placed on a clean plate and served with a glass of cool water. The large family's home being presentable can be a problem if regular chore time is not a part of the day. Things get messy quickly in the large family's home, and it can be embarrassing. Lastly there's our attitude. A hospitable attitude should be one of love. It's an attitude that makes the guest feel special. When a guest is over, the normal household routine stops and centers around making guests feel welcome. It is not "show and tell time" for our family.

Let's set up monthly goals to get us to the place of having a hospitable home. Start with the end result you desire and work backwards:

December: The house is open for guests. There are meals and appetizers in the freezer (even if you bought them at Sam's Club). House chores are done regularly throughout the day. Any Christmas craft activities are welcome for guests to participate in also. Invite all the people you had over during the year for a variety of hospitality events. Have families over for a craft day and potluck supper. Hold a Christmas tea party. Gather friends for carolling and then a snack supper. Plan to have guests after an event (such as a music program).

November: Invite guests over on the spur-of–the moment twice this month. Be prepared for anything. Maybe have your husband do the inviting so you don't chicken out.

October: Pick a Sunday and prepare for guests. Plan a good crockpot dish that's tried and true. Make all the Sunday food the day before. After church, look around for strangers or visitors and invite them to join you for Sunday dinner. Practice makes perfect. Keep working on hospitality so that you can be able.

September: Look around your church: Who are the lonely? Invite a grandma for an afternoon tea or a college student for an evening meal and a family game. These people will bless our lives just as you are blessing them with warm hospitality.

August: Do you have neighbors that you don't know? Invite them over for an evening. What do you do when new neighbors move in? Make a plan for when that happens. A fresh pie or cookies would be a great treat on moving day. Don't get so caught up in your own life that you miss these opportunities to spread good cheer.

July: Plan an outdoor party. Prepare ahead. Send out invitations or phone a couple of weeks ahead of time. Make a frozen dessert. How will you serve the food? Where will everyone sit? How will the small children manage eating outside? How will you keep things safe for guest's children? What are some group games everyone can play? Think ahead and write down your ideas, plan for them, and have fun making it a great day for your guests! Do a yard clean-up, as you don't want a guest to trip on a hoe while playing kickball and end up at the ER. Put some fresh planters out or make some flower arrangements with your children for the tables. Don't forget a back-up plan if the weather turns bad. Is your garage a Plan B option?

June: Does your church ever have foreign missionaries visit for a few days that need a home to stay in? Work on preparing your home for this type of opportunity. Create a plan for having overnight guests. What will you serve for food and drink? Where will they sleep? Will this displace your children, and where will they sleep? Prepare your children for overnight guests by talking over these plans and teaching manners (treat others like you would like to be treated). Let your church leaders know that your home is open for missionary guests.

May: Invite an older couple from church or neighborhood that you would like to get to know better. Instruct your children ahead of time that there is much to be learned from your guests and that they should stay near to them, serve them, ask questions, and converse with them. Your children should not ignore them or run off to do their own thing until permission is granted. Instruct and role play for this ahead of time, making it part of your school time.

April: Invite a family for dinner that you would like to get to know better. Have your children plan activities or games to do with the guest children. Work on having a play area that guest children will enjoy also. Discuss with your children how to handle sharing or putting away very special dolls or objects. Encourage your children to play group activities such as games. Make a notebook or folder of game ideas and their instructions.

March: Plan a tea party with your best girlfriends and their daughters. In the room where you are having your tea party do extra cleaning and decorating (we're working on the embarrassment factor here). Set the date for the end of the month and then plan backwards for it. Spend time on your Office Days, Cooking Days, and Cleaning Days to plan and prepare for the event. Do this every month with the thought, "I'm working on being more hospitable this year, therefore, I need to improve our chore time, cleaning, and food prep."

February: Invite your best friends over, the ones you have over when the house is a mess. Only this time, pull out all stops, set the table beautifully and then serve them your best food and drink.

January: Prepare your household management skills for being hospitable. Regular chore times and a weekly cleaning day are a strong start.

As you start doing hospitality events, you will grow more and more able to be hospitable, and soon it will become old hat. Hospitality will become an automatic function of your home. You and your family will learn systems that work best for serving people outdoors and in, planned and spur-of-the-moment.

Practice makes perfect: The more you hostess events, the easier it will get. Remember, the most important thing is not you, your home, or the food. The most important thing is the guest and making the guest feel comfortable and welcome. Take your eyes off of yourself and put them on the guest. Usually guests don't feel comfortable doing nothing or having their hands empty, so either put something like a drink in their hands or let them help you with preparations. Ask them questions about themselves to get the conversation rolling. Relax and your guests will be relaxed. Smile and laugh.

Being prepared for guests helps you to be able to focus on guests rather than the necessary work. With this plan, you are working at preparation skills one month at a time.

Keep your hospitality ideas, systems, recipe and drink lists, and conversation starters in your Home Management Book (make a tab for Hospitality). When you get a little befuddled, you can pull it out and remember "Oh, yes, this recipe looks great and is simple; it will be easy to serve for ____."

If you enjoy a reward system, then reward yourself with a décor item, a table service item, a book about hostessing or recipes, or a special tea blend for the next event. It doesn't have to be expensive, just something that helps you feel like a more competent hostess.

This goal planning system can be applied to any goal, running a 5k or having regular hospitality being just two examples.

Planning out your goals and resolutions puts feet under them. Soon, if you put your step-by-step plans into practice, you will be so improved that your New Year's Resolutions will not be the "same-old, same-old" ones. You will not give up on setting them, and you will be reaching higher.

CHAPTER 3
Systems

Systems are essential for the right functioning of any endeavor. But not all systems work well. Some are good systems; some are bad.

The family that doesn't clean a table until right before the next meal has a system. The family that piles up mail but never sorts it has a system. These are, of course, bad systems.

A good system is one in which the work is done completely and efficiently. In our house, some of the systems are getting implemented some of the time by some of the people, but not all of our systems are being properly implemented by all of the people all of the time. Like any family, we have system breakdowns. This is natural in a home full of flesh-and-blood people of different stages of growth and development. Add in a bad cold that takes a month to work through a large family, and there are a lot of system breakdowns!

Yet good systems throughout the home are a blessing to all. From dishwashing to laundry, from cleaning the toilets to bedtime routines, each system plays an important part in a family's routine. This does not mean that there is no room for creativity in our life; it simply means that when we do something, we follow an order of events. If we have strong, well-working systems, they improve efficiency and give us more time for creativity.

When improving a system, it really helps to identify its components and write them down. Then put them in an order that improves the speed of the system.

For some systems, you will want to post the completed order of events at the place where the task is performed as a reminder of what needs to be done.

Each system that is reordered must be taught to the family. Explain to them that the new way of doing things will be a better and faster way. That means that they will get more time to play or read their book! Explain also that God wants us to do our work heartily as unto Him (Colossians 3:23). I know from experience to start slowly if I want to make things "stick." Focus on one new system at a time. Work through this method while teaching a new thing:

1. Show them how to do it, demonstrate the protocol.

2. Watch them do it, giving correction.

3. Let them do it unsupervised with you checking later, and give further instruction if needed.

4. Require independent work with occasional checks; if they begin to be sloppy (they are human), then start over.

"Systems don't work if you don't work the systems" is a quote that my husband brought home from the corporate world. A system may be good, but if you don't use it, it will be ineffective, so work to not only establish effective systems in your home, but to diligently implement them. When you do this, you and your family will be blessed.

CHAPTER 4
Self-Discipline: It Starts with You

That which we persist in doing becomes easier—not that the nature of the task has changed, but our ability to do has increased. —Ralph Waldo Emerson

You can have wisdom on how to rightly live and have the most refined set of goals and well-tuned system in the world on how to get there, but if you don't pursue your goals and implement your plan, your ideas are next to worthless.

Getting from goal to execution requires self-discipline. Self-discipline is making yourself do something that you don't want to presently do. John MacArthur says it this way, "Biblically, self-discipline may be summarized in one word: obedience." Our sin nature groans at this thought! It is so easy to give in to the flesh and do what it wants to do right now.

Yet when we stop to consider the consequences, we really don't want what our flesh wants at the moment. Chocolate fudge brownies with ice cream won't help us wear those clothes that used to fit. Self-discipline means delaying gratification. When we have a goal, we must delay the gratification for the instant fleshly thing in order to achieve long-term reward and blessing.

Learning self-discipline starts with keeping our eyes constantly on the goal. As Christian mothers, our goal is to be God's goal. We first must be seeking His kingdom, and we do that by studying His will for our lives as Christian women. We learn about kingdom living in the Bible and by praying for His help through the Holy Spirit. The Holy Spirit is given to counsel us on where we need to put off the old man through repentance, and we must confess our sins and turn from them when we are convicted of wrong behavior. Guided by God's Word and the Holy Spirit, we can overcome our weaknesses and live disciplined lives for Christ.

Slowly but surely, as we fix our eyes on Christ and put aside our selfishness, we will become more kingdom-oriented. Sometimes we will move forward quickly in one area of the Christian life while, at the same time, being blind to sins in another area. That is why we must be so gracious with each other; God is working on us all in different ways. None of us have arrived yet. This said, when we keep our eyes on God's goal—godly womanhood—and regularly seek His wisdom, we will gain His character over time. We will also begin to see the people of the world as He does and respond with patience and mercy. Being Christ-like is the goal.

When we have God's Word in our minds and are sensitive to the Holy Spirit, we will gain control over our selfish fleshly desires. We must not give in to our emotions but surrender them to God daily through a life of prayer. God tells us to pray without ceasing for a reason. It is hard to give in to temptation and pray at the same time!

Gaining self-control over emotions is found through the renewing of the mind. When you hide God's Word in your heart, you will replace selfish thoughts with His thoughts.

> *Do not be conformed to this world, but be transformed by the renewal of your mind, that by testing you may discern what is the will of God, what is good and acceptable and perfect.* —*Romans 12:2*

I have found help in memorizing Scripture relevant to my emotion and praying for wisdom in using my tongue. Bad thoughts need to be replaced with good. For example, when we understand that God gives us trials and that we are to count them as joy, our outlook will improve (James 1:2). Our perspective will be righted when we embrace a heart of gratitude. Being thankful for everything conquers a self-pitying spirit (1 Thessalonians 5:18), so make a list of thanksgivings!

Gaining self-control in different areas happens with small steps and small victories. When we need to discipline ourselves to overcome a large thing, it can help to start out with small steps. Choose something for which you need more discipline, and once you have conquered it, add a related thing. Soon the small things will add up to be a big thing that you are disciplined about. This starts by saying no to yourself and then resolving to do the hard thing—to finish the work you've laid before you, to do what you say you are going to do, and to be timely and organized.

Forming good habits make self-discipline easier to learn. A habit is something that you regularly do. Choose a small thing such as keeping your bedside table tidy, and do it every night before lying down. Make it a habit. Then add to it. Put a prayer list on your bedside table, and every night after you tidy your bedside table, pray over the list. Once that is a habit, add another task before tidying the bedside table, such as tidying that part of the room. When you have strong habits that are beneficial to you and your family, it becomes easier to deny self-gratifying impulses.

These things can sound huge to an overwhelmed mom who is drowning in work. I know—I've been there—and you can get past your discouragement! Start with small things and add to them. Practice makes perfect. Someday, when you fail to be disciplined in an area; it will be easier to regain that discipline. You did it once; you can do it again! You can do it with His strength, and there is joy in His strength.

The same principle applies to our children, and it is critical to teach them self-discipline while they are little. Require them to do small chores when they are small, and as they grow, increase their responsibility. When they are required to be faithful in small things and know the importance of their work, they will gradually learn to be self-disciplined. When they are self-disciplined in one area of life, it will carry over to other areas. It requires faithfulness on your part as a parent to check on your children's work and require it to be done right. Just remember to guide and correct them with an attitude of encouragement.

If we want our home to be characterized by order and tranquility, we must lead by example. It starts with us. In seeking to implement the goals we have established with our husband's lead, we must demonstrate self-discipline and set the tone of being more like Christ who "stedfastly set his face to go to Jerusalem" (Luke 9:51) when He knew this meant His sure and painful death. Christ was self-disciplined to carry out the plan His Father gave Him, and so we must we be as mothers if we hope to have a thriving and orderly home.

May we be more like Jesus in the example of self-discipline we show our children!

More Like Jesus Would I Be

More like Jesus would I be, let my Savior dwell with me;
Fill my soul with peace and love—make me gentle as a dove;
More like Jesus, while I go, pilgrim in this world below;
Poor in spirit would I be; let my Savior dwell in me.

If He hears the raven's cry, if His ever watchful eye
Marks the sparrows when they fall, surely He will hear my call:
He will teach me how to live, all my sinful thoughts forgive;
Pure in heart I still would be—let my Savior dwell in me.

More like Jesus when I pray, more like Jesus day by day,
May I rest me by His side, where the tranquil waters glide.
Born of Him through grace renewed, by His love my will subdued,
Rich in faith I still would be—let my Savior dwell in me.

—Fanny J. Crosby

CHAPTER 5
Attitude is Critical

A Matter of the Heart

Keep your heart with all vigilance, for from it flow the springs of life. —Proverbs 4:23

You've met them: The large family that appears to have it all together. You've admired their example; you've even learned important lessons from them that have helped you in your journey to be a better wife and mother. In key areas, they've been a benchmark for you to measure your progress on how a together-family operates.

And then you've lamented the unexpected: when this outwardly-exemplary family fizzled out and fell away from godly living.

The Prophet Jeremiah gives us this sobering truth: "The heart is deceitful above all things, and desperately wicked: who can know it?" (Jeremiah 17:9, KJV).

As wives and mothers, it is critical that we not just have it together on the outside, but that we regularly examine our hearts before God and renew our minds with His Word—that we say with Psalmist, "With my whole heart have I sought thee: O let me not wander from thy commandments" (Psalm 119:10, KJV).

Otherwise, we become poster children for those hypocrites Christ identified during His earthly ministry: "This people honors me with their lips, but their heart is far from me" (Matthew 15:8).

Phariseeism will only last so long before it catches up to us if we do not get our hearts right with God. This doesn't mean that we will always have the perfect attitude—we must do right even when we don't feel like it. Yet when our hearts dramatically drift from being rooted in things of Christ for an extended length of time, we become hypocrites and set ourselves up for a potentially disastrous fall.

Guard your hearts against this by daily confessing your sins and by staying sensitive toward your own bad attitudes. Don't become callous in your heart toward God.

Perfection

Do you see others as perfect? As if they have it all together? Do you try to be perfect and fail?

I *know* that others aren't perfect. Only Jesus was perfect. I know that in my head. But there is a big part of me that wants life to go according to my standards of perfection.

My idea of perfection tends to be centered around the perfect day, perfectly respectful and obedient children, being the perfect wife, having the perfect home, the perfect landscape design, a perfectly weed-free garden with perfect fruits and vegetables, perfect meals—and of course all that would be due to me being the perfect person. I want to be perfectly kind, perfectly gracious to all, perfectly patient, perfectly everything. Is this wrong to aim for?

We must first recognize that attempts to attain perfection in our own strength will fall short—"all our righteousnesses are as filthy rags" (Isaiah 64:6, KJV). Even Job, who was one of the most faithful, godly men who ever lived, did not measure up to God's perfections, and when he compared himself to God, he proclaimed, "Therefore I despise myself, and repent in dust and ashes" (Job 42:6).

If we vaunt ourselves in our accomplishments, we err. It's only by God's grace and mercy that we can do anything right, and we should give glory to Him whenever we excel at any pursuit.

Your salvation is not dependent upon your "perfection"; the Scriptures refute this thought (See Romans 1:16-17, for example). Jesus, the perfect Lamb of God, is our righteousness, and His covering over us is the only way we can stand before God. Yet if you are a Christian, you are to seek to be like Christ. Paul instructs us to put off the old man and put on the new (Ephesians 4:24).

While perfection in human terms will not happen in this world, we as Christians should seek to emulate God's perfect character. We are to work towards that goal, not just give up and say, "I guess I won't even try"; "I could never _____"; "Why bother"; or "I can't." Matthew 5:48 tells us, "You therefore must be perfect, as your heavenly Father is perfect." We cannot walk around with our head hanging with defeat. We must continue to strive.

Seeking to be like Christ involves many important character traits. Our God is a God of love (1 John 4:7-8), for example, and I certainly don't love others like He does. I love Self: Me, Myself, and I—me, me, me. But I am to take my eyes off myself, see others with His eyes, and love them as He sees them.

Our God is slow to anger (Numbers 14:18). Not so with me, as I can get irate pretty quickly and sin in my anger, which the Scriptures condemn. "The wrath of man worketh not the righteousness of God" (James 1:20, KJV).

I can also ignore sin in my children because discipline is hard work. It seems easier to avoid conflict. I'm lazy. But the Bible says, "Go to the ant, O sluggard; consider her ways and be wise" (Proverbs 6:6). I must persevere in doing what God has called me to do and not be indolent.

I could go on all the day looking at each way that God is perfect and I am not. Just a little bit of this exercise causes me to see myself as the worm I am and brings me to repentance.

Jesus is our righteousness; everything we do apart from Him, even the things that go "perfect," are as filthy rags (Isaiah 64:6). We are to repent of it all, be filled with the Spirit, and "press on toward the goal for the prize of the upward call of God in Christ Jesus" (Philippians 3:14). He is perfection, and we are called to be like Him: to aim for perfection (2 Corinthians 13:11).

Yes, we are to be perfectionists. We are to perfect being Christ-like in all areas of life. We can look around us and learn from others, but the goal is not to be like our imperfect friend. Our goal in perfection is being like Jesus.

> *Do not be conformed to this world but be transformed by the renewal of your mind, that by testing you may discern what is the will of God, what is good and acceptable and perfect. —Romans 12:2*

This world tells us to "let go of perfection"; "don't even try"; "you're hurting yourself and those around you through your quest for perfection." There is a grain of truth to this. If your goal in perfection is your own glory rather than God's glory, then you will hurt those around you. Yet if your goal is to let the light of Christ's glorious perfection shine through you, God will be pleased. Well-behaved happy children, pleasant and beautiful homes, and healthy, gourmet meals are things which are not bad goals if they are pursued to bring glory to God rather than Self.

When the world tells us to quit being perfectionists, we need to respond in God's terms and strive to be perfect like Him.

Obedience Is a Choice

In our family, we don't permit our children to say, "I can't." This is a habit that we deal with early on with them.

They can do things if they choose; it's a matter of obedience.

Last night I had to have a talk with one of my little daughters. In this situation, she was simply being stubborn and willful about saying her bedtime prayers, She was refusing to do it by whining, "I can't"—unacceptable speech for this house! We don't even think those words around here. It was time for her to understand that.

The conversation went something like this, with a little girl voice whining and a determined Mama answering with firmness:

"I can't."

"You will."

"But I can't."

"If you can *say*, 'I can't,' then you can *say* your bedtime prayers."

"I can't."

Mama, sensing the opportunity for a teaching moment replied, "In this house, we do not say, 'I can't,' we say, 'I'll try my hardest' or 'I'll do my best,' but we do *not* say, 'I can't.' Do you understand?"

"Yes, Mom."

And then she said her prayers like she does every night.

The situation last night reminded me of a recent conversation that my husband Matt and I had with another mom of a big family. The setting was mealtime with a lot of people present, and we were discussing large families. The mother asked Matt and me if, in response to the hecticness of mealtime, we ever said, "I just can't do this anymore. I can't do one more meal."

Without thought, we both responded, "No," and I added that sometimes we have to get really firm, requiring everybody to sit down at the table and be quiet. After being firm and even sometimes saying, "No more talking," then it's okay, and peace and order returns. But saying, "I can't" is something we don't say. "I can't" gets replaced with praying without ceasing.

When I have to have the "I can't" talk with an older child, we also discuss our thought life. I tell them that it's a mind habit to quit, and that they need to replace the "I can't" thought with an "I'll try my hardest" thought. Usually the child then says the verse or starts singing the song, "I can do all things through Christ who strengthens me." A defeatist attitude is replaced with an attitude of determination and calling on God for help.

Even if the end result of the child's effort is not perfect, doing the best job possible is worthy of great praise and usually is rewarded in some way or another. Satisfaction in learning or even trying a new skill is also a reward. Skill builds on skill, and soon trying new things and the determination for success that goes along with it results in a confident, can-do person. But it starts with those little conversations with little people who let those "I can't" words slip out.

We don't say, "I can't." We say, "I can do all things through Christ who strengthens me" (Philippians 4:13).

Follow Me

I once heard a speaker at a mother-daughter retreat tell us mothers to get in line with Jesus and that our daughters would follow our lead. If our children see us being Sunday Christians, then they won't take Christianity seriously, and church will just be a Sunday social club. By contrast, if they see us confessing, repenting, reading the Bible, and living according to its precepts, then they will do the same. We must live a life that says, "Follow me, girls!"

As mothers, we are on a pedestal in our daughters' little-girl eyes, and we must do as Paul did and say, "Be followers of me." It's a big responsibility, but it is our calling. We are mothers and must live an exemplary life, leading the way for our daughters. Of course, this doesn't apply only to daughters but to our sons as well; it's just that our daughters will identify with us more as ladies-in-the-making.

The scary thing is that our girls will follow us or react to us no matter if we want them to or not. That is why we need to follow Jesus and not the prevailing wind of the day. We must put out of our lives those things that influence us and our daughters away from being noble women of God.

What we watch, listen to, and read has a great pull not only on us but on our daughters as well. Given this fact, it's important to ask: What magazines do you have lying around your house? What books are on your shelves? What music do you listen to? What shows and movies do you watch? What web sites do you visit on the Internet? We might think that such things don't influence us, but they do, as advertisers can tell you.

Ouch, ouch, ouch!

These influences change our attitudes, our thoughts, and in turn what comes out of our mouth. And who is it that we talk to the most? Our children. They are watching and imitating us.

Are you talking to them about things that will draw them closer to the Father? Are you whining and complaining through your pity party? Are you showing them a fence-riding Christian who lives a double life? Do you say one thing and do another? Do you threaten to leave or even joke about it? If you're a homeschooling mom, maybe you threaten to send them off to school.

Do you use the TV to keep your children out of the way? Are you relieved when your children are gone from the house for a day, or a few days? Is the law of kindness on your tongue? How often do you sigh?

Oh, these are hard-hitting questions, and we are all guilty of sinful thoughts that are further expressed in actions!

Don't quit! Don't give up! Get into God's Word. Make it part of your daily life, apply it, and set the example for your daughters. You don't need to say, "Follow me," just live in a way that you would want your children to go, and they will follow.

In conclusion, we must recognize that our attitude is critical. In all our efforts to strive toward good and profitable goals, we must not lose sight of this. We must keep "[our] heart with all vigilance, for from it flow the springs of life." (Proverbs 4:23).

CHAPTER 6
Where Does the Time Go?

So teach us to number our days that we may get a heart of wisdom. —Psalm 90:12

The Mystery Exposed

Fourteen hundred and forty minutes are yours every day. Have you ever wondered where the time goes? Have you ever asked yourself, "What did I do all day?"

Do you sometimes feel like you are "sitting and spinning"? You keep trying to make progress but it does not come very quickly. Do you feel as though you dawdle around all day and never accomplish much to bless your family, your church, and your neighbors?

I've been there! The first two years of parenting, I felt much that way!

Here is a helpful exercise that will expose the minutes of your day and get on track. Write down everything that you do and an approximate time for how long it took. Start right now and continue this for a couple of days. The longer you do this, the more you will see progress in getting to where you want to be, but do this for a minimum two days. If you journal, you can record your exercise there, and if not, just use a standard notebook and pen.

It will help to keep a watch or clock right beside your time log. Do not write only the big things but write down interruptions—everything. If you change a diaper, write down how long it took. If you helped somebody with a math problem or three pages of math, write it down. If you stop at the sink and drink a glass of water, write that down. Tonight when you go to bed, review it and commit to doing the same exercise tomorrow.

This will show you where your time goes and what you are doing with it. It will show you places in the day where you can be more efficient. You might see that if you lined up your day a little better, you will be able to save time and do more. You will see opportunities where you can multi-task. You might also find that you are trying to put too many things into your day, and that this is why you cannot get anything done. That is my current time-use problem. Are there things that you can delegate? Maybe you need to excuse you and your family from some outside activities. There are so many "good" things to do, and it is very easy to over-commit our families and ourselves.

Take a step back and revisit your priorities and goals. How does reality fall into line with your primary priorities? This exercise can be enlightening and expose things that need to be cut out of your life. When you cut something out, it doesn't mean that you can never do it again, just that this is not the season for it. If you streamline your daily routines better, will there be more time for what you need to do and what you desire to do?

Continue this activity for a few days and start writing down notes to yourself about places in the day that can be improved and how you will improve them. Watch your children, and write down what each of them are doing during the day. Just take a quick glance around and quickly write down who is doing what. This will help you identify time-wasting children. Are they wasting their time and yours with bickering about chores? Write down the time their bickering takes and show them how they are using the minutes.

This exercise will also help you to see a child who is taking lots of your time and determine whether this is truly necessary or not. I am not suggesting that you cut your children short on love and affection. Different children need different things in different ways. However, some children cost you time because of their character flaws.

Think about what you can do in changing your reaction, your disciplining of this child, or restructuring this child's day so that the character flaw is overcome. Maybe you do need to keep on doing what you are doing with this child. Writing down what is happening and journaling about it will bring things to light about you and your children that otherwise would go unnoticed except in your ever- increasing frustration at the situation or child.

Another very helpful thing to do with this time-logging exercise is to write down everything that you eat and drink. Patterns will emerge in your days that you see are unhealthy. You will not want to write down that you ate six spoons of cookie dough at 4:30 PM. Begin to brainstorm and journal about what you can do to ward off your hungry belly at 4:30. A handful of raw almonds would be a bit healthier. Write down how much you are eating. The last time I did the exercise, I was amazed at the amount of food that I was eating. Did I really need that much? I discovered that I did not. I started to pay attention to my body and learn to recognize again the sense of being full. I began to serve myself smaller portions and eat more slowly.

Journaling minute-by-minute exposes reality. When you think you have done enough itemizing of your days and thought about what is truly happening, write a realistic plan for your days. Match up what you want to happen with what is really happening. If it takes you ten minutes for a diaper change, then that is reality. Leave enough time in the events of your day to encompass diaper changes, settling of disputes, switching the laundry loads, and wiping up the spilled milk. Plan for interruptions.

Some of us tend to be idealistic and think that we can do everything, do it all well, and do it super-fast. Others among us don't attempt to do anything but depend on others to do everything. Every person can find value in taking stock of what really truly happens with his or her day. The over-achievers will see that they are letting first priorities suffer. The under-achievers will see that they can step it up a notch and be more helpful in the broader community.

Everyone benefits when exposing the reality of our days. We all learn where we are weak, where we are strong, and how we can further bring glory to God in our homes and families.

For everything there is a season, and a time for every matter under heaven. —Ecclesiastes 3:1

CHAPTER 7
The Interrupted Day

There will be times in life when your days do not go as planned. The constant barrage of interruptions have the ability to upend a day. Sometimes you can make a recovery. Sometimes you need to spread a task out through the week to get back on track. And sometimes it's one thing after the other, and life spirals into chaos. You "lose." Or at least it appears that you lose, but in reality God gives many lessons in trials.

The key thing is attitude. Keep in mind that you should focus on doing something that you can do something about, and let the rest be. There is always next week. Next week, Monday is Laundry Day again. Next week, you can clean the laundry room, work on the ironing and mending, and clean the top of the equipment. The world will not end because the current Laundry Day does not go according to your wishes.

By planning a routine for your work, you can rest assured that you have inadvertently also planned for these interruptions. "So Laundry Day isn't working out this week, next week we will get to it." Later this week we will make an extra effort to make sure that we do "4 Loads by 4." Cycling through different tasks assures that all things get done eventually. Some weeks will be stellar, some not. A routine brings peace of mind. You can say with confidence, "We'll get back to this."

In looking at my calendar, I can see ahead of time when a week is full of events that are going to hinder our daily work. Thus, by looking ahead, I can plan to do extra work the week before, and I can also knowingly try to work extra-fast during that busy week to make up for time lost. When those two things fail, I can still relax inside and say, "We will get to it later." Getting uptight and upset accomplishes nothing but damaged relationships with those I take out my frustration on.

Interrupted schoolwork goes the same way. It's part of the beauty of homeschooling that we can double-up the day before or the day after. The children can take their work along in the van. They can work in a waiting room. They can do it on Saturday. We can add weeks to the "school year." It's good to make goals; they give us direction and a target, but our plan to reach a goal should not be a whip for us or for our children.

Plans are a guide, not a master. A plan serves you. You do not serve the plan. A plan helps to get the work done in an efficient way. It gives you time and freedom to do things you might think that you can't do. When an opportunity that will disrupt your day presents itself, you can say with confidence, "We'll do five loads of laundry by five the rest of the week." Or, "I have enough things stocked in the freezer and we'll clean the fridge next week when Kitchen Day comes around again." A plan gives you confidence. You know how to plan ahead and you know how to recover from an event.

An interrupted day is God's plan for the life of a mother:

> *The plans of the heart belong to man, but the answer of the tongue is from the LORD. All the ways of a man are pure in his own eyes, but the LORD weighs the spirit. Commit your work to the LORD, and your plans will be established. The LORD has made everything for its purpose, even the wicked for the day of trouble. Everyone who is arrogant in heart is an abomination to the LORD; be assured, he will not go unpunished. By steadfast love and faithfulness iniquity is atoned for, and by the fear of the LORD one turns away from evil. When a man's ways please the LORD, he makes even his enemies to be at peace with him. Better is a little with righteousness than great revenues with injustice. The heart of man plans his way, but the LORD establishes his steps. —Proverbs 16:1-9*

We cannot know what He wills for us and for our children ahead of time. But when interruptions come, we can say with confidence, "This is God's will. He must have something to teach me, or the children, or maybe He is blessing me and the children with this." Or "Somehow, God is being glorified in this event. I need to live obediently and not grump about it or fight it."

Being upset about interrupted plans is, in essence, fighting with God. Yes, a season in life can be really awful. Sometimes it's a full-blown trial. It stinks; it hurts; it always seems so inconvenient. A lot of times the interruption causes more work.

The key is for us to remove "Self" from the center of our world and put God there instead. Serving Him is the most important thing. When we depend on Him, He equips us with the grace to deal with interruptions.

CHAPTER 8
The Psalms–Your Spiritual Multi-Vitamin

I love reading the Psalms. There is a Psalm for most every feeling, thought, and event under the sun. Reading a chapter of Psalms every morning and night is a sure cure for many ailments of the heart and mind! Going to sleep with a Psalm in mind is a wonderful way to sleep. Reading one upon rising puts a completely new perspective on the day. It is a wonderful practice to read a chapter to the children at breakfast. I want the children to hear and know about the wonderful God we serve and how He cares for us in all of our human trials.

It seems that every attribute of man and God is written about in the Psalms. The imagery in the poetry helps us to see God's fullness in a way that speaks to our hearts. To think that we have the world's greatest poetry, written by the inspiration of God, right here in our homes, at our fingertips. Who needs curriculum for teaching poetry? Read the Psalms!

The Psalms comfort us with the knowledge that God is in control. He knows us, and in spite of the ugliness in our lives, He loves us. A friend told me once that Psalm 139:5 is a description of a hug from God.

You hem me in, behind and before, and lay your hand upon me.

In our humanness we cannot grasp God's bigness and sovereignty, but the Psalms show us a glimpse of it in a myriad of ways. They teach us to look around at His creation and know that it is no random action. God's creation is too beautiful, too detailed, too huge and beyond our feeble comprehension to understand.

There are bad things going on in the world all the time, but it is for a season; God will bring glory from ashes. He does it all the time in small ways; someday we will see it in a huge way! We will never be able to understand the whys of evil things, but we can rest in the fact that we are His sheep and He is our shepherd. He has a plan for us, whether that is to take us home with Him unexpectedly, to transplant us to another region, to cause some kind of crisis that causes us to fall upon Him for help, or to use us to bring comfort and hope to a dying world. He is God, and He will do what He wants. Our duty as His people is to be obedient to His commands to love our neighbors as ourselves. We are to follow the example of Jesus and lay down our lives, our self-centered ugliness, and bring glory to Him in whatever way is at hand.

The Psalms teach us these things. They give us a great picture of God and His attributes. They give us comfort in times of distress. They teach us to rely on God and His sovereignty. They give us peace that passes understanding. They cause us to love God more.

My counsel is this: Start reading the Psalms to your children everyday for a spiritual multi-vitamin!

The "I'm Stressed" Psalm

O Lord, my heart is not lifted up; my eyes are not raised too high; I do not occupy myself with things too great and too marvelous for me. But I have calmed and quieted my soul, like a weaned child with its mother; like a weaned child is my soul within me. O Israel, hope in the Lord from this time forth and forevermore. —Psalm 131

CHAPTER 9
Give Your Children a Work Ethic

The principal cause of boredom is the hatred of work. People are trained from childhood to hate it. Parents often feel guilty about making children do anything but the merest gestures toward work. Perhaps the children are required to make their beds and, in a feeble and half-hearted fashion, tidy up their rooms once a month or so. But take full responsibility to clear the table, load the dishwasher, scrub the pots, wipe the counters? How many have the courage to ask this of a ten-year-old? It would be too much to ask of many ten-year-olds because parents have seriously asked nothing of them when they were two or three. Children quickly pick up the parents' negative attitudes toward work and think of it as something most sedulously to be avoided. —Elisabeth Elliot

A Christian Work Ethic

I grew up on a farm, my husband grew up on a farm, and we are raising our children on a farm. Not a hobby farm or an acreage, but a working farm.

My lineage of descent, and my husband's, is that of farmers. When I read about chores for kids in the parenting magazines at the dentist office, they list feeding the dog, and taking out the trash—I have to chuckle. Scraping hog floors didn't make the list? Farm kids work hard. Physically hard and, more often than not, dirty work. I had it easy because I had two brothers in my family to do most of the physical farm work. I made meals, cleaned the house, and froze my hands feeding bottle calves. I pulled out fence and rolled up barbed wire back in the day. Feed the dog and take out the trash? For someone used to farm life, that's an easy task.

Hard physical work builds character. Once you have done hard work, everything else comes much easier. And what is character? Character is having the ability to see beyond this second in time and to persevere beyond what feels good. It is learning the self-discipline to make your body do more than your feelings want to. It is training the mind to overcome the flesh. It is one thing to read about character in a book and aspire to do hard things. It is another thing to practice it. Practicing character traits happens with work.

When my ten-year-old complained about sweeping the kitchen floor every day, he was told, "You are going to get some pigs, and you will have to scrape hog floors. After that you will never complain about sweeping the kitchen again. Sweeping floors will be easy."

We bought pigs for a 4-H project, and he was assigned to feed, water, bed, and scrape their floor. He had to wash and groom them to show. By comparison, sweeping the floor in the house became easy. He also made quite a bit of money, won some ribbons at the county fair, and ate plenty of bacon, sausage, and grilled pork chops for a year as a bonus. He built character and saw the reward. As a parent, you should seek these kind of character-building opportunities for your children.

Boys especially need physical work. Chopping wood and tending the fire is excellent work for a young boy, even if it's just for a regular campfire night in the backyard. Have your boys dig a hole for a water garden. Teach them to prune the trees and bushes and hoe a garden. The character built in physical work will transfer into many areas of life.

Hard work, when properly cultivated, will contribute to the good of the family. That is one danger of the sports culture as it tends to promote separation of the family unit—each child going his own way and robbing the family of time together during the evening when Dad is home. It's far better for your children to do hard work with Dad.

Discipline is being able to force yourself to do something, in spite of how you feel, over and over until it becomes a habit. This is a huge battle for those who did not have regular chores, but it must be won.

The Christian work ethic that was once the hallmark of American culture seems to have been lost in the last couple of generations. We post-modernists think that we are too smart to work. This is a wrong perspective.

Look around at the children of today—obese and dull-eyed. Do they have the life skills and character traits it requires to live on their own in a home with other people? The culture is failing to teach children to work, to think, and to see outside of themselves. It is a gi'me culture. Gi'me this and gi'me that. The current culture, which thinks of itself as Christian, has failed.

It is important for our children to learn household habits at an early age. Our children will live in a house their whole lives. More than likely, they will be living with other people. It is necessary to know the routines that need to happen in every household automatically. It should not be a hugely taxing effort to know what it is they are to do next. They need to learn to see the work and have the ability to dive in and do it. Household habits need to be ingrained into their life.

Just like brushing teeth before bed is a habit that you teach, you also need to teach them to spend a couple of minutes tidying their room. These kind of small routine tasks taught throughout the day to your little children become part of them, and when they are grown, they will carry them into whatever living circumstances they are in.

Move beyond taking the trash out and give your children some character building work. Start when they are two, three, and four with little things like moving the laundry from the washer to the dryer, carrying a little basket or dishpan of folded laundry to be put away, and wiping the table with a wet sponge. Little children love to please, and they want to do what you are doing.

Do not swish your children away to be entertained by the television or toys; include them in your work instead. Give them a broom or a wet washcloth. Talk to them while you work, and tell them why you are doing what you are doing. Explain to them the value of work and the joy that comes from a job well done. Praise them and brag about your busy little workers to their father when he comes home. Do not allow them to whine!

As your children grow, give them more difficult jobs, and grow those little muscles. Encourage them and tell them to do their best. Do not expect children to do the quality of work that an adult can do, but do encourage them to do excellent work. Watch their spirit and gauge whether it needs inspired and bolstered or whether they are starting to cheat and slack. Usually a word of warning is all that is needed to turn a slacker around, if you nip this tendency in the bud early on.

Sometimes you will need to examine how you can make a chore more efficient and enjoyable. For instance, a poorly sized or broken tool is disheartening. Do your best to improve poor work environments. Is the child truly tired, or does she just simply dislike physical effort?

As a family, study and memorize Scripture about work. Proverbs is full of great commentary on the subject! This will help improve everyone's work ethic. If a child slips on a job that you know he is capable of, then have him return to do the work again. Set a goal such as going for a treat when the work is done well.

Take breaks, but do not let your children lie down on the job. Lying or sitting down while work is being done around them is unacceptable. "If you do not know what to do, then ask" is a phrase frequently heard at our house.

Teaching the children never ends. Just as soon as a character shortcoming is addressed in one child, a different one will crop up in another. Each child will need to learn each task. The good news is that the older children will help teach the younger ones attitude, character traits, and the chore. Be sure to teach the older children well!

When the children are done with a task, teach them to come to you and ask, "What can I do next for you Mom?" You should reply, "Oh! Are you done with _____ already? Good job! And thank you for coming to me and offering more help! I sure am glad to have a good helper like you!" Always be encouraging, inspiring, and thankful.

Everyone likes to be thanked for their help. When you visit others or you're at a social event, teach your children to be helpful there also. Teach them to ask the hostess, "Is there anything I can do to help you?" and hopefully the hostess will have them set the table or get chairs or at least thank them. Teach the children that when somebody else asks them for help at church or an event, they should willingly and cheerfully hop-to-it. Better yet, train them too see work and begin helping without being asked. This is teaching them servanthood. It starts with you and your example to them.

I have heard it said that "children should not be required to work because they will be working the rest of their lives"; that "childhood is the one time in life that they can just play and be children." If you embrace this perspective, you will set your children up for failure. If children aren't taught to work when they are young, then they will find it hard to work the rest of their life. They will grow up with an entitlement mentality. They will expect everybody around them to take care of their every need while they sit back demanding it to be hurried. I've seen it up close and personal, and it's not pretty.

Work is what we were created for, and it is a joy when done with the right attitude. This is the ethic we must encourage in our children.

This said, my children are not perfectly willing workers all the time. We are always working on something with someone. Even when we think something was taken care of years ago, it might crop up again.

God is still working on me in different areas of my life. Sometimes I'm a slow learner, and sometimes I have to relearn lessons that I thought were conquered! But I can't quit. In teaching my children His ways, He teaches me. My duty is to teach them His ways and one of His ways is a work ethic based on Scripture.

As you seek to cultivate a solid work ethic in your family, I would encourage you to read, discuss, and memorize the following Scripture verses. I have also found it helpful to post them above the kitchen sink, on mirrors, and other places where they can be viewed and memorized.

- Proverbs 6:6
- Proverbs 10:26
- Proverbs 13:4
- Proverbs 14:23
- Proverbs 18:9
- Proverbs 20:4

- Proverbs 20:13
- Proverbs 21:17
- Proverbs 21:25
- Proverbs 22:29
- Proverbs 24:30-34
- Proverbs 26:13-16

- Proverbs 27:1
- 1 Corinthians 4:2
- Philippians 4:13
- Colossians 3:22-23
- 2 Thessalonians 3:10
- 1 Timothy 5:8

We Work Before We Play

A quote we often use is: "We Work Before We Play." For our family, playing includes building tree houses, reading, and writing. In fact, I include many "fun" things in the homeschooling/education category of life. Just because a child is doing a good thing that looks like work instead of what they are supposed to be doing, does not make the wrong of disobedience right. It is still disobedience.

This is not so much of a problem with little children as it is with older ones. I often write this quote on their chore charts and schoolwork assignments. The middle part of the day when a lot of the chores and schoolwork are completed is when they start to slip away to their "play".

Establishing a solid worth ethic in your family takes focus, but the reward is great—children who are prepared to take on the responsibilities of caring for their own families someday.

CHAPTER 10
Repeating Yourself?

It is hard to do anything with children when they are disobedient. They aren't fun to play with, they won't help with the work, they are impossible to teach, and have fun getting a sitter! It is paramount that you work on the character trait of obedience in your child before you attempt to do anything else.

We all fall into the repeating habit without even realizing it. "Put the cushions back on the couch."

Said a bit louder, "Put the cushions back on the couch."

Louder yet (maybe he didn't hear), "Put the cushions back on the couch!"

We often don't even hear ourselves say it the first three times. Then at the fourth time we lose it and realize that we have been repeating ourselves. "How many times did I say that?"

We moms are busy people. We're great at multi-tasking. But child discipline isn't something that can be multi-tasked. We need to stop and focus. We need to train ourselves to hear ourselves. It's hard—no doubt about it. But repeating ourselves is training our children to continue in disobedience.

Pray for wisdom as you address this problem. Ask God to help you hear yourself. Ask God to show you how to focus and train each child. They are each one unique, and they respond differently to discipline.

Train the children that when you give them an instruction, they are to respond, "Yes, Mom." That signals to you that they heard and will obey. If they didn't respond, then be sure that you were looking at them with the instruction, that eye contact was made, and that they really did hear.

If all of those were the case, then you must discipline them for directly defying you. You are the parent; you are your children's God-given authority, and you must train them in the nurture and admonition of the Lord.

One approach I've used is to role play first-time obedience in a fun way with variations on games such as Mother May I?, Red Light Green Light, and Simon Says. This said, be sure to explain to your children that obedience is not a game, but serious—sometimes even a matter of life and death.

As mothers, we can find ourselves in a poor situation when we are multitasking while giving instruction to a child. Our "mother ears" are picking up what is going on with other children, or the pot bubbling on the stove at the same time that we are disciplining a child. Again, it is learning to focus. Men are great at it. When they are focused on a task, it seems at times that somebody could be burning the house down, and they wouldn't know it. When men focus their attention in loving or disciplining a child, it is beautiful. We need to take a lesson from the men here!

Part of the solution is training the children not to interrupt us. They are not to demand your attention from another room. If they need you, they should come to you (unless someone is burning down the house). When they come and you are busy with somebody else, they should lay their hand on your arm as a sign that they need you and wait patiently until you can give them your full attention, just like they should do when you're at church or a party and you are talking to your friend. This is something you need to deliberately work at training. Role play it over and over for several days. As the children grow, the little ones will usually pick it up from the older children, but you may find that if you haven't deliberately given the lesson for a few years, that you will need to teach this lesson to the next set of children coming up.

Perhaps you are instructing a child and there is bickering going on in the next room. Assuming there's not a major crisis, focus and finish with the first child. Then go to the bickering children and give instruction and discipline there.

If you can make it work with your schedule, get up before the children and spend some time reading the Word and in prayer. Fill your head with good things. Deliberately choose to keep junk out, for it will drag you down and steal your inspiration and joy.

If you have a friend whose child-rearing standards are different, and who contributes to your pity-party or brings you down in any way, then it's time to get some space from her. Misery loves company, and you need to choose encouragers to be with, not the miserable. Also, don't be the one who drags others down; be an encourager! Once you and your children are stronger, then spend limited time with those that need your encouragement. I say limited time because bad influences will undo your children (Proverbs 13:20b).

Keep the fun and love in your home by being focused on teaching obedience.

CHAPTER 11
Teaching a New Chore

"Inspect what you expect" is an often quoted saying for those in management and very handy for moms to keep in their heads!

There are five classic steps for teaching a new chore to children:

1. Tell them

2. Show them

3. Do it with them

4. Supervised practice

5. Independent practice

I would encourage you to put these things on a sticky note and place it above your kitchen sink for a season until you have the steps down.

Do not expect children to do a chore well when you have only done the first two steps with them. It can take a short or long time to get from Step One to Step Five, depending on the child and the specific chore.

Make it a fun time by gathering all the kids for the telling and showing steps, then use the timer to see how fast each person can do the new task. Celebrate with a treat!

After telling, showing and doing, write the steps on a card and tape it near the job site. This aids in supervised practice for the reader. If you are teaching a non-reader, you will have to spend more time supervising. This will be work for you in short run, but in the end, you will have a team of cheerful diligent workers that clean the house in no time flat.

This brings me to the most important point: attitude.

You should not treat your children like slaves or your personal minions. The goal is to raise a godly seed.

Do everything without complaining (Philippians 2:14). If you complain, your children will complain. Don't complain about your children; that is the biggest joy-squisher of all! It is terribly demoralizing and will destroy your relationships with them. Don't complain to your friends about your children, don't complain online about your children. Simply do not complain! It is a bad habit you need to break. When you catch yourself complaining, turn it around into a praise.

Do your work as unto the Lord (Colossians 3:23). If you are working as unto the Lord, your children will notice your cheerful attitude! You can't be grumpy and whiny when you are doing your work as if Jesus were right there beside you and you were doing it for Him. Keep the words, "as unto the Lord", in mind. It is another new habit to replace grumbling.

A cheerful heart is good medicine (Proverbs 15:13). When you work cheerfully with your children, it is contagious and spreads joy among your family!

A crushed spirit dries up the bones (Proverbs 15:13). Do not wound the spirit of your children. Take care of them with your words, your smile, your singing, your stories, and your joy. You take care of their minds with homeschooling, you take care of their bodies with good food and medical care—take care of their spirit too!

Do more than the minimum required, "so as to walk in a manner worthy of the Lord, fully pleasing to him, bearing fruit in every good work and increasing in the knowledge of God" (Colossians 1:10).

When we do a task, we should do it wholly and completely. It is one thing to be short on time for one reason or another and to give a task "a lick and a promise". It is another thing to consistently not do a job in a complete and thorough manner. Teach your children to do a job from start to finish, left to right, top to bottom, inside to outside.

If you have a child that is rushing their work and not doing a complete job, you need to require them to do it again. Not in a way that picks on him or is mean but for their own sake. If you allow them to get away with incomplete work, you are setting them to be a lazy worker for their whole life. You really do not want your child to struggle with employment or with keeping a home and caring for your grandchildren!

Train them now to love work. Show them by your actions and attitude how to work properly. Work brings satisfaction. Work is serving God, and little ones learn this when they learn to do their first chores.

CHAPTER 12

Rejecting Me-Centeredness, Redeeming Time Alone

Feelings, like thoughts, must be brought into captivity. No one whose first concern is feeling good can be a disciple. We are called to carry a cross and to glorify God.
—*Elisabeth Elliot,* Discipline: The Glad Surrender

Motherhood

Being a mom is a huge responsibility. It is an immeasurable honor and duty to receive this little bundle of personhood and protect, nurture, lead, cultivate, nurse, shield, teach, provide for his numerous needs and give account to God for it all in the end.

Motherhood is a life of sacrifice; it is a life poured out for our children. So what are we to do to get some space from it all? When we are honest with ourselves, we know that it is not "Me Time" we need or a "Girls' Night Out". Children are not a burden to escape or endure; they are a blessing that drives us to Christ because we are incapable of parenting well without Him. God is who we need. While there are helpful strategies we can employ in order to have a more peaceful day with our children, the number one thing we must do is to deny Self and cling to the cross.

Morning

Disruptions can set me on edge. I like routine, just like little children. Some variety is fun; it adds spice to life as they say. But when I have a pattern to the days, a certain order of events, a way of doing things, peace reigns in the home. The interruptions of children during the day are to be expected of course. "Mom I need ____." "Mom how do I do ____?"

Settling squabbles, correcting behavior, giving instructions, kissing the boo-boos, those things are part of the routine. But when my morning routine gets severely disrupted, it can wreck my day. If things don't go the way I want them to early on, I can quickly get a stinky attitude. Some days I can go back to my room and start all over and that helps. But others start off like a shot out of the cannon, and the battle rages on all day long. I need to check my attitude on the fly. I think this is where that verse "Pray without ceasing" comes into especially good use. These are the days when the scripture verses stuck above the sink or on the mirror help tremendously.

For a long time, I had a verse stuck over my sink that helped me control my voice: "The wrath of man worketh not the righteousness of God" (James 1:20). Thanks to that verse, I would catch myself murmuring and realize that I was angry about little things. Little things are part of life with little people. I had to get over my habit of an irritated attitude. Really, I was making an idol of Self, as usual. I wanted things to go my way.

I love mornings. I love the morning routines that I create as the seasons change. In the winter, I like a cozy time by the fire with my coffee and Bible, making breakfast for Matt, the house silent. That early morning silence is a balm to my soul. In the warm seasons, I like to do that on the deck watching the sun come up. A person might call that "me time", but really it is time with God and time with my husband. It becomes "me time" when my attitude toward not having that time turns stinky. I can't make an idol of my early mornings.

God doesn't give us a beautiful start to every day. When the children are up early, I read the Bible aloud to whomever is present. That is a beautiful thing! To read the Bible aloud in the early morning to your children is living the Sh'ma (Deuteronomy 6). It is good for the whole family to appreciate God's gift of beauty and quiet in the morning.

Afternoon

Nap time is a good opportunity for everyone in the house to have a Quiet Time. We use it here for reading alone, doing a quiet craft or project alone. I personally have a hard time napping during the day unless I'm completely exhausted. I prefer to have a longer night by going to bed early. After I have a baby, my mother-in-law comes over in the afternoon to sit with the children and insists that I lay down. I protest but do it anyway and sure enough, I collapse for a couple for hours. If you're an afternoon napper, go with it!

If you aren't a napper, Quiet Hour is a good time to do those things that you need a quiet house for. Each of us is different and needs quiet for different tasks. I generally like quiet when I'm doing something that I need to really think about. If we have a project that we need to do without any interference from little children we do it during nap time. As soon as the little ones are down we race the clock until they get up.

There was a season in my life where I voraciously studied God's Word. I got up early and studied before the children were up and did more when they were down for naps. There are seasons of life that fit different methods of Bible study or devotions. Don't get hung up on a time or a method.

Keep your focus right by honoring God with your Quiet Time. Yet don't let Quiet Time itself become an idol.

Evening

Your bedside table is a place to keep those most important things to rejuvenate your life. Your Bible and a prayer journal should be there and ready for late evening and early morning routines. The key is in being ready for opportunity.

Do your best to keep regular bedtime routines for the benefit of everyone's health. Doing the same thing every night with the children helps them to settle down and relax. Children love to know what is going to happen next; it makes them feel safer. Structure makes for peaceful evenings. A pleasantly-structured evening with the children means that you and your husband will likely have the opportunity to have a quiet time together later on.

When Do I Take a Shower?

There are seasons in life when this is a very real and valid question. One season for me was when I had a hard-working, rarely home-husband combined with a handful of little ones and a baby. Another season was having a needy baby who wouldn't settle down at night and who got up at the crack of dawn to eat for an hour, combined with two-handfuls of children going five different directions all day and each one needing something from Mom right now, all the time.

Sleep is a wonderful blessing that fixes many things. A long hot shower runs second to that. Those two things make a huge difference in whether the day is great or one in which you just want to crawl in a hole and cry. I personally don't like to take a shower in the middle of the day—during nap time—but there are seasons when that is the most reasonable time to do it. Don't get hung up on things. Be flexible, and take a shower when the opportunity arises.

Relationships

Being home alone with children can be lonely at times. As a young mom, I missed the daily interaction of friends that I had experienced from kindergarten through college. It was strange to me to be alone every day. I remember that the highlight of my week was going to a Bible study with other moms. I learned to make Jesus my best friend. He was faithful and there every day for me. That said, I also succumbed to entertaining myself every afternoon with the soap *All My Children* and dreamt more than once that I was part of the stories. Erica Kane was my best friend. It was a double life and I eventually overcame my addiction by taping this verse to the television.

> *Finally, brothers, whatever is true, whatever is honorable, whatever is just, whatever is pure, whatever is lovely, whatever is commendable, if there is any excellence, if there is anything worthy of praise, think about these things. —Philippians 4:8*

Once Erica left my life, and I replaced the bad habit with a good one—studying God's Word—I became more content with the relationships I did have.

Who did God put in my life? First, my husband and children; I could do my best to be what they needed. Second, I had a lot of family around. Third, I had the people in my church. I had to learn that relationships aren't about me—that's a selfish love—but about being Jesus to others. Serving others through the strength God gives those willing to work with Him. Studying who Jesus is and developing a relationship with Him was a far richer life than serving my desire for entertainment.

It was not easy to give up Erica. I learned that I could watch her once a month and still keep up, and then I gradually got so disgusted with the show that it became easy to not watch it anymore. There truly is victory in Jesus.

> I was brutish and ignorant; I was like a beast toward you. Nevertheless, I am continually with you; you hold my right hand. —Psalm 73:22-23

Our husband is God's gift to us for a best friend. We should balance and complement each other. He is our leader, and we are his helpmate (Genesis 1-3). Together we create a family that will impact the future in tremendous ways either for the good or the bad. We must bless each other in our specific roles.

As the years go by and our children grow up, they too become our friends. You will love to listen to them, talk with them, and do things together as friends do. They will be the ones you think of when you want to share an experience you've had, when you see a sight, discover something or hash an issue with. That is the reward of training them well as little children, helping them develop their unique gifts, teaching them thinking skills, and spending time developing loving relationships with them. It will happen that when you decide to do a thing you will want it to be with your family.

The family is the most important earthly relationship to develop, and it starts in the early days of marriage and bringing up children. What you do with each day, how you react to each other, how you train your children, and what you teach them will be your family legacy.

You can't let the days go by willy-nilly with no direction. You must give thought to your actions and how those actions will change the relationships you are involved in.

Friendships

The Bible has plenty to say about friendships and gives us multiple examples of good and bad ones. It is clear that God intends for us to interact with each other in the Body of Christ, although sometimes it is hard to see how that works when we are so busy with our own families.

When the children were small, I would get together with another mom or two and all of our children. Of course, the children love these times, and even though it's a bit hard to have a lengthy conversation when there are constant interruptions, the encouragement and fellowship was very precious. Now that there are more big kids, it is easier because they organize games, kiss ouchies, and help keep the peace. These are good times for all. Our children are learning to interact with others not in their family with parental supervision, and Moms have an opportunity to visit face to face.

I have also started getting together with a friend for lunch on a monthly basis. That might not sound very often but believe me, the month flies by and it's time to have a lunch date again. The children have a special lunch at home under the watchful eye of an older sibling, while I slip out for a short set amount of time with my friend. The meal with my friend is refreshing, but even more so is the time of mutual exhortation and prayer with my sister in Christ.

Good intentions don't accomplish anything, that's why planning a certain day every month helps a lot in actually getting a hospitality event accomplished. Before I planned for friendship, long periods of time were going by without seeing local friends face to face! It's not an intentional dropping of friends, it simply requires thought and planning.

Our family has also established a family Hospitality Night. I schedule an evening or a Sunday afternoon to invite another family over. Getting together as families is a rich time for relationships and growth as families together. The input of the fathers into the lives of the families during this time of fellowship simply cannot be measured.

Friendships are vital to the life of the Body of Christ. They warm the heart, rejoice in victories, and give empathy, understanding and support in trials. Friends are great to chat with and to have fun with but my best friend must be God and after that my husband. Nurturing the children comes next. These are the priority relationships that the Lord has given us, and these are the ones that we will have with us all of our lives. After God, husbands, and family comes the church. We are to extend hospitality to other believers, edifying each other. If our friendships are taking away from those priorities, then we have adjustments to make. Don't let other people take precedence over your husband and children.

On the flip side: If you are so alone that you have no fellowship with other Christian moms, then you need to work on finding like minded sisters in Christ and building relationships with them. We need the support of other Christian moms, especially those older moms that have gone before us.

Seek out wise Godly women and invite them over; ask them for advice in the stage of life you are in. As you grow in maturity, do the same for the younger moms coming behind you. There is a lot of support for moms on the internet, but nothing takes the place of real, live, local friendships. Look for these women in your local church and your homeschool support group. Be wise and discerning in the friends you choose.

> *Let no corrupting talk come out of your mouths, but only such as is good for building up, as fits the occasion, that it may give grace to those who hear. —Ephesians 4:29*

> *So then let us pursue what makes for peace and for mutual upbuilding. —Romans 14:19*

> *What then, brothers? When you come together, each one has a hymn, a lesson, a revelation, a tongue, or an interpretation. Let all things be done for building up. —I Corinthians 14:26*

God might have you in a season of aloneness as he did with me in the early days of my marriage. Be content with what He has given you and use it to His glory! He is the potter and we are the clay; He is shaping and molding us into His image. Jesus is your best friend, and in His time and His way, He will supply your every need.

Time to Read

Books allow us to visit with those knowledgeable on a subject that we want to know more about. They teach us and take us on travels around the world and through time.

Books can build us up, inspire us, encourage us, and be our mentors. They can also cause us to grow discontent with our husband, family, friends, home, finances, and more. We can escape our own reality with books.

It's therefore important that we focus on God-honoring books, not trash. We need to be wise with our choices and read with discernment. Even Christian literature can have wrong teachings or feed desires that are not godly. Our time as mothers is limited, and we must use that time to the benefit of the lives we serve, not to escape. Anything we use to run from the situation God has us in is an act of discontentment and not counting our trial as joy.

Constantly seeking knowledge is not always a good thing either (it hurts me to say that!). We need to take care of our work and relationships with those around us first. God wants us to come to Him with our needs, not escape through a book.

I love to read and learn new things. When my children were little, I would read a chapter and then do work, read, work, read, work. I liked to think about what I had just read while I worked. This system was useful for a long time until the workload grew larger, the homeschooling hours grew longer, and the accumulated chatter of children drowned out the voice I was reading! These days I read before sleeping and while nursing the baby. A little bit at a time, and I find that I've read quite a stack of books.

Being a mother is an awesome responsibility and an incredible experience. The blessings that come with motherhood far outweigh the trials, small and large, that come along with it. The world would have us think that we are burdened by our families and that we need to do certain things in order to retain sanity. Reject this thought. By keeping our focus on Jesus, ordering our days in peaceful ways, and building relationships with others that bless the whole family, we can find refreshment in ways that honor Him.

CHAPTER 13
Life with Littles

How Little is Little?

How little is little? That depends on your family. If you have nobody over the age of six, then your oldest children, even though in another family they would be the Littles, are the Bigs in your family. I have a friend whose oldest child is the same age as one of my children. Her child, as the oldest, is very mature and a mother hen towards her younger siblings. My same-aged child does not have the same sense of responsibility in part because of the older siblings' catering, and in part because of my failure to give chores that encourage responsibility.

"How Little is Little?" depends on how you are training your Littles. Children don't instantly become helpful when they hit a certain age; it is a result of the developmental training process that you employ at each age. Make work fun, do it with a right attitude, as unto the Lord, and as children grow, they will gradually pick up new skills and slowly become more helpful. Every six months that passes means a huge difference in the ability of a child.

A two-year-old can help unload the dishwasher with your encouraging help, help you switch laundry loads and fold clothes, and stand at the sink with you and wash dishes. It might look more like play, but they are learning through watching and doing with you. Two-year-olds cannot stay on task long or be held responsible for regular chores. Two, three, and four-year-olds are in the preparatory stage for doing regular chores. They love to help do work; they love to accomplish something; they love praise; they love to do things with you.

Enjoy this time of life with them, include them in your work, and teach them how to work. Encourage them to be helpers by saying things like, "Come help me mop," and give them a little mop rag. Then thank them for their wonderful help. Say, "See how fast it went when we worked together?" and "Daddy will be so happy to see a clean floor and know how hard you worked to make our house clean"; "Look how clean it is!"

When somebody spills something on the clean floor, teach the children to handle a spill with grace as you hand them a little wet towel to quick-mop it with a smile and not a sigh. A good attitude on the part of mom, who teaches that good attitude to her children, makes for a happy home.

Little children can learn to work much more easily if their day follows a routine. If you train them, through doing it with them, to make their bed every morning, it will be a work habit. They aren't coordinated enough to make a bed to look beautiful, but encourage them to do their best. Teach them, "If you pull the sheet tight at the top, it makes a neater line." And "When you are done washing your face, grab a paper towel and wipe down the counter." Say little phrases such as these to them every day while you do the work together, and they will learn. When these little children are big, you will hear them saying the same things to the next set of little children in your home. This is your reward for training your oldest children well. Little children can learn helpful work habits and learn to do them with excellence!

After making the bed, they should go to the bathroom, wash, and brush with you there beside them or just with your direction. They will get into the habit of doing that little chore every day. If they are accustomed to rising and sitting in front of the television, then that will become their habit. Isn't it much better for them to rise, make their bed, dress, and do personal grooming for their early morning routine? Little children can do this if we are helping them to do it.

Ease into Homeschooling

When the little children are accustomed to routine and order and taught basic chores and skills with your encouragement, when they are taught to obey their mother and father, then the next step of teaching them life skills becomes easy. It becomes easier to teach a new skill by simply adding it on to another thing you are already doing during the daily routine.

Do you have a time of day when you read to the children? Tack on a few minutes of phonics with Alphaphonics or The Victory Drill Book. While reading aloud, have the children narrate back to you a little bit at a time. Gradually increase what they narrate. Does your preschooler help set the table? Show him on paper what 5 plates plus 1 plate reads like. Do you already play outside? Get down and find a bug, and then look it up and read about it.

Learning is not only found in books and tests. Teach your children to teach themselves by providing them toys, activities, and experiences that foster curiosity, imagination, creativity, and a love for life and learning. This can be done with a baby, toddlers, and preschoolers before they ever enter "school age." These life skills can be introduced by you, right now, in how you structure their day and the things you encourage your children to do in their day. You are not passing the time babysitting; you are mothering. Do not think of the preschool years as merely entertaining them, but as years when you can teach and train them to be godly offspring.

Content Yourself with Healthy Brain Food

Life with Littles involves a fair amount of physically hard work. It can lack mental stimulation that we, as women, crave. We feel that lack and will look to fill it with something.

My oldest children were little before the days of the Internet, so I didn't have to battle getting caught up in online discussions and the like. If you are looking to online friends for encouragement, tread carefully and wisely. The women of old got in trouble going from house to house gossiping. We don't need to leave our houses to fall into the same sins. And I would suggest using a timer at the computer so you don't fall into the cyber abyss. It's a little scary how fast time flies when you are sitting in front of that screen.

For safer, better mental stimulation, I recommend reading books. Not fiction, but how-to, theology, philosophy, Bible study, and other books that provoke thought. These types of books can be read one chapter at a time and then thought about while doing physical work. How-to books can also promote creative action. Of course, you can find helpful articles on the Internet, too, but you have to watch out for the abyss which can sap your time as well as your emotional and spiritual energy.

What you put in comes out. If you sow into your mind things that promote discontent—argumentative online debates, television sitcoms or irrelevant reality shows, foolish novels, and worldly magazines—then you will reap discontent in your life. This can happen online and offline as well. Examine your heart to see if it is focused on God and serving Him or on yourself. Do not allow yourself to be discontent, but look at all things with thanksgiving and challenge yourself to overcome trials with biblical responses. Look at the long physically hard days as the blessing that they are. This is the school of sanctification. God is growing you.

Hide God's Word in Your Heart

List the good things that come about through each trial and do what you can to improve each hard thing. Improve your attitude towards it by choosing to see it as a growth opportunity. Look and see how God's Word instructs us about that particular trial, learn how to handle the situation better, and try to understand what God is teaching you through it. Look at the trial as a challenge to be overcome, and the next time that trial or one similar comes around, you will be better equipped to handle it.

As the years go by and you become stronger, things that were trials at one time become easy. The physically hard work of this stage of life is making us strong for the future. We learn to rest in God and depend on Him for the strength we need for each day. We learn to seek Him for wisdom in how to handle all the things that wear on us. We learn to pray without ceasing and make Him our best friend in the lonely days of little adult interaction.

Even as you learn to lean upon the Lord through Scripture and prayer, be sure to train your little ones to do the same. The everyday choices we make as moms affect the lives of our little children. What do you want them to have stored in their heads from these days?

"Thy word I have hid in my heart, that I might not sin against thee!" —Psalm 119:11, KJV

We can work on this daily with our little children. They are like sponges and can memorize easily. Add a time of day when you do memory work with your Littles. Do it after a meal, or make a little circle with them on the floor, and spend a few minutes reciting a verse. Another easy way to learn Scripture is through song. Place into your day a time when you listen to Scripture music. This can be when you are folding laundry together or washing dishes. Sing along with it while you work. Little children can learn hymns. Hymns are rich stories of the Christian faith that will help your children throughout their lives. Choose a time of day when you practice singing a hymn and teach them great truths of God in this easy way. Hide the Word in their hearts!

I Can't Get Anything Done!

Now, you ask, how am I to add all these things into the day when already I can't get anything done? Do you currently have a plan? If not, that's your problem. Without a plan for the day, you are aiming at nothing and hitting it every day. If you have a plan that's not working, then your plan needs to be modified. There are times in life that certain things do not fit in and must be let go for a season.

What are the most important priorities to your Christian family? These are the things that must be emphasized on your daily plan. Examine your days and see how the different things that must happen can be made more efficient, more streamlined, and better organized.

A very successful way of examining your day is by writing down every single little thing that you and the children do from the moment of rising until you fall asleep at night. It is an inconvenience to do this but it will help you become better at managing your home in the long run. What this exercise will do is expose areas of the day when you and the children are wandering aimlessly. I'm not saying that there is no place for wandering aimlessly, but let's do it in the yard on a lazy summer afternoon, not while going about the daily routine of life with Littles.

Efficiency sometimes gets a bad rap in the creative crowd, but what being efficient does, in its proper place, is allow you more time for creative endeavors. Sometimes being efficient in this stage of life means letting some things go. Paper plates, paper napkins and plastic silverware might be the answer for a season. Hiring or bartering for a cleaning service. Staying home instead of being on the go, go, go improves efficiency and contributes greatly to a healthy and happy home life. There is a place for going out and experiencing new things with the children but try to make it the exception to the at-home life and a small part of the daily and weekly routine.

Is the tyranny of the urgent ruining your days? Try to identify what the tyrant is so that you can manage it better. Sometimes it is an especially needy child. What can you do to meet this child's needs better? The needs for sleep and food are typical culprits for irritable Littles. Or does this child need to learn respect and obedience? Identify the need and address it. Sometimes the tyrant is a time of day. Does your lunch need to be earlier? Are you waiting too long before having nap time? Do you need a snack time scheduled? Is there a part of the house (bedrooms, playroom, bathroom, kitchen) that is a problem? Spend a day or two studying the problem and thinking about what would make it more pleasing to your home life. Interruptions are part of life, but you must be diligent so that the interruptions do not take over and become the tyrant.

Less is More

Less is more with Littles. They do not need every toy under the sun. What will be most helpful to them—and you—are open-ended imaginative toys and activities. Aim for classic toys that will stand up to use and be passed down through all of your children. These teach their brains to grow and think. Minimize the sheer amount by de-cluttering the toys that don't get played with, the flashy, noisy toys that give you a headache (mom doesn't need that!), and of course all toys with missing or broken pieces.

Place some in storage and rotate them by week, month, or season to further pare down the volume. Keep the remaining toys in a way that the children know where they are kept and can put them away with ease when told to. Teach them, "Everything has a place and everything in its place." You will need to help them put away their toys to train them how to do it and to train them in work. They were born with a sin nature just like me and you, and as parents we need to help them learn self-discipline and a work ethic. It starts with teaching the littlest ones to put away their toys. What you will see happen with less toys, but perhaps higher quality toys, is that they will play longer and with more imagination as their brain grows and stretches. Instead of a toy being interesting for ten minutes and laid aside, they will often play with it for hours or days in untold ways.

Toys for little ones should be kept near to where you are working. Then you can keep on top of mishandling and disagreements. A playroom that is too far away from the kitchen or main part of the house will leave the children unsupervised. Toys in bedrooms contribute to disastrous bedrooms. If you keep the bedroom chores to the minimum of making the bed and clothing storage, cleaning maintenance will be far easier on you and the children.

Before lunch and nap time, hold a ten-minute-tidy session. Sing a silly song about picking up toys and make it fun and quick. Once again, have a ten-minute-tidy time before Dad comes home so that he doesn't walk into a mess. Help out his peace of mind by doing the quick-pick-up. If the toys come out again before bedtime, have another pick-up before the bedtime routine. Pick-up times should be able to happen in ten minutes or less. If it takes longer than that, then it's time to have another de-clutter session or box up more for the toy rotation. If a child has an especially interesting toy project that he doesn't want disturbed, then be kind and respectful, and store it out of the way or pick-up everything but that spot where his project is.

CHAPTER 14
Baby Balance

After nine babies, I think I've done every schedule, non-schedule, and modified version. Our ninth baby was born at 26 weeks gestation age, and when he came home from the NICU, my singular goal was to get as much nutrition and antibodies in his body as I could. I let him nurse whenever he was interested and for as long as he wanted to eat. This was typically every three hours except for a session in the early morning when he ate every 30 minutes for about two hours. The rest of the day he slept in our arms. I wanted him to sleep because babies grow when they sleep. If it was in my arms, so be it.

While in NICU, I read all the literature on premature babies I could get my hands on, and it was demonstrated in study after study that babies who are held skin to skin are more physiologically stable and grow better. In the NICU, I held him as much as I possibly could. When we came home, he slept with me and my body was in tune with him. When he stirred, I turned to nurse him. During the day we held him all day long, and he slept in our arms. Our baby grew and was healthy, and that's what was most important.

It reminded me of the days of my first baby. With our first I nursed "on demand" as I was taught at the hospital and through the literature of the La Leche League. When you have one baby and are home alone, you have no extra arms to hold the baby or other little children to entertain the baby! It is a unique situation that normally only happens once in a lifetime. Our first baby was, in retrospect, a very easy baby. He quickly settled down into a routine of his own. He took naps without sleep props. He weaned himself at 14 months.

The second baby was the same, although he was a big hungry boy. He did not settle into a routine as predictable as the first baby. He did take two naps a day and slept well at night but also preferred to eat every two or three hours. As an older baby he was too busy playing all day to eat and did his nursing during the night. When he finally started eating food, he quickly dropped nursing which happened at 14 months.

We did the early 90's version of a popular parent-directed feeding method with the next three babies. I had plenty of milk for these babies until nine months, and then I had to supplement and eventually switched them to the bottle. I was a slow learner. With our sixth, seventh, and eighth babies, I nursed on demand for the first several weeks, never tried to cut out any nighttime feedings, and never went to a four-hour schedule. Instead of putting them off in the late afternoon and evening, I fed them every two hours. These three babies nursed exclusively for the first year and I never had a problem with my milk supply. In the second year, I nursed before meals and offered them food until they weaned themselves which was 18 months with Baby #6, 26 months with Baby #7, and 24 months with Baby #8. All of these babies took a late afternoon nap until 6-9 months, a morning nap until about 15 months, and an afternoon nap for years. They all slept about 12 hours at night. Baby #9, whose Corrected Age is six months as I write this, eats every three hours, has a morning nap, afternoon nap, and late afternoon nap. In the late afternoon and evening, I feed him every two hours or however he cues.

The biggest value in the parent-directed method is the sleep, eat, wake cycle. Learning to see the cues for being tired, which happen approximately one and half hours after waking from the last nap, is a benefit for mom and baby. Then the baby takes an hour and half nap, which I found that they easily do, which allows Mom to attend to the things she can't do while the baby is awake. After a nap, the baby is well-rested, hungry, and will have a good nursing session. It is good to have days when you know what to expect, and a well-rested baby is a happy baby.

When the baby is awake, there is plenty of time for holding and playing with them. If you use the same routine for laying a tired baby down to sleep by himself from day one, he will learn to go to sleep by himself. It is key to lay him down before he is overtired. Watch the clock for that hour-and-a-half mark and for cues such as rubbing the head, ear, eyes, and tired eyes along with grumpy vocalization. Very early in life establish a go-to-sleep routine (song, prayer, story, etc), it becomes a signal to the baby for sleep. Swaddle a new baby for their comfort and sleep but allow access to hands if they want it. Some babies suck on their hands to go to sleep; some do not care.

If a baby wakes in his nap, it is probably a burp. Pick him up quietly, pat his back until he burps, lay him back down, and he will normally go back to sleep. When the baby wakes up after his hour and half nap, go to him immediately with a happy face, change his diaper and, feed him. Then he can play. In the late afternoon, the nap will be shorter. A schedule is a tool for you and your baby. Do not be a slave to the schedule or to the baby. This is parenting with grace.

Listening to your baby's communication signals takes a bit of practice, but if you watch and listen you will learn them. This learning process with each baby is one of the joys and challenges of mothering! Baby's "talk" with their eyes, their facial expressions, their hand and arm movements, along with vocalizations. Babies will grunt, squirm, search for you, suck on their hands and root when they are hungry. Do not put off a tiny tummy that digests breast milk quickly—it will disturb their health and development.

Christian mothers must pray for wisdom and be discerning about the cries of their baby. There is a cry that babies will make in a nap that we do not need to run to, and that is the little cry they make when they are disturbed and will go back to sleep. Matthew does this almost exactly 45 minutes into his nap. If this cry is immediately run to and the baby is further awakened, then he will miss out on sleep. Babies grow when they sleep. Quietly check on the baby to see how awake he is. If he looks uncomfortable, try to ascertain why. Often the wakening is a burp. Quietly put him up to your shoulder, burp him gently, and lay him back down. He will often sleep another half an hour or more.

If your baby consistently wakes up while sleeping—and it's not because he's hungry—raise one end of his bed to aid in digestion. Reflux hurts! Tummy sleeping aids digestion and if you are concerned about SIDS, there is a monitor available that is a mat under the mattress and will sound an alarm if there is no movement for 20 seconds. Letting a baby cry is potentially ignoring hunger, reflux, apnea, teething pain, and the unknown. It also disturbs the development of trust and attachment. Pray for wisdom in understanding the needs of each baby and reading their cues.

This is a walk of grace with each child. When we miss their communication signals we get an unhappy baby. In my experience of both having babies in my room and not (#s 3 and 4 were in the nursery with a monitor), it is easier to get to know your baby's cues when the baby is nearby.

Be the humble God-centered family. As Christians we must not polarize each other with parenting practices. There is a right way, and that is God's way. God is just and merciful; He convicts sin and extends grace. If I am convinced my way is God's way, then I need to be willing to back my view with all of God's Word, correctly interpreted. Everyone comes to the parenting philosophy discussion with the accumulated baggage of our own childhoods, encounters we have had with people and churches, books we have read, classes we have taken, teaching we've had from the medical establishment, and more. We need to be thinking people and test everything we experience and encounter against the Scriptures. We can't take a scissors to the Scripture either! We aren't perfect people and we need to be humble in that regard with each other. Discussing parenting with Christian friends and mentors is a valid way to hold each other accountable to God's Word.

Mother's Milk

Studies show, and it is my personal experience, that mom's milk supply is lower in the late afternoon. If your baby is hungry, then feed him; don't put him off if you can help it. You will know when he is hungry if he is fussy and is sucking on his fist. Learn to read your particular baby. If he is still hungry, then you need to learn how to increase your milk production. If he has trouble nursing, talk to a lactation consultant. Newborn babies need to eat frequently.

Breast milk is valuable in a myriad of ways. It is the perfect food. Breast milk is full of nutrients and antibodies to everything in the mother and baby's environment. If at all possible do what you can to make your milk nutritious by eating good food and taking supplements. I learned in the NICU that different moms have different fat concentrations in their milk. Some nursing mothers need to feed their babies more frequently—that is how their particular breasts work. Keep your production as high as you can so that you will have enough milk for as long as you can. Your baby still needs all the complex nutrients and immunological factors in breast milk as he grows older and into his toddler years.

Here are factors that affect milk supply and ways to increase it that I learned while pumping for Matthew in the NICU:

- Herbal teas such as More Milk Plus and Mother's Milk.

- Fenugreek-two capsules three times a day.

- Alfalfa tablets or liquid.

- Brewer's Yeast tablets.

- Oats and/or rice in the diet.

- A tall glass of water or herbal tea each time you sit down with the baby.

- Nutrients that you might be low on include protein, zinc, essential fatty acids (primrose oil, flax oil, cod liver oil, borage oil, walnut oil).

- Nurse/pump every two hours; nurse and then pump.

- "Power Pumping"—pump for ten minutes, rest for ten minutes, on and off for one hour, once a day.

- Pharmaceuticals used to increase milk supply are Reglan and Domperidone

- Going longer than three hours between nursings or pumping is detrimental to milk production—even affecting how much milk you will produce in the future for an older baby.

- Babies may need to eat more frequently in the very early morning hours and again late in the afternoon.

CHAPTER 15
The Family Dynamic

God settles the solitary in a home. —Psalm 68:6

Many moms of today grew up with busy childhoods of simply busywork. We got up, rode the bus, went to school, rode the bus, did homework, ate supper, watched TV, went to bed, and did the same routine every day for years and years. Some of us led even more busy lives by being involved in every activity possible that took us away from home every evening and weekends—sports, dance, clubs, youth group, drama, etc. Some of us were blessed enough to have chores before and/or after school and on Saturdays. Some of us had moms who did all the work while we were gone. If the family is not at home, the house doesn't get messy and honestly, the cleaning just doesn't take that long.

We tend to raise our children as we were raised and clean like our mothers cleaned; throw several more children and homeschooling into the mix, and the old system of mom doing all the housework breaks the system and breaks the mom. Are you burned out with school or housework? If so, don't throw in the towel! You can do this! Your family is a dynamic group of people with different strengths and weaknesses. You need to put all these people on the same team—the family team.

Planning

First you're going to need to make a plan to identify what is working and what is not in your home. Think through each aspect of your home life and schedule. If you need to, take a sample of three to four days, writing down what each member of the family is doing each hour during the day. Now take this list to your husband. Remember, he is the head of the family, and God has given him unique wisdom and insight. He needs to lead, and you need his help, maybe more than either of you realize.

The Family Meeting

Next, gather the whole family. If your husband is interested in leading this family meeting, fantastic! If he would prefer to delegate that duty to you, be sure to communicate to the family that you are his ambassador, his vice-regent. Then, have your children help you make a list, perhaps on a white board or a large piece of paper, of all the responsibilities and duties necessary for taking care of the needs of the family. Some of these would include laundry, ironing, cooking, dishes, mopping, cleaning bathrooms, and so on. Making a pie chart or a graph or a similar visual aid to show the children that if everyone in the family takes some of the responsibility, that everyone has a lighter load than one person would have trying to do the whole thing. You can even have a test run.

Pick a section of the house and divide up the cleaning. Set the timer for five minutes. Have four people work for five minutes (one dusts, one sweeps or vacuums, one puts away odd items, and one wipes surfaces). When the timer goes off, everyone will stop and marvel at what was accomplished in five minutes by all four people instead of one person spending twenty minutes by themselves! When the children see how this works practically, their heads will be brimming with ideas!

Next, have ready a list of all the things that need done in each room of the house: Daily, Weekly, and Monthly. Have each room's list on its own laminated paper or sheet in a protected sleeve. For starters, you want the lists fairly simple, so that the tasks don't seem overwhelming. Talk through the lists with the family so they understand what is expected. Let everyone know that each person needs to carry their own weight, and then ask for volunteers. When the volunteers are exhausted, you will need to cheerfully assign the rest of the duties.

Babies and toddlers of course cannot clean by themselves, but they can learn by watching. Assign them to a buddy who can include the little ones in his work and have them do little but important things like pick up the trash. Preschoolers can work very hard when supervised by cheerful older siblings. If the preschoolers are the oldest children in the house, then it is best that you bring your preschoolers along with you in whatever you are doing. Show them what to do, and let them do the work with you. You are training these children so that they can train the next set of little children when they are the big ones. It will take you longer to do the work, but it will pay big dividends down the road.

When you go into each room, show the children the paper that has listed the things that need to be done. Assign each item to the smallest person capable of doing each item. Teach this method to your big children that are a mini-team with little children. It might be easier for you or the big kids to do the work, but if you keep it up, the younger set will grow up being slackers expecting everyone to do things for them. You don't want that!

It probably won't all sink in to them until you are actually coaching them through the work. The first few days and weeks will be challenging. Praise and reward children as you go. Challenge and motivate those who are struggling. Remember: This is a long-term investment!

Working along side any child of any age, encouraging them and teaching them, is a wonderful way to get to know a child better, and it greatly encourages them to work harder and more diligently. They get a better picture of why they are doing what they are doing. Working along side a loved one is fun, enjoyable, encouraging, and doesn't seem like work at all. When work is done alone, it can be lonely and dull. Of course a lot of times work does need to be done alone and this is when they need to be taught to enjoy work for work's sake, to do it for the family, to do it heartily as unto the Lord, to sing or whistle while they work, and to work quickly and efficiently in order to get it done. You can teach these things to them when you are working side-by-side. Start this when the children are little, and they will teach it to the next set of little children.

Just Do It

"Just do it!"—I know the phrase hardly means anything anymore but really, that is what a lot of work boils down to. It's another thing that we need to teach our children, gently of course.

Try not to yell, "Just do it!" Teach them that it's an attitude. It's determination. Demonstrate it for them. No pity parties allowed. Set a good example. When you sigh while washing dishes, they will learn to do it also. Sometimes it takes great effort: You have to force yourself to defrost the deep freeze or gather the supplies to paint. Then once you're actually doing it, it flows and goes forward, and soon you're done and you realize that getting up the momentum to do it was far greater than the effort to do the task!

If You Don't Work, You Don't Eat

Teach the children that the Bible says, "If you don't work, you don't eat" (2 Thessalonians 3:10). Every member of the family needs to know that they are needed and valued. If one person does not do their part, either the family fails to function as well, or someone else has to double up. There are many natural circumstances which will allow you to demonstrate this. Use these circumstances with humor, and the whole family can get the point without one member feeling humiliated or embarrassed.

Flexibility

There are days when things just don't go according to plan. Sickness, weather, a late night, and unexpected needs are some of the things which call for an extra measure of flexibility. When this happens, just adjust! Change your plan, or take a break. Gather everyone together, offer some encouraging words, pray, take a nap, get a drink or a snack, or read a story. Take the time needed to get everyone back on track, and then get back on track!

Sometimes one person's area needs to be cleaned fast, such as when you see unexpected company driving down the lane. Then everybody needs to pitch in together to do a quick tidy of the public area of the house, starting with the view from the front door. This is something to practice for so when it happens in reality, everybody knows what to do and how to do it fast. Whining, "But it's not my job" is unacceptable at anytime because everybody should help each other, but when doing a Quick Tidy, it's especially unacceptable. You don't have time when company is walking up to the house to go discipline the whiner, so prepare ahead of time with practice runs so that there is no whiner. A helpful saying we have around our house is "We are a family, we love each other, we take care of each other, and we help each other."

CHAPTER 16
Your Own Personal Spa

Wherefore I perceive that there is nothing better, than that a man should rejoice in his own works; for that is his portion. —Ecclesiastes 3:22, KJV

I hesitate using this language a little bit, because I want to be careful not to borrow from the world or create an appetite for something which is often used to indulge selfishness and personal gratification. And yet, the Scripture is full of images of a job well done resulting in glorious celebrations! So, with that caveat, I want to exhort you to take dominion over an oft-neglected area of your home and then rejoice and celebrate it's dominion! If you are like me, you probably leave your bathroom first thing in the morning and don't return until you are ready to fall into bed at night! Maybe your master bedroom has even become the storage area for all those things you have not had time to put away. But this is the sanctuary for you and your husband! This is your marital retreat where you are restored, refreshed, and re-energized to serve your family again! So, let's get going and turn the storage room into a personal, restorative spa.

How to Clean a Bathroom Super-Fast!

First, take a big drink of water and maybe even a snack for energy—something healthy like a banana or an apple. This is also an exercise workout, by the way.

Next, grab your kitchen timer. We're going to do a series of 5-minute jobs.

While you're getting the timer, grab the dish soap and a rag. Next, get your window cleaner and a couple of paper towels, the toilet bowl cleaner, and the broom and dust pan. Grab one of your children to help carry the load. Ready, set, go! Fast as you can we're going to get this ugly task over with and never let it get this bad again!

1. First, fill the bathroom sink with hot water and squirt in your soap.

2. Squirt the toilet bowl with the cleaner, but don't swish it yet; let it soak.

3. Toss the dry rag up into corners of the bathroom to catch any cobwebs.

4. Pick up all the dirty laundry, the bath rugs, pull off the curtains if they're dirty and take it all to your laundry room. While you're there, throw the curtains in the washing machine.

5. Collect the trash, including any empty shampoo containers in your shower.

6. Sweep the floor and empty that into the trash, and then haul it out.

7. The five minutes should be up, and you might be panting with exertion. Open the window and take a big breath of fresh air.

8. Set the timer again for 5 minutes. This is the second set.

9. Put away all the things that you have sitting around. And say to yourself 5 times, "I will put things where they belong not leave them out to make a mess." (Next time you catch your children leaving something lying around, say it to them too.)

10. Take your wet rag and wipe the counters and any other level surfaces that have been collecting that sticky bathroom dust.

11. The third 5-minute set will help the light shine in and around your bathroom.

12. Wet the rag and wipe around the windowsill, the casing, and the window, if it's really dirty.

13. Grab your window cleaner and wipe the window and mirrors.

14. That was easy wasn't it? And doesn't it look brighter?

15. Set the timer again for 5 minutes.

16. Does your sink water need changing? If so, do it.

17. Rinse out your rag well and give it a good wringing. You're going to spend this set dusting. Yes, you are going to use a wet rag to dust. That bathroom grime can be sticky, and it needs some help to get it off sometimes.

18. Wipe off all of your nick-knacks and anything hanging on the walls. Then move down and wipe the cabinets and the floorboards.

19. This is the 5th 5-minute set. Can you believe you let the bathroom get this bad? Yuck! Never again! This 5-minute workout is for the shower and tub. You do not need a special cleaner.

20. What's on your walls? Soap. Get it wet and give it some elbow grease.

21. If your water softener is out of salt then, yes, you will need something strong. It might take you an extra 5 minutes and some deep breathing with your head out the window when you're done.

22. 5 minutes for the sink, toilet, and floor and then you're done!

23. The sink should be pretty clean by now, just wipe the faucets and the bowl so that no toothpaste is left glued on.

24. Next is the toilet. Swish it and flush. Then wipe it starting at the top and go to the bottom. When you get to the bottom, keep on wiping, moving to the floor.

25. Wipe the floor all around the toilet working your way backwards out the door.

You have just had a 30-minute workout. There is no need to exercise today! Do some stretching and thinking now. How could this job be easier?

For starters, when things are not very dirty, they are easy to clean. It takes more time to clean up an ugly job than it does to maintain. Now I know your time is valuable to you. You would probably rather get your exercise some other way than cleaning the bathroom, wouldn't you? And walking into your master bath all clean and pretty would be like having your own personal spa, wouldn't it? Start thinking of the master bath as if it were a spa made just for you.

To maintain it, do a cleaning job every time you go into your bathroom. Make it a lifelong habit.

Here are a couple more.

Every time you wash your hands, wipe down the sink and counter. Keep a towel for this purpose under the sink. When you take a shower, do a quick wipe of the shower walls. It's an easy thing; the hard part is starting the habit. To help you with the thinking process of starting the new habit of keeping your bathroom clean, write down every task that we just did. Post this list on your mirror and every time you are in the bathroom, do one task. Pretty soon, you won't have to look at the list on the mirror; you'll just automatically be doing the work.

All of the things I had you grab and carry to your bathroom? Put those in a bucket under the sink. Put a broom and dustpan in your closet. One set of cleaning tools for each bathroom. If the tools are accessible, you will be more liable to use them!

Creating the Spa Atmosphere

Take an honest look at your spa. You're going to be spending time in there every day anyway, so make it a place where you will be able to unwind from the day. There is something about sitting in warm water that causes your muscles to relax. When the house is quiet and we are relaxed, we can contemplate, dream, remember, and just be.

How can you make this room be that place you go to at the end of the day to unwind? How can you make this room more beautiful? What is your favorite color? What color would you like to be surrounded by while taking a leisurely bubble bath? Think about bathrooms you've seen and appreciated and ask, "Can I do something similar here?" Make a list and a plan to make your bathroom more personal and spa-like. It can be as simple as a bud vase and some new bath soap. Do you have a feminine night gown to wear after you've lathered your skin with lotion? Toss out the T-shirts and boxers.

A bath sounds like a luxury you think you can't manage in this stage of life, doesn't it? You're wrong. You can do it every night. Let me tell you how. First, tuck your children in bed, feed the baby and put him to bed.

- Start the tub.

- Straighten the bathroom, do a quick cleaning job, light the candles.

- Lay out your night clothes and your clothes for tomorrow.

- Get a glass of water, cup of tea or whatever suits you fancy to sip while you soak.

- Wash and soak until the water starts to cool and get out before you get cold (15 minutes or so).

- Drain the water; hair, teeth, contacts, lotion, put on a nighty.

- Rinse the tub, straighten the bathroom.

- Go to bed.

Do you see that it doesn't take much longer to add a bath to your bedtime routine? I promise that you will go to bed much more relaxed than when you don't bathe, that you will fall asleep more quickly, and sleep better.

If you're a morning shower person, then keep on with that if you want. The nighttime bath is about more than getting clean. Its purpose is to relax and rejuvenate.

Now you will never be embarrassed about your master bathroom again. It is a retreat that you will want to go spend time in. During the day when you get tired or frustrated, you will remember that tonight you will return to your spa and enjoy a long soak in your tub, surrounded by candles. A fresh and fluffy towel is waiting for you as well as some lotion to rub into your tired feet.

You no longer have a grungy mess—you have a spa. Enjoy!

> *Behold, you are beautiful, my love, behold, you are beautiful! Your eyes are doves behind your veil. Your hair is like a flock of goats leaping down the slopes of Gilead.*
> *—Song of Solomon 4:1*

CHAPTER 17
Dress for Success

[H]er clothing is fine linen and purple. —Proverbs 31:22

First, Get Dressed

Every mom has had them—those days when you don't get dressed until the baby goes down for his morning nap. Or a day when one mess or mini-crisis after another results in you realizing that it is two o'clock and you haven't brushed your teeth yet.

Don't cry! No pity parties allowed. Put everybody in a safe place, go back to your bedroom, and start the day over. Get dressed, wash your face, brush your teeth, brush your hair, make yourself look presentable. Look in the mirror and smile, and laugh a little at yourself—there are worse things! Pray for wisdom, strength, and courage.

Gather your children, smile at them, and read a story. Put on some cheerful music, then sit them at the table to color, and put supper together. Help the children put the coloring projects away, and straighten the house together.

Tonight, take a bath and go to bed early, but before you go to bed, lay out your clothes for the next day. Get dressed as soon as your feet hit the floor in the morning. You'll have a better day!

What Not to Wear

Moms bend over a lot to help their little children zip a jacket, pick up a pacifier, whisper instructions in a small ear, and do a hundred other things. There are a few clothing items that just won't work with those kind of situations. Wide neck blouses are out for you. Everything stays in place just fine until a squirmy baby starts to climb up your neck. Got the picture? And midline shirts creep up when you bend over, exposing your backside and climb up when you redo your pony tail. Snap up shirts, that's right: the children will unsnap. And the same with zipper sweaters. Are you getting the idea? Here's a good rule of thumb: Always wear camisoles!

Not all skirts are created equal. Choose longer skirts while shopping. When you are wearing a loose swishy skirt that might have been long enough without a breeze, the wind will certainly blow it up while you are holding your little ones' hands, and God didn't give us a hold-the-skirt-down hand. Wrap around skirts fall open when you sit down, as do skirts with a walking slit up the front. This is not a huge problem if your hands are free to deftly pull yourself together, but when you are also handling a couple of little children, you can easily make a spectacle of yourself. It's just best to leave those skirts on the no-list, or at least the not-while-I'm-shopping list.

Heels can be dangerous to wear while carrying babies, are not good for your feet or back, and really what is the practical purpose of them? Save yourself some grief and get sensible shoes. Check the tread of the shoes you buy—slick- bottomed shoes are . . . slick. You will fall on your bum and drop your baby. There are plenty of stylish shoes that will not damage your body or cause you to accidentally hurt your children.

What to Wear

When you are a wife and mother, you should dress like a wife and mother, not a teenager. When I was a young mom, I wore whatever was comfortable or whatever looked cute on the mannequin. The mannequin or catalog model was not shown bending over retrieving a pacifier. When you are trying clothes on, move around and make sure that you can maneuver in different positions and still be modest. It is wise to ask your husband, "Does this look 'hot' or 'beautiful'?" "Hot" is for your husband alone.

Scriptures to consider when choosing your clothing for your wardrobe: 1 Peter 3:3-6, Isaiah 47, Proverbs 5:15-23, Song of Solomon 4, Deuteronomy 22:5, 1 Peter 3:4, 1 Corinthians 6:12-20, Galatians 5:13, 1 Timothy 2:9-15.

Mom-smart clothes should be easily cleaned. The blouse that has to be dry-cleaned is better suited for a night out with your husband than for Sunday. It seems that Sunday, when you want to look your best, is the day that you get spit up on, snot rubbed on your shoulder, and the baby has the biggest blow-out diaper of the week. Clothing that does not let your skin breath is a poor choice, for motherhood is often hard, sweaty work. Long sleeves get in the way and wet while you bathe children, wash dishes, and wipe counters. Choose short or ¾ length. An apron is your best friend in the kitchen. They are an easy thing to sew, and you can routinely find home dec fabrics on sale to make them inexpensively.

Clothes to wear while nursing can be a trick to find. Two-piece outfits are appropriate; you can pull the top up and if it's loose, still have your mid-section covered. Fitted shirts tend to climb up. Button downs work well and can be more modest with a camisole. Cut lengthwise nursing slits in the camisole so that you don't need to pull it up. Layers help with modesty but are of course hot in the summer. Jumpers work but can be awkward, depending on the style.

Nursing covers are so handy. Numerous styles can be found online or you can make your own. Choose lightweight fabric for the summer and warm flannel for the winter. When the baby starts to wave his hands around and be grabby, tuck the bottom of the cover between his head and your arm to keep his arm inside.

I am of the camp that thinks that a baby should be able to matter-of-factly eat anywhere. Our over-sexed society is sick and wrong to be offended at a modestly nursing mom but not at immodest cleavage exposure which has become so commonplace. Breasts were made to feed babies the perfect food. Nursing babies are a fact of life. It is sad that people have not grown up around and are not accustomed to babies or specifically breast-fed babies. Historically speaking, the last fifty years are not normal.

That said, we need to be discreet and modest as mothers when we are obviously causing someone to be uncomfortable. You can choose a part of the room that is not front and center, you can use a nursing cover, and your clothing choices should enable you to show as little as possible. I have found that it is most difficult to nurse newborns modestly. It is easiest on many levels and best for the new baby to simply stay home as much as possible.

Breast pads are essential to avoid milk spots on your clothes. Keep a hefty supply on hand. Washable pads are a good investment. My favorite kind are a special soft wool.

Avoiding Frump

We all detest the idea of being frumpy. Clothing style is a very personal choice. It is an expression of our unique personalities—casual, sophisticated, artsy, sporty, scholarly, etc. Some love the details of trims and appliqués; some prefer belts, bags, and shoes. Frumpy happens to moms because their body size goes up and down with pregnancy and nursing without their clothing sizes being updated accordingly.

At any given time, we have four sizes of clothes in our closet and know better than to purge them because we are going to wear one of those sizes sometime in the next year. When we have four different sizes of clothing in our closet we inadvertently wear the wrong size with another piece that may or may not be the wrong size, producing a sloppy look. Add to that the fact that an item doesn't look quite as good as it did before being stretched out with pregnancy, a small spit up stain on the shoulder, and an old jelly stain on the sleeve.

Don't cry! We can plan for this. It starts with being honest about our bodies. Yes, your size goes up and down with pregnancy, postpartum, nursing to nine months, nursing beyond nine months, nursing the toddler, nursing the toddler and being pregnant.

Fact: Our bodies change and they are not the bodies of models.

Fact: We all have our personal clothing style.

Fact: Our life at home is hard on clothes.

Dresses are more forgiving in sizes going up and down and still looking good. Ill-fitting knit clothes are bad news and tend to cling to pregnancy weight. Tunic type shirts and peasant blouses hide the mommy tummy and let it grow when you are pregnant, prolonging the need to get out the maternity shirts. Yes, ill-mannered people will assume or ask you if you are pregnant, but after having a baby every other year, don't they do that anyway? Let them be and carry on. Just be sure your blouse is attractive and fits your shoulders.

Small print causes large people to look larger. Dark colors make a person look smaller. Long skirts and dresses make a person look taller and thinner. Only the very thin can wear gathered waists, as they make the mid-section look bulky. To help avoid the problem of wearing the wrong size, keep the things that do not fit you put away or organized in your closet so that they are not within your easy reach.

If you are unsure of what style of clothes express yourself the best, then order a selection of catalogs and/or window shop brand stores at an outlet mall. Take note of brand names, and pick one that suits your unique taste. We're all different, so what you like, your best friend might not. You will probably find your tastes change over time, or your favorite store might change their style away from what you appreciated. By choosing a store or brand name to shop from, you will find your closet getting a unified look where items coordinate and work together in a pleasing manner.

Buy good quality fabrics with strong seams so that they stand the test of time. When buying knit shirts, get ones with seams on the sides to avoid twisting. When working at home, wear clothes that are easy to clean and hide stains. Whites are a mistake unless it's your under layer. You will tend to not work if you are wearing clothes you are afraid of staining. Prints hide stains. Denim of course is heavy duty but often not feminine. Work out clothes are comfortable but are typically not made to stand up to the test of time and look bad quickly. They are also not feminine. Save them for your workouts. Sweaters are warm but sometimes the bulk can be confining. Cardigans open easily and are thus handy for nursing; ¾ sleeve lightweight cardigans are my personal favorite. Wool is warm but needs special care. Special care typically doesn't get special care as the number of children climbs higher. Matching shoe and handbag color gives a "together" look to your outfit.

We live in a society that promotes androgyny. Stand up for the way God made you as a woman by choosing feminine clothes.

Good posture makes anything look better, so walk tall, shoulders up, back, and down. And smile from the eyes. Spread God's love to all you meet.

Jennie Chancey's comment on feminine dress says it well: "Our foremothers settled this land, built houses, planted gardens and tended animals in long skirts and beautiful dresses. Even their aprons were wonderful to behold! Surely in our day of microwaves, washing machines and vacuum cleaners, we can do our chores with as much feminine flair as they. Personally, I feel it is uplifting to the spirit to go through each day in womanly attire. Let's dignify our work by dressing appropriately and beautifully for it!"

Closet Organization

Your closet probably contains the following categories of items: winter, summer, everyday clothes, going-out clothes, workout clothes, Sunday clothes, maternity clothes, postpartum clothes, nursing baby clothes, losing the baby weight clothes, lost the nursing bosom clothes, early pregnancy clothes which might be the same as the postpartum clothes. Whew!

The task of organizing this mess involves five steps:

1. Collect all the clothes in season that truly fit you right now. Put the things you hate and never wear into the give-away box. Put the rest in the main part of your closet.

2. If Step 1 did not involve maternity clothes, collect them and put them into a box. Do not keep the maternity clothes you never wear, put them into the give-away box.

3. Sort the rest of the clothes by size and put them in boxes, one box for each size.

4. Sort through the socks, underwear, and nightclothes, discarding what you never wear.

5. Each time the season changes or your size goes up or down, do this task again keeping only what truly fits you in your closet.

Planning What to Wear

A large part of this book is about planning, organizing, and making your life more efficient so that you can spend more time loving your family and doing things that bless those around you. I am going to propose an idea that the free spirits among you might not appreciate. That's OK; you don't have to do it, and the world will still go around. Some of you will really appreciate it and find it an effective tool for making your days go better. I'm sure that there will be people in the middle who will take this task part way but not fully, and that's OK too. We are unique and have different personalities and styles. This task will help you with your week's work and make your mornings flow better. You will sleep better knowing that you have a plan for the first part of the morning that will make your day go more smoothly! Yes, you can do this task and it will bring peace not only to your mornings, but to your Laundry Day. And not only your Laundry Day but also your closet. Organized clothes make for more orderly laundry days and a thinned down closet. Your husband will look at you and say, "Excellent!"

Here's what I suggest that you do: Plan each day's clothes with the day of the week. An outfit for Laundry Day, Kitchen Day, Town Day, Office Day, Cleaning Day, Gardening Day, and The Lord's Day.

If you think about it, you might already have clothes that you wear for cleaning or when you leave the house. I am asking you to take it a step further and choose an outfit for each day of the week. If you are the kind of person who really enjoys clothes, or a free spirit, then you might want to choose two or three outfits for each day.

Match the clothes for the day's work. For Cleaning Day choose clothes that will work well for cleaning; short sleeves, clothes that are comfortable to move in, clothes that won't show dirt, etc. For Kitchen Day choose short sleeves again and an outfit that goes well with your favorite heavy-duty apron. For Office Day, choose clothes that make you feel business-like, something that will put you in the frame of mind for taking care of expenses, numbers, pencil pushing, phone calling, etc. Think about your week, look at your clothes, and organize them by what you do each day of the week. Make them complete with accessories and an idea of what shoes to wear with each if you have to leave the house.

This task should have pruned out more of your clothes to put in the give-away box. Do you see that now you know what you are wearing each morning when you get up? You will avoid the frumpy look by having given thought and planning to your clothes. Be mentally prepared for the work of the day by knowing what you will wear.

> *Strength and dignity are her clothing, and she laughs at the time to come. —Proverbs 31:25*

Part Two

CHAPTER 18
Your Home Management Book

Do the Next Thing

> *Whatever you do, work heartily, as for the Lord and not for men, knowing that from the Lord you will receive the inheritance as your reward. You are serving the Lord Christ. —Colossians 3:23-24*

The purpose of creating a Home Management Book is to help you manage your new life of habits. When you don't know what to do next, check your Home Management Book; it will tell you. It is for those days when you are learning new habits; for the day after a sleepless night; for your husband and children when you are unavailable. It is the protocol for how your house functions.

Each component of the days listed here is detailed in further chapters. This chapter is a broad overview of the system.

The Tools and How to Use Them

You will need the following items:

- A three-ring-binder.

- 8 ½"x 11" paper.

- Page protectors.

- Sticky notes.

- A pencil.

If you want to build this with a day planner that you're already using or with an unused planner sitting on your shelf, that is great! However, I truly think it is best to make your own. You can be far more creative and better able to personalize it for your life, your family, and your home.

If your current life is crazy-busy and you are overwhelmed, do not worry about working on this book, except on your Office Day (See Chapter 30). Put the components of your home management book together over time. Start using what you have built right away, but put it together slowly and deliberately. When we move carefully and methodically, one-step at a time, our new habits become stronger parts of our lives.

Once you get this in motion, you can print your papers out from the computer or just do some writing on the paper at first and then organize it better later. You need page protectors because you need to protect the pages from PB-J-fingered children. You will use the sticky notes on the pages for adjustments on the fly. Later, you can pull out the pages with sticky note adjustments and redo the pages.

Take seven sheets of paper and, at the top of each, put the name of the days of the week. We are going to set up our household management like our grandmothers before us did. Monday is Laundry Day, etc.

There is beauty in order and rhythm. When we know what to do when, and our families know what to do when, it brings security, peace, and comfort. A secure and happy family is true beauty. If the order of days does not suit your family's life, then arrange your days according to your unique family situation.

Why set up days of the week? Can't I just see the work and do it? Sure! However, there are many overwhelming days when we don't know where to start. We tend to get distracted, starting one task, and halfway through, moving to another and then another. When the day ends, we look around and see several things started and not finished.

What a Home Management Book does is build efficiency into the work. Not to the exclusion of flexibility and loving people, but the more efficient home management systems are, the more smoothly life flows.

You know those embroidered towels that you see at estate sales and in antique stores? Our grandmothers and the foremothers before them knew the value of ordering their work, and though they had fewer tools at their disposal than we do now, they accomplished more than most women do today. What has happened in the last couple of generations?

As women began to be blessed with an array of tools to free their time to be more efficient, they were also exposed to teaching from early feminists who told them that they were too smart for housework. One of the myriad of results was that the majority of women lost the home and family skills that were once commonplace among homemakers. They stopped passing on the accumulated homekeeping knowledge of many generations to their daughters and instead encouraged them to be independent and to pursue work for a paycheck. Feminist ideology stole the joy of homekeeping that women once embraced, and the art of homemaking was, to a great extent, lost as a result.

Thankfully, there is a backlash against feminism and a return to more traditional homemaking going on in America today. You can see this with the enormous popularity of Martha Stewart's books, magazines, and television shows over the last twenty years. Women are seeking the lost skills that past homewives once had.

One of the forgotten homemaking practices that is being rediscovered is that of devoting particular housekeeping tasks to a specific day of the week. Our foremothers understood the wisdom and efficiency of this approach. Emilie Barnes, who has written many books for the Christian woman and her home, was the first to encourage me to order my days this way, and I must say that living by this system works well.

Significantly, God did not create everything in the universe in one day. He took six days to do it in an orderly manner instead. He divided His creative work among the first six days of the week, focusing on creating specific parts of the universe and specific animal kinds on specific days. Then he rested on the seventh day. He didn't have to do it like this, but He did, and it is prudent for us to do the same. Focusing on one area of the home on a weekly basis keeps it under control. We are not so tempted to postpone certain housekeeping tasks forever when we have a day set aside to tackle them specifically.

Your days will not always go according to your schedule. God has given interruptions as a blessing to you and those who interrupt your plan. What your Home Management Book does is give you a reference point in managing your home. When you are done with the interruption, go back to your reference point and do the next thing. With a plan in hand, you are working with direction and managing your home in an orderly manner.

The heart of man plans his way, but the LORD establishes his steps. —Proverbs 16:9

Monday is Laundry Day

Commit this day to your laundry equipment. Start the day as soon as you can—even get up earlier than normal on Laundry Day—and set the timer for switching your loads. Fold as soon as you pull the clothes out of the dryer. Allot some time to mending and ironing between loads. Mending and ironing are chores that can be done near your homeschooling children so that you are available to them.

Tuesday is Kitchen Day

Commit this day to your kitchen. Use this day for extra baking, making yogurt, starting sprouts, freezer meals, etc. Also, spend some time cleaning in the kitchen. Remove the clutter and wipe the counters. Clean out the refrigerator. If you do it every week, it is a ten-minute job and never gets disgusting. Organize your cupboard of plastic containers. Clean and organize one drawer, one cupboard, and one pantry shelf, working through your kitchen as the weeks go by. This might sound like a lot of work that will take copious amounts of time, but actually, it is not so bad. Use your timer and see how long it really takes! If you have big kids, give each one a task and have them race each other or the clock.

Wednesday is Office Day

On this day, work on fine tuning your Home Management Book, plan menus and grocery lists, balance the check book, pay bills, file papers, plan vacation, etc. If you need to make phone calls, do it on

Office Day. Schedule an appointment with each child to review schoolwork. Clean and organize one drawer or cupboard.

Thursday is Town Day

Use this day to schedule appointments and music lessons as much as possible. Do your shopping on this day. Plan your driving route and the route in each store ahead of time. Work on speed and efficiency. If you have little children, try to do all of your errands right after breakfast when they are freshest, and get home before lunch and nap time.

Friday is Cleaning Day

During Afternoon Chore Time, add vacuuming, dusting, and some Deep Cleaning work. When Afternoon Chore Time happens every day, the house stays picked up. Minimize the clutter, and the house is much easier to dust and vacuum! After the whole house is dusted and vacuumed, then do Deep Cleaning in one area. By rotating the Deep Cleaning areas through the month, each area gets a regular deep cleaning.

Saturday is Gardening Day

Work in your flower and vegetable beds, mow, pick up the yard, and sweep the deck, etc. on Gardening Day. In the winter, clean the walks, plan your gardens, and order seeds. Clean your vehicles and the garage. Once again, if your family does these jobs weekly, they never become huge ugly monsters. Dedicate time in the day to prepare for the Lord's Day. Lay out clothes, shoes, and tights. Pack the diaper bag. Put food in crock-pots and make the salad.

Sunday is The Lord's Day

Rest in the Lord. Enjoy your family and friends.

Your Morning Routine

Write at the top of each page your Morning Routine, every little bit of it. If you are using your computer, copy and paste it on the top of each page. You will do this routine every morning for the rest of your life; it will become an ingrained habit, much like brushing your teeth. Of course, at some point, you might decide you need to drop a habit, or add a new one, but for the most part, you need to focus on the same routine every day.

Your Evening Routine

At the bottom of each page, put your Evening Routine, every little thing that you need to do before going to sleep. Writing down the details of your Evening Routine helps establish them and aids tremendously in having a good morning.

Meal Time Routines

In the middle of each page, put The Noon Hour and towards the bottom, The Dinner Hour. Your routine in these hours include the Table Chores.

You need to establish habits that go with meals. Write Meal Routines and Table Chores big and bold on a poster in your kitchen to help your family master the new habits you have established. If they don't remember what a chore involves, you can direct them to the poster.

Filling Out the Rest of Your Day

Write down the order of activities you want your family to do during the day. This will be determined by the age of your children. A family of children under the age of eight will have a very different day than a family of elementary and young adults. A family that includes all three age groups and a baby will have another schedule. I use the term schedule lightly; we need to be flexible and roll with the punches the day throws at us. An order of events to follow is a better description. Put the least important things at the end of the schedule so that it is not a crisis if you drop it.

A few things you will want to include are:

TABLE TIME

Do this after the breakfast table chores are done and before everyone starts going their own direction. Include Bible Study, reciting memory work and catechism, practicing reading, learning manners, and other group activities that need to be done at the table.

WORK ON PHONICS WITH YOUR NON-READER

Large families usually have at least one child in the process of learning to read. Spending 15 minutes a day with these children goes a long way toward the goal. Make it fun and break it up with reading an easy-reader on alternate days.

ONE HOUR OF QUIET TIME

You need a break to nap, read, write, think, and the children need to learn to be quiet and do something alone for a while. The older children will learn self-discipline and respect for others during Quiet Time. The little children will get their well-earned nap.

READ ALOUD TIME

At our house, this is everyone's favorite part of the day. I find it best to do it after Quiet Time so that I don't fall asleep reading!

AFTERNOON CHORE TIME

Your family may choose to have it at a different time of day or break it into two separate times. It's important for our family to do a serious house pick-up time before Dad comes home from work. He likes to come home to a haven of peace and harmony, the smell of supper in the air, a happy wife and content children. Because you are the mother/teacher, you might not notice the disarray and clutter that accumulate during the day's activities, but walking into it cold can look like a picture of chaos! Create a haven of respite from the world for your husband.

CHAPTER 19
Laundry Day

One unhappy temper, one unbending will, one unloving unsympathetic heart, may becloud and embitter the sunniest and sweetest home on earth. —Octavius Winslow

Manage the Monster

Do you have a Laundry Monster living in your home? Do dirty clothes grow mold and mildew in your hampers? Do your children have clean and dirty clothes mixed around on the floor of their bedrooms? Are there huge heaps piled around your washer and dryer? Believe me—I've been in that spot in the past and still have the battle with the beast when the rest of life crowds out the regular duties of home!

Four Loads by Four

In addition to Laundry Day, every day you will need to do loads like baby clothes, diapers, bedding, muddy work clothes, etc. On Cleaning Day, you will need to wash sheets and towels. These loads should be done by 4 o'clock so that the children can put these clothes away and you can focus on getting the house ready for the evening.

Yet one sure thing will keep the Laundry Monster from growing any larger than a yipping dog. Assign a day of the week to laundry. In our house, it is Monday.

Add a daily plan of Laundry Day to your Home Management Book. Doing this helps to focus effort and put a big dent in the never-ending job of laundry. You know how big the mountain can be for the large family. Colossal. Copious.

When I had only a few small children, laundry had the potential to depress me. Yet those days were nothing compared to the amount that can pile up in a heartbeat in these days with nine children and one farmer husband. I have three adult-sized people, in addition to myself, who seem to delight in seeing how much manure they can cake on their clothes. If it's not manure, then it's grease and oil from the shop. The next day it might be dried-on cement. Add to that a passel of girls who like to change clothes as the mood strikes throughout the day (we're working on that), as well as children who seem to wear food rather than eat it, including a peanut butter and honey-smeared toddler. And don't forget the baby with regular diaper blow-outs and banana gunk!

A look into the future tells me it will get worse before it gets better; the children will grow! I have seen the heap under our clothes chute nearly as tall as I am and I say aloud, "How can this be? We just did laundry?!" I think "Laundry Monster" is a mild term in this situation—"Monumental Massive Mega Mammoth Monster" is more appropriate. I'm not exaggerating. I laugh at my old self who used to get so despondent over five measly loads waiting to be done. Perspective is everything.

You tame the beast and your beastly attitude by making a commitment to your laundry. Act as if you are joined with the washer and dryer. They are your new best friends. You will not leave them nor forsake them all the day long. This is an important point that I believe is the key to managing your family's laundry. It changed my life.

Early in the morning—wake up extra-early—meet with the washer and dryer. Feed them their first loads. Set the timer and clip it to yourself; tie it with a ribbon or a shoelace around your neck, stick it in your pocket, or duck tape it to your wrist! You will have to time your loads, as some will dry faster than others, and you will learn how to adjust your timer accordingly. The point here is that as soon as your timer goes off, you run—yes, you are also exercising—to the washer and dryer and take care of the laundry. You will switch loads and fold clothes each time the timer beeps.

When you are done folding a load, look around and ask, "What can I do to make this area look nicer?" Wipe the laundry equipment, sweep the floor, catch the cobwebs—these are three good ways to help improve the cleanliness of your washroom. Is there clutter collecting on top of the washer and dryer? Put it away in its proper place. What can you do to keep clutter from collecting there? How about a little basket for all the things that people leave in their pockets? If you do one little clean-up chore after each load, the room will stay clean. Between loads, work on mending and ironing. Take these two tasks to the same room the children are working in.

How do you hold a Laundry Day and homeschool your big brood? When you leave the room where they are working, instruct them to keep working and try to figure things out for themselves. When you return, praise them for their diligent work, help them with their questions, and if they were rotten, then hand out consequences. Use Laundry Day to wean your children from needing your constant instruction and hand holding. They need to be able to learn how to learn something for themselves, for they will not have you teaching them their whole lives.

The discipline to be self-teaching is an important skill they need to have for a successful adult life.

Laundry Day helps facilitate this. There have been times when I had a child "tomato-staked" to me because he couldn't behave without me with him every second. I take a long soft strip of knit material and tie it to the child's wrist and to my own. When a child is tomato-staked to me, I give him work to do with me. The tomato-staked child also gets lots of love and instruction, which is what a tomato-staked child needs the most.

When the children are old enough to help more, have them take turns switching loads, folding, and doing a clean-up chore. Start with the oldest and run down the line of children. When it comes time for the little children's turn, go with them and teach them how to run the equipment. Use a permanent marker to indicate the most commonly-used setting on the equipment. For the older children who are able to do laundry alone, make a big poster explaining how much soap and water, specific temperatures for certain loads, clean-up chores to do, and whatever else your particular laundry situation calls for. Make a stain treatment book available for them in the laundry area.

How old are your laundry helpers? I know of two families who give the laundry work to the resident ten-year-old. When the next child in line turns ten, that child gets the laundry work. From these two examples, I think it is safe to say that a ten-year-old can do laundry unassisted. My current seven-year-old can switch loads and run the equipment without assistance. I can send her to switch loads and know that it will be done right. We work on it all together all the time, but the elementary-age girls are chiefly responsible for keeping the loads changing. If a family member wants certain articles of laundry done, then that member does a full load of laundry for himself. My boys who wrestle and lose four pounds of water weight in a wrestling practice are chiefly responsible for all of their smelly wrestling clothes.

Anything less than a full load is subject to severe punishment in this house! A large family makes a lot of laundry, and many hands make light work. When each member contributes to the good of the family, he or she builds self-worth and confidence in the ability to do a life-long chore. This is education. Fill it up for the good of all.

Part of holding a regular Laundry Day is the chore of putting things where they belong. When your children "arise and call you blessed" because they have clean clothes, you will say, "Please bring all of the dirty laundry from your bedroom and bathroom to the laundry area and sort it." You need to say this every day of their life with you until they say, "I know, Mom," and it happens. At that point, they have finally gotten it. Every morning of the week, dirty laundry goes to the laundry room. If they do not obey when you tell them this little sentence, it is direct disobedience and should be disciplined in whatever manner your family disciplines direct disobedience. It is a habit that every single person should learn and carry along all through life.

This means discipline on your part in checking up on them regularly: "Inspect what you expect." Make it a habit of yours to take a little house tour with the children every morning. You have to keep doing this, or things will slide into mess, and then you'll have the Laundry Monster taking up residence again.

Make a five-minute bedroom pick-up as part of their morning routine to keep the laundry off the floor. Clean laundry needs to be in drawers, on shelves, or hung up. When all you have is Littles, you will need to do this with them. Talk to them about what you are doing and why you are doing it. Hand them the laundry to put in the basket or throw down the laundry chute. Make laundry a fun game as you identify colors, count items, and so on. Help your children to lay the clean clothes on the shelves or hang them up. This teaches them order and organization. Of course, it would be faster to do it yourself at first, but your end goal is self-sufficient, self-disciplined adults, and it starts with these baby steps. It can be hard, but the pay off will be great.

When these things are not done, the result will be a huge laundry monster that seems to have the ability to eat the house alive. The other result: You will not be blessing your children with the ability to care for themselves if you don't teach them responsibility when they're young, and they will grow up to be slovenly adults.

On Laundry Day, your goal is to do as many loads of laundry as possible until 4 o'clock. At 4 o'clock, your family should be doing their Late Afternoon Chore Routine. Part of that routine on Laundry Day is collecting full baskets of folded clothing, putting clothes away, and bringing the basket back to the laundry area. If you have older children, they should be doing these things either instead of you or with you. If you have all little children, then make an effort to find little baskets or plastic dishpans they can use to carry their own clothes.

If you are a morning person and love to see clothes waving on the line, then make it a goal to have all of your loads of wash flying in the breeze by noon. We save a step and fold our clothes directly off the line into the baskets. Doing this outside gives you exercise in bending and stretching, gets fresh air into your lungs, and a bit of sunshine for Vitamin D. It is also a beautiful thing to hear the birds sing and the children playing nearby. If you have a baby, take him out with you on a blanket while you take down the laundry.

It is easier and more enjoyable to do laundry when the whole setup—from clothing storage to cleaning and folding—is efficient. Efficiency saves you time, and we all appreciate more time.

The specific steps to make your laundry and clothing system reach maximum efficiency is going to vary, depending on the house you live in. What works for one will not necessarily work for another. Ask for ideas when you're with other ladies. Browse through the laundry, shelving, and storage aisles of home stores to look for solutions to improve your laundry workflow.

Here's the setup and strategy we use in our laundry room at this point in time. Our Laundry Room is the unfinished portion of our basement and is beside a walk-out door. This makes it easy to hang out clothes. We keep the boys' clothes in this area on shelves.

Across one side of the room, we hung a one-inch pipe for hanging shirts, drip-dry clothes, and out-of-season coats, jackets, snow pants, etc. We put a laundry chute from the second story, through the first floor mudroom, that empties beside the laundry equipment in the basement. The laundry chute is an eight-inch PVC pipe. The laundry chute has helped keep dirty laundry from lying around the main floor and the second story (yes, I have people who take off socks and leave them lying about).

In our Laundry Room, we have big shelves that hold large clear plastic containers of out-of-season clothing and sizes that aren't currently being worn. I only save the best clothes from one season or child to the next. I have discovered that my perception at the end of a season is not that great. I still think something is nice just because it was at the beginning of the season. I have to be very strict with myself when putting clothes into storage; I have a lot of storage space but also a lot of children. There's not room to keep everything and keep track of it. Keeping only the nicest things saves time, effort, and prevents children from wearing clothes that are too bedraggled.

When you begin ironing and mending on Laundry Day, you won't likely knock out the whole backed-up stack at once, yet consistency is the key to success. On Monday, iron for a certain amount of time (love the timer!), then mend for a certain amount of time. After a few weeks of this, you will be caught up on your ironing and mending. If you stay disciplined to committing Monday as Laundry Day, you will stay caught up. If you can, do the ironing and mending near the children while they are doing their schoolwork.

It is helpful to have the members of your family learn to take their clothes off right side out, socks un-balled, and layers removed from each other. Sometimes gentle reminders are all it takes, but there are times when the consistently-guilty culprit needs to be brought to the scene of the crime and instructed to undo their dirty laundry themselves. Explain to the family that laundry in this state does not come clean, and show them an example of the balled-up sock that is still filthy after being washed and dried. I have found that showing the "why" of certain things we do helps to reinforce the "what" and "how."

Start this when they are little so that it will carry on when they are older. Explain to them that keeping their laundry right side out is being considerate to others, that it is good manners, and that it is their Christian duty to consider others more highly than themselves. Teach them this when they are little when you are undressing them for their bath. You'll be glad you did later in life!

Four by Four

Having a regular Laundry Day will be a big help in keeping the laundry under control but, of course, laundry occurs all the time. As soon as eleven people change clothes at the end of each day, there are three new loads. Add in baby laundry, towels, and sheets, and the laundry will about bring you to tears. But don't let the Laundry Monster win! Keep the upper hand by having a daily goal in addition to keeping a Laundry Day.

Our goal is Four Loads by Four. In the summer when we get up with the sun and hang out laundry, the goal is Four Loads by Noon. I love it when I have a load on the line before breakfast. Some weeks we do well to keep loads going each day, and because of our daily goal of four by four, we get a light day for Laundry Day! Some weeks we are especially busy, and our daily goals aren't reached, which makes Laundry Day another battle to be fought—and won!—with the Laundry Monster.

I Love to Do Laundry

This might be a very strange and foreign thought, but learn to love doing laundry. Replace all the bad feelings and ugly thoughts with Scripture and God-pleasing thoughts. Do the laundry as unto the Lord. You wouldn't complain about doing His laundry, would you?!

Less than a hundred years ago, women in developed countries were still standing over a fire, stirring their boiling clothes. There is a local woman in my area whose mother died from the burns sustained when her dress caught fire on Wash Day. Even today there are women around the world who do their wash by hand in a river nearby their home.

We have it easy by comparison: We throw the wash in a machine and walk away. In addition, we have easy access to so many beautiful and comfortable clothes compared to those who came before us.

Live gratefully, and take care of the blessing God has given your family! Thank Him for each person whose laundry passes through your hands. Thank Him for the sun and breeze. Thank Him for the clouds that bring rain. Thank Him for soap and clear water. Thank Him for the day He made and blessed you with. Thank Him for strength for the tasks ahead.

> *The Lord is my strength and my shield; in him my heart trusts, and I am helped; my heart exults, and with my song I give thanks to him. —Psalm 28:7*

Laundry Tips

- Time how long it actually takes to fold a load. You will be pleasantly surprised!

- Keep stain-treat handy and use it on clothes before they land in the dirty basket. Keep it in each bathroom to be used when the clothes are taken off.

- Put bibs on your little children while they eat.

- Never buy white shirts, pants, or dresses. If you do, avoid eating and playing while wearing them!

- It pays to read labels and follow instructions. Teach your helpers to do this also.

- Read labels before you buy a garment. Save yourself effort and don't buy high-care fabrics.

- Use vinegar for your fabric softener—it rinses the soap out, softens, is inexpensive, and is better for those sensitive to scents.

- Hang up towels immediately to keep from smelling musty. Wash them in hot water and put vinegar in the wash and rinse to help keep towels smelling fresh. Hanging them out in the sunshine will also help, but it makes for stiff towels. When worse comes to worst, use bleach, but be aware that it will ruin the color.

- Remove clothes immediately from the dryer when the timer buzzes to eliminate wrinkles. If you miss the buzzer, throw a damp towel in to help unset wrinkles. There are also spray-on products that will release wrinkles.

- Fold the laundry all together as a family and listen to audio stories.

- Mark clothes to be passed down with dots or Xs—one for the first wearer, two for the second, three for the third, and so on (if they last that long). This aids in keeping things sorted correctly while folding. This is the number one tip regarding laundry management that the Large Family Logistics web site receives from moms of large families.

- Use small baskets or dishpans for little people to put their clothes into for carrying to their closets.

- Iron clothes with a hint of dampness in them or sprinkle with warm water to aid in ironing.

- Label your linen closet shelves to assist the people who put away or remove linens.

- Sunshine brightens whites, fades stains, removes smells, and kills germs.

- Wipe your clothesline before hanging out to prevent black marks on the laundry.

- Be efficient when hanging your laundry by pinning side-by-side garments with the same clothespin.

- Before you hang up clothes or move from washer to dryer, give them a good snap or two to remove wrinkles.

- When hanging up wet button-up shirts, stretch the wrinkles out by pulling with your hands from the top and bottom and the sleeves from the body of the shirt.

- Do not overload the washing machine, and teach your family this. The clothes will not come clean because the soap and water cannot circulate around and through the clothes.

- Sort your clothes by color and weight to get a longer life out of them.

- Mend tears before washing to eliminate the fabric from unraveling in the wash.

- Wash lightly-soiled colored clothes in cold water to keep them bright.

- Blue jeans bleed for their whole lifespan; do not wash them with other clothes.

- Wash whites and very dirty clothes in hot water to remove soil and kill germs.

- Wear old clothes or aprons for dirty jobs that will stain clothes as when pitting cherries, cutting peaches, gardening, and painting.

- Fresh blood will come out if immediately rinsed in cold water. Heat will set the stain. Hydrogen peroxide removes blood stains.

- Grass stains come out with a vinegar pre-treat or when allowed to soak in a bucket of water with an enzyme cleaner.

- Grease stains come out with a citrus-based pre-treat.

- Bodily fluids come out after pre-treating with a bacterial enzyme based "pet stain remover". This also works great for carpet, furniture, and car upholstery.

- Keep softener salt in your water softener!

Make a Laundry Protocol Poster

Making a Laundry Protocol poster will aid your family in knowing how to use the equipment and will help them know how to wash certain loads.

At the top, in large letters, write "Laundry Protocol." Under this heading, write specific instructions for Detergent Use in your machine. Check your owner's manual and the detergent box for specifics.

Explain sorting categories. Then make a column for the days of the week. The second column is to correspond with the days and will explain which laundry to do on each day, including a couple of days off. Don't try to do laundry on your Town Day or The Lord's Day.

In the third column, write how to wash each particular load and which cleaners and settings that you want used on a particular load. Some things that are obvious to us as moms due to our experience are not so obvious to the uninitiated. Help your young apprentices with specific instructions on how to do the job well. For example: Friday, Towels and Sheets, Use hot water.

Hang the poster near your equipment. Then take your helpers to the poster and read through it with them. Ask them if they have any questions. If, while doing laundry, they ask you how to do something, refer them to the poster. Teach them to think. Maybe something is not clear on your part and needs to be modified. The poster is your teacher's aid in helping get everything done that needs done and done well.

Victory is Yours

Each home is different, each laundry set up is different, and each household's laundry is different due to the activities that the family members participate in. One house might have toddler food, the next grass stains, the next red clay, and the next chicken manure. One house might have the laundry room in the garage, the next on a back porch, the next in the kitchen, and so on.

Take the ideas here and use them to get your creative juices flowing and make a system that works for your family in your home. The bottom line is to do the laundry and keep on top of it. Work at it daily—early morning, late morning, noon, and early afternoon—then stop and put it away. Between each activity that you schedule in your day, switch loads and fold.

Learn to love laundry, study how to do it correctly, and make it an art! This is how you gain victory over the Laundry Monster.

CHAPTER 20
Kitchen Day

The kitchen is key to effective home and time management.
—*Deniece Schofield's* Kitchen Organization Tips and Secrets

Kitchen Organization: The Countertops and Island

When you walk into your kitchen, what's the first thing that catches your eye? If you're the home manager, it's probably the work that you need to accomplish. What does your husband see first? When you have guests, what do they see first?

The counters can quickly be a catch-all clutter collecting point. Even if all the dirty and clean dishes are taken care of, the food put away, and the papers stashed, the counters can still be cluttered with decorations and appliances that we think we need to have out.

How do we keep these areas clean and clear of clutter? Just like everything else in home management, we need to be diligent, and we need to train our children to put things away where they belong: "Don't lay it down, put it away!" Catch your children doing the trick, and tell them to put it where it belongs. I'm sure you know the saying, "Everything has a place, and everything in its place." Say it over and over again to your children. If you have severe offenders, then institute appropriate punishments and rewards.

During Afternoon Chore Time, one of the chores for the Kitchen is to clear the table and counters of all clutter. It's not a bad job when we are all practicing, "Don't lay it down, put it away!" When we are lazy and let things pile up, it can be a real drag to put all that "stuff" away.

When my husband comes in the back door at the end of the day, the first thing he sees is our kitchen island, dining room table, and the floors. If all went well with our Afternoon Chore Time, what he sees is pleasing to the eye: the table set for supper, the counter clean, supper smells in the air, and the projects and toys put away. But there are evenings when he walks in to find schoolwork, food prep spread all over the kitchen, and a floor of crumbs, papers, and toys. This is not a peaceful haven of rest for him at the end of the day. He feels like he's coming home to more work. It can make the difference between a pleasant relaxing evening for him and our whole family or chaos. Our evenings are so much better when the work has been done in a timely fashion before he walks in the door.

The next time that your kitchen is completely clean and your countertops cleared to what is your normal standard, leave the room and then come back in, pretending that you are seeing things through your husband's or your neighbor's eyes. You might find that you can make things look a bit tidier by doing this trick. Is there still some unnecessary clutter out? Do you really need to have that appliance out? How often do you really use it? Is there room for it elsewhere?

Look for your kitchen's natural focal point, and do what you can to enhance the beauty of it. It might be the light, it might be a window, it might be a countertop, or it might be the cupboards. Something that might not catch the eye at all in one kitchen can become the focal point of another. Each kitchen design is unique and has its strong points of beauty and eyesores that should be minimized. Find what it is in your kitchen and enhance that area. It might be as simple as keeping it clean and shiny.

How do you avoid paper piles in your kitchen? Start with identifying what the paper is and where it came from. Sort your mail over the trash can, and immediately dispose of the junk. Put the bills in a place that you have just for bills. Put the magazines and newspapers at the place where they are read. When they are finished being read, pitch them. For papers that your husband needs to see, have a specific place (a pretty basket or attractive box) where he will find them. Have your children keep their schoolwork and books in a specific place, and require them to keep their things in that place. Put an end to the habit of stacking stuff on the kitchen counters.

Do you have men-folk who come in and empty their pockets of tools on the closest flat surface? In our house, I emptied the drawer nearest to where my men's "dumping ground" was. In that drawer, I placed baskets: one basket is for pliers, screwdrivers and other tools, one basket is for money, another basket is for the small things like nuts and bolts, golf tees, pencils, etc. Also in this drawer are the flashlights which seemed to lie around in odd places by the back door. By keeping a drawer for their "stuff", it keeps it out of sight, and they know where to find the things that they dumped the day before. They are actually learning to empty their pockets into the drawer and sort it into the baskets. At some point, clean this junk drawer out. Assign better spots for things, put things away, replace broken baskets, and dispose of the true junk.

By keeping your counters and island free and clear, it is more pleasing to the eye and makes a nicer workspace for you to be in. Clearing the clutter from the kitchen is not a once-and-forever job; it's something that needs to be evaluated every few months. Clutter creeps up on us, and we need to keep our eye on it so that it doesn't take over. Clutter makes our daily work harder to do because we have to fumble around it. Train your eye to constantly evaluate the clutter factor in your most important workspace.

Kitchen Organization: A Start

I once read an article about a woman who, with her husband and six-year-old daughter, moved for various reasons from a 1500-square-foot apartment into 150 square feet of living space on a sailboat. Yes, they were going to live in the sailboat. The crux of the article was about making choices and simplifying life. They had to pare down their "stuff" tremendously, and this alone helped to simplify their life.

This woman's new kitchen was the size of a shower stall. She had one gas burner, a toaster oven, and a tiny refrigerator/freezer. The thing that struck me at the time, and motivated me to do a big clean out in my kitchen, was that she had only two knives, a chopping knife and a paring knife. She then went on to describe how she loved to cook and found that with the barest minimum of utensils she could still make great gourmet meals because she was focusing more on the ingredients rather than the process of using all the gadgets that a person thinks they need to cook with.

After reading this article, I immediately got a box and went to my kitchen and starting pitching in all the things that were overflowing my drawers and cupboards that I never used—especially the knife drawer. While reading the article, I realized that I only use maybe three knives on a regular basis. I do have favorite knives for certain things, but I rarely use them.

I quickly realized that there was a plethora of things in my kitchen that were simply taking up space and making my life more complicated. I did not need to risk my fingers scrambling in the knife drawer or waste minutes digging in the gadget drawer for the few things that I actually used. I quickly filled a box with stuff to give away. I kept the box on my counter for a month or so just in case I had acted hastily. As I came across other things in the drawers and cupboards, I added to the box. I don't think I pulled a single thing back out. This box went to Goodwill and then, throughout the last year, I kept on purging the kitchen and adding to the give-away-box I keep at the back door.

If you're not ready for a complete organizational overhaul in the kitchen, or if you're short on time, just setting a give-away-box at the back door is a good start.

Creating Efficiency

When I started paying attention to how many steps and movements I was making in the kitchen, it caused me to think of better ways to arrange things. In my kitchen, the refrigerator is at one end and I had the knife drawer at the opposite end, yet I do most of the cutting in the middle. By simply moving the knife drawer directly under the cutting area, I have saved many steps. A change like this may not seem significant, but multiply this several times around your kitchen, and you will find yourself enjoying your time there more and being faster with your work.

You make three meals a day, 365 days a year in the kitchen. That's a lot of time and energy! Given this fact, creating an efficient kitchen is one of the biggest ways to save precious time in your life. When things are simplified and set up efficiently, creativity has a place to bloom. Your family will appreciate your more cheerful attitude and want to join you. By creating an efficient workspace in the kitchen, you will make it easier to teach and train your children in cooking, cleaning, and managing.

Managing the kitchen and meals is one of the biggest tasks of being a keeper-at-home. It can be easy to be overwhelmed by this due to inexperience, but just because you were not taught how to manage a kitchen is no excuse for throwing up your hands in defeat.

Think of all the other things you have had to teach yourself. Learning never stops in life unless you stop seeking to educate yourself. I have seen people not try and heard them say things that indicate they think they can't learn anymore or that they can't be good at something. It's simply not true. We can always try new things and learn new skills with God's help and a bit of determination. As women, God has made us to be helpmeets to our men and to be busy at home (Genesis 2, Titus 2). What He has assigned He will enable us to do. He is Jehovah-Jireh, God the Provider.

So how do you start making your kitchen more efficient? It comes by observing and thinking while you are working in the kitchen—how many steps am I taking?, how many times am I bending over?, reaching up?, digging through a drawer?, scrounging in the back of a cupboard?—and then by making informed adjustments.

Now's the time to begin the process. Observe yourself for a week as you work in the kitchen. Keep a paper on the fridge, and write down ideas for improving organization and workflow as they come to you. Then begin to implement these improvements. You'll be glad that you did!

Kitchen Centers to Improve Efficiency

1. Cutting and Sink Center: knives and cutting boards, coffee and coffee maker, dish washing tools, colander, drinking glasses, pitchers, juicer, liquid measuring glass, plant watering can.

2. Cooking Center: pots and pans, cooking oil, rice, pasta, cooked cereals, serving dishes, platters, trays, timer, teakettle, tea.

3. Mixing Center: mixer, bowls, bread pans, baking ingredients.

4. Serving Center: dinnerware, flatware.

5. Refrigerator Center: Ziplocs and containers for leftovers, a marking pen, sack lunch items.

Use the Kitchen Centers list above as a springboard of ideas for your unique kitchen. Think about things that you make often, and set the kitchen up so it can be done quickly. If you do a lot of juicing, then create a Juice Center. If you make salads every meal, then create a Salad Center.

Put the items that you use most in your daily cooking between your eye level and your hip level. If you have children that do a lot of cooking, then take that into consideration. I recently moved my mixing bowls to a low spot to stop my children from climbing the counters every day.

If you have cake pans that you use every year or two and don't want to give away, store them in a high cupboard or a back corner cupboard. I cleaned and organized a shelf in my basement's unfinished area for my infrequently used items. I plan to sew a simple curtain to hide it and keep the things from getting dusty.

There is no perfect kitchen anywhere; there will always be a spot or an area that irritates you. Some of these centers will overlap in your kitchens, and that's okay. You might want to keep two of the same tools or knives in your kitchen—one for each center to save you some steps. Some of you might have a kitchen that is so tiny that centers are nearly impossible, but at the same time, it's so tiny that you aren't taking any steps but simply turning around and around. My kitchen is long, and that presents challenges. The bottom line is to arrange things for the greatest efficiency possible.

As the years go by and your cooking changes, you will find that your kitchen needs to be rearranged again. I found that, as I started making double and triple batches of things, I needed to bring my biggest pots, pans, and baking dishes to the front and center and move the smaller things to the back.

A word of counsel: Do not walk into your kitchen and start tearing it apart right away. Take a few days to observe yourself and think about things. It could be that you already have things set up in an efficient way in your kitchen, and it only needs a little bit of tweaking. If it's not broke, don't fix it.

The Kitchen Day

This is the day when you do the big tasks and clean in your kitchen. Set aside a day for this for the sake of efficiency. If you keep your focus in the kitchen for a day, it will help out your family's health, grocery budget, cleanliness, and general well being. Big families make big messes. They also require a lot of food, and making a lot of food makes a lot of mess. Small families may be able to go longer times between certain cleaning jobs, but if you haven't figured it out yet, the life span of a clean area is greatly reduced in large families.

To start with, write out the weekly cleaning chores for the kitchen. This is the day that you and the children do those chores. If everyone does one or two tasks from the list every week, the kitchen stays clean with little effort. Each task can be done in just a few minutes, if it's done weekly. But if tasks are left undone for weeks on end, it will take much more time to get things back into shape.

WEEKLY KITCHEN CLEANING CHORES

- Wipe appliances.
- Clean stove hood.
- Clean top of stove.
- Organize and clean one drawer.
- Organize and clean one cupboard.
- Organize cupboard of plastic containers.
- Organize and clean one pantry shelf.
- Remove counter clutter and wipe counter.

- Wipe appliances that sit on counter.

- Clean out refrigerator.

- Clean top of refrigerator.

- Clean kitchen window.

- Scrub kitchen sink and faucet crevices.

- Scrub dish drainer.

- Mop Floor.

- Dust.

- Cobwebs.

KITCHEN DAY EXAMPLE

The night before Kitchen Day, soak dry beans. In the morning, before breakfast or during breakfast table chores, drain the water off. Put the beans in the crockpot, cover them with water, and cook on low all day. During Afternoon Chore Time, turn it off and cool, then put the beans in freezer boxes or containers and freeze. This is an easy and inexpensive way to build a healthy pantry.

Early in the morning, put chickens and vegetables in a big pot to simmer all day. In the late morning, when you're making lunch, pull the chickens out to cool and, after lunch, debone the chickens. Then freeze the meat in Ziploc bags and put the bones back in the pot. Simmer the bones all day. During Afternoon Chore Time, cool the broth; strain; and put the broth in freezer containers. Chicken broth is handy in many recipes and one of the healthiest things for your family when made from scratch.

In the morning, set out ground meat to thaw. During Afternoon Chore Time, make meat loaves, meatballs, and/or brown and freeze.

In the morning, while the children are doing their independent schoolwork, start bread dough and let rise. While the children are doing Table Chores after lunch, shape the loaves and let rise. During mid-afternoon, put the loaves in the oven.

During your family's Read Aloud hour, you read while the children mop. You can also listen to audio stories while you do the kitchen cleaning chores. My children tend to work faster when they are listening to a story and not talking to each other.

Do not feel that you have to do everything, every single week. Take inventory of your freezer to see if you need to restock your browned meat or chicken broth.

Do not think that your little children can't be helpful in the kitchen. They can mop and wipe appliances and cupboard doors. They can debone a chicken. Little children think work is fun! Don't send them off; put them to work with a smile!

Floor Mopping for the Large Family

This might sound a bit crazy, but I like to mop the floor. I haven't done it for awhile (my kids have been doing it), but really, I like it.

In the past, I had a Swiffer. I think they are made for mopping floors that don't get dirty. At my house, the pads just seemed to make mud. When I ran out of pads, I used a micro-fiber rag on the Swiffer, and that was a little better. But the Swiffer was eventually de-cluttered. I have used sponge mops before, and I rate them as okay but they also have a tendency to make mud.

The best mop I have owned is from Don Aslett's Clean Report catalog. It has different kinds of heads you can put on it, and it swivels nicely. But you have to bend down and wring it out. If you're bending down, you might as well bend all the way down and just mop the floor with your hand. With his mop, you still have the problem of the dried-on food spots or stickers someone stuck onto the floor. One solution is to let them soak and come back later, but I have a lot of those spots on the floor. Am I supposed to flood the whole floor and come back in ten minutes to mop it?

Here's my solution.

Nap time is the most logical time of day to mop. Those children who are not napping when you mop can gather their things, visit the toilet, find their "spot", and stay parked for the mopping and drying time.

When I do the mopping, I put on some relaxing classical music and fill a bucket with soapy water. I use Wood Wash from the Don Aslett catalog, a terry rag or micro-fiber cloth, and a dish scraper for the stickers and other things that need scraped off. I get down on my hands and knees and start mopping at one end and finish by the toilet in the mudroom. Then I dump the dirty water down the toilet. It takes me twenty minutes when working alone. If three or four of us mop together, it takes less than ten minutes.

To do it more perfectly, according to Don Aslett's cleaning books, you need two buckets: one for rinsing the dirty rag, the second for the soapy water that you wash with. In my view, this approach is generally more hassle than is necessary. I don't like the mud that the sponge mop or Swiffer makes, but I'm not so picky that I'm going to use two buckets. When the floor is very dirty, however, I do use the two-bucket method and even change the rinse water because it turns black so quickly. That happens more often in the summer during canning season. Plus I live on a farm and have a mudroom that is called a mudroom for a reason. The two-bucket system is good for a muddy mudroom.

I find mopping to be relaxing because the house is quiet with everyone doing an activity elsewhere or sleeping; the music is relaxing; and I can just mop and think. I like to have that quiet time, though the mopping is over before I know it. Then I find a quiet spot to read until the floor has dried.

Now, in my quest to multi-task and teach my children how to work, my method the last few years has been to have the big kids mop while I read aloud. With four of them mopping, it gets done in a flash. They start at one end and race each other to the middle. They also point out to each other when they miss a spot. The mop bucket is behind them, and they go from it to their mopping spot on the floor, moving backwards towards the bucket. I sit on a nearby chair and read. This system has been working great.

The Spot Mop Method: When someone spills something (which usually happens at least once a day at our house), we mop not only the spill area, but also everything that can be reached within an arm's length. Using this method, the floor can be kept decently clean for a while. Another version of this method is to walk around with a spray bottle of soapy water and a wet rag, looking for the dirty spots. This is a good method to have a child do when you are receiving surprise visitors!

Building up Help in the Kitchen

Assign a day of the week to each child. The "special" child for the day gets extra privileges and is Mama's right hand in the kitchen. By assigning each child a day in the kitchen, they learn how to cook! My children love to cook and try to cook on days that aren't "their day," and this often turns into a squabble! They often get excited about a recipe and are told to save it for their special day. Ingredients that they need are added to the grocery list.

The child assigned for the day is required to be in the kitchen during meal preparation. Involve the child in the recipe making and, if they can, let them do it alone! Start this when they are little, and by the time they are 8, 10, and definitely by age 12, they will be able to make meals alone!

Show no fear! When your children want to make cream puffs, and you think the recipe sounds too complicated, let them do it! Tell them to follow the directions of their recipes exactly. I tend to be a "dump cook", which is good and bad. The good is that a dump cook can make something out of nothing and no recipe. The bad is that a dump cook tends to rewrite the directions to a recipe (to simplify, substitute ingredients, or speed it up) and can end up wrecking it. I have learned the hard way that when the kids want to make something that requires exaction—baked goods—and they have a reliable recipe, I should get out of the way! If they see a recipe made on a TV cooking show, let them get the recipe off the internet and make it. Help them out with collecting the ingredients and being their dishwasher and supporting role in the production. Then sit down and enjoy the food!

Little Children in the Kitchen

Oh, little children are fun to have in the kitchen! They are so delighted and curious about everything! Of course, sometimes they can be in the way, especially when you are hurrying, but try not to squish them. Give them something to do:

- A container of beans or rice and various measuring cups and spoons. Have them transfer the beans from one bowl to another. This increases coordination and teaches fractions. A funnel is also fun.

- A cheese shaker full of toothpicks. Put the toothpicks on a plate and have the child put toothpicks in the holes of the shaker. This activity increases finger dexterity.

- Securely stand a child at the sink, perhaps while you are washing dishes, and let them play in the water with a funnel and slotted spoons.

- An older preschooler can play with little cups and pitchers and learn to carefully pour from one thing to the next. When she is done, hand her a rag, and she can wipe the cupboards and mop the floor.

- Stacking plastic cups is fun for a toddler.
- An older child can layer different color beans in a jar. After everyone has admired his art project, soak the beans in water, and cook them for soup.

CHAPTER 21
Office Day

The heart of her husband trusts in her, and he will have no lack of gain. She does him good, and not harm, all the days of her life. —Proverbs 31:11-12

She considers a field and buys it; with the fruit of her hands she plants a vineyard. —Proverbs 31:16

She perceives that her merchandise is profitable. —Proverbs 31:18

She looks well to the ways of her household and does not eat the bread of idleness. —Proverbs 31:27

Assign a day of the week to your Home Office and add it to your Home Management Book. The goal is a Home Office where you, the Home Office Manager, tend to the business side of home life. From menu plans to financial investments, anything to do with paper, pencils, numbers, money, and planning, you need to take seriously and respectfully in an orderly manner.

If your husband takes care of some of these responsibilities, then dub yourself his Office Assistant. Keep his desk in order, file his papers, and attend to the things he assigns to you. My husband has traveled with his work for nearly all of our married life, so most of the business tasks have been my duty. Once again, untrained for this job, I made many mistakes along the way, learned too many things the hard way, and created personal coping strategies that I will now share with you.

We live in a paper age. Paper, paper, everywhere. When we don't take time to deal with all the paper in our lives, it turns into a monster—The Paper Monster. While whole books have been written about this pesky creature, I'm going to share with you the simple way I've found to kill him.

Take one day of the week and spend it at your desk, not surfing the net or reading e-mails, but use the time rather to get the finances and paper under control. Call it Office Day. At first you might spend hours putting things in order, but eventually you will come to the place where you will spend only half an hour a week paying bills and taking care of the paperwork.

Ordering the Paper Monster Out of His Lair

If the thought of a whole day fighting this monster is overwhelming, then break it up into chunks. Spend ten minutes tackling one paper pile. Then go read a story to your children. Come back to the desk and spend ten minutes straightening a drawer. Then go get a drink of water and look out your kitchen window for a bit. Then tackle another paper pile.

Just work slow and steady. You do not need to kill the monster in a day, just wound him. Let him know that his days are numbered. You're coming back next week—same day, same place—and sooner or later, he is going to die, and you will be the victor. You will be a Home Office Manager, and you will be great at your job, ten minutes at a time, one day a week, for the rest of your life.

Every time you clear an area or clean out a drawer, claim it as yours—it no longer belongs to The Paper Monster. Do not let anything be placed there to clutter it up again. Put a vase of flowers, framed art, or a picture of your children there to claim the spot. You will not lay paper there again. The paper has its place—you now keep it in its place, whether it is the trash can, a lovely basket or a file.

Once you have the paper under control, clean out the desk drawers, cupboards, shelves, and other areas that are part of your Home Office. Do not get overwhelmed—do this slowly, one place at a time, ten minutes at a time, taking frequent breaks. It make take weeks to gain victory over the mounds of paper lurking here and there, but conquer this beast and get the Home Office up and running.

Some of the paper deluge we need, some of it we want, and some of it we don't know what to do with. There's auto, legal, receipts, taxes, and so on. There's travel information about that area where we vacationed a few years ago, just in case we want to go back to the same place. There's research on that theological topic that you studied once upon a time. There's information on all the paint colors and brands that you used in your house when you last painted, set aside for the looming day when you need to repaint. It seems we can file forever.

Our family has found File Solutions (www.filesolutions.com) to be a huge help in our Home Office. With this solution, you won't be fumbling through all your file drawers anymore. You can send your husband or children to find something or put something away. This is a time-saving, efficient, and attractive system.

Quick Fast Paper Recovery

Looking at paper piles can be depressing, but do not fear! Most of it can be tossed into the trash. When you're climbing one of those mountains, grab a trash can and two boxes. Throw all junk mail, catalogs, newspapers—anything that doesn't have to do with money or important papers to file—into the trash.

Put all the bills into one box labeled "Bills" and all the rest into the other box labeled "File". Pay all of the bills that you can and put the invoices into the File box.

File the papers into gallon-sized zip bags labeled with the pertinent year. I suggest zip bags because you probably have some handy in your kitchen. Each day, keep putting your papers to be filed into these bags. This is a temporary situation. You need files to properly control your paper by topic. When you get the mail each day, sort it, and put your important papers in a zip bag labeled with the current year.

Put your bills that are waiting to be paid in a gallon-sized zip labeled "Bills" until you get a Bill Paying System in place. Remember, the zip bag filing is temporary. Do not grow accustomed to it. It is a stepping-stone to your new life of regular filing.

To take dominion of this area, you will need to invest in a filing system. At office supply stores, there are desk top files and file boxes with hinged lids and handles that you can purchase. These are a very inexpensive alternative to the cabinet type file drawers. You will also need to buy hanging files and manila folders to slip inside the hanging files.

For paper from last year and beyond, keep only the most important documents, the ones that might draw interest from the IRS. Sort the papers only by year, not by topic. You have too much else to do to file more specifically now. Put the zip bags, labeled by year, into a box. Label the box with the years included, and put it in storage. If you ever need information from those years (not likely), then you can sort the papers further at that point. Your most important goal at this early stage is to get your current papers under control.

What Order Looks Like

Now that everything is clean and neat, work on getting your plans in place:

- A menu plan of 31 meals that you can reference for meals.

- A home book for writing down decorating ideas and pasting in pictures.

- Lesson plans and your own family's homeschool scope and sequence plan.

- Financial goals and the plans to reach those goals.

- Garden and landscape plans.

- Plans for anticipating expenses.

As Home Office Manager, you will now be more calm and relaxed because you have an orderly place to plan your work and reference your plans. The Home Office will be a rock in your house—the hub from which you run your daily operations. It will be a well-ordered reference point from which you plan and set forth orders.

Little by little, you will continue to gain control of this area of life. Once you have your base operations established, you won't know how you got along without it! With structure and routine, you will know what to expect. You can anticipate surprises and plan for them. Based on my experience, it is well worth it to dedicate one day a week to the Home Office.

Office Day Tasks

- Do each one of these things every Office Day:
- Balance Checkbook.
- Pay Bills.
- File Papers.
- Plan Menus.
- Plan the Route for Town Day.
- Plan Lessons.
- Schedule an appointment with each child to review schoolwork.
- Save your Internet research and shopping for Office Day. Keep a running To Do list for the things you will look up on Office Day.
- Write a letter to a friend.
- Write your non-essential e-mails today.
- Clean out one desk drawer or cupboard.
- Clean desktop.
- Restore books to shelves.
- Gather library books and put in vehicle.

Setting up Your Desk

Because a desk is a level surface, it can quite easily become a collective dropping ground. When people see a pile of papers there, it can become a magnet to place another paper on the pile rather than going the extra step to put that paper where it belongs.

Make a daily effort when you sort the mail to not allow paper piles on your desk. Keep a basket or stacking files for papers that you need to file. Do not put junk mail or bills in this basket. There should be space on your desk for you to spread out your work. You should have some sort of container to hold your pens, pencils, and a letter opener conveniently located on your desk. Put a pretty coaster on your desk for you to set a water glass or cup of tea when you sit down to work. A small vase for a garden flower is also a nice touch. The point is to keep it cleared and make it look nice so that it will invite and inspire you rather than look like a big pile of paper drudgery.

Stacking horizontal files make a handy paper system. You can slip papers into the appropriate file every day. Use three files, and label them "Action", "Pending", and "File".

The "Action" file is for things you need to take care of within a week. Schedule time on Office Day to go through this, and leave it clean for the next week's worth of paper.

The "Pending" file is for invitations that require action, mail order receipts for things that haven't arrived yet, tickets, etc. Go through this also on Office Day, take action on the items, and throw out the unnecessary.

The "File" folder is where you put things that need to be filed when you have time to do it now. Every Office Day, file the papers that you've placed in the "File" folder during the week.

This same system can be used for a home business.

Managing Your Desk

Holding a weekly Office Day will keep things under control. If you sit there every day to check e-mail or if you keep your date book on the computer, be sure to not leave a pile of debris behind you. Make it a habit when you stand up to take your glass back to the sink, have a child put away the toys he brought you, put the burp cloth in the laundry, hang your purse on its hook, straighten papers, throw away the junk mail—clean up behind yourself!

Give yourself a rule of only a certain amount of objects to clutter the desk. These are the five things that I limit mine to:

1. A glass of water.

2. A pencil holder (this also needs to be de-junked regularly).

3. Stacking files.

4. Computer monitor and mouse.

5. Baby's pacifier and burp rag.

Managing Your Calendar

Check your calendar twice every day, when you wake up and before you go to bed. For a large family, it is wise to have a calendar on the wall so that everyone can reference it and know when and what things are going to happen. You will have a happier family when they know what to expect. Require that everyone put their events on the wall calendar. Some moms do well with a calendar on their computer and/or PDA; some are "paper people" and like to have a date book they carry with them. Everyone is unique; the important thing is that you have a system that works for you and your family.

I have one calendar on the wall for events and a second calendar beside it with house and garden projects I would like to have done by certain dates. Doing this informs everyone of the work expectations for each week.

Managing Your Computer Time

Ha! Are you laughing at that title? Those rabbit trails can be pretty long sometimes, can't they?

We first were "connected" to the Internet in 1998. Back when we got online, Matt traveled a lot during the spring, summer, and fall, and the children were 7, 5, and 3 years old, and I had a baby.

Discovering the online world was a breath of fresh air in my days of Alphaphonics, macaroni and cheese, Barney, and homemade baby food. Through it I discovered oodles of homeschooling resources including "classical" education, enlightening theology articles, and research on home products which helped in building our house.

I learned tons about cooking on the web. I was in at least one online group that focused on freezer cooking. I spent about a year on a crockpot group, and, for a little while, I was on a group that sent out a recipe-a-day. I also spent about two years as part of an online group that discussed the recipe/nutrition book, "Nourishing Traditions," by Sally Fallon and Dr. Mary Enig.

I learned much on the Mothers of Many Young Siblings (MOMYS) digest over the years. I also discovered the Managers of Their Homes (MOTH) book by Teri Maxwell on the Internet when baby #4 was about 18 months old. In 2001 or so, I joined the Patriarch's Wives group and learned from Stacy McDonald and the wise ladies there.

There are so many things that are edifying, but too many at once start to take a lot of time. Through the years, as we added children and the homeschooling took more time, I discovered the need to manage my computer time better. Staying up late was a bad idea for me because it gave the next day a bad start, so I cut out the computer time after supper. Then I decided that I should stay off the computer until our schoolwork was done and I had read and played with the little children. When the gardening season came around, I would drop groups or go "no mail" for the season. When we were busy with a unit study, I would do the same.

Despite the time constraints, it is nice to have that brain stimulation, learn new skills, research curriculum, and meet great people from all over the world. When you're in the middle of a project, it is such a cinch to punch in the right words and get just the right information. The Internet is a great thing, but it can be a time stealer, and as mothers with a lot of responsibility, we cannot afford to have our time stolen.

Here are a few practices that have helped me manage my time on the computer more efficiently:

1. Do your work first: kitchen, bathrooms, floors, meals, school. "We work before we play."

2. Multi-task by nursing the baby at the computer. Do not burp your baby for an excessively long period of time.

3. Use a timer, and give yourself a certain amount of time for e-mail and the Internet each day.

4. Take one day (Office Day) to do any research and to allow time for the inadvertent rabbit trails.

5. Categorize your browser bookmarks by person who uses the computer and subject.

6. While you're categorizing bookmarks, make one for Daily and one for Weekly. In the Daily folder, put those bookmarks that you like to read daily. It's the place to put the blog feeds you read every day and your online banking site. In the Weekly folder, put the occasional reads.

7. Subscribe to favorite sites, whenever this option is available, and you will get a notice when it is updated. That saves you time (especially if you have a slow connection) from visiting it and then discovering that it's the same thing you read yesterday or last week.

8. When doing a web search, use a good search engine like Google. Don't read only the heading and click or scan the blurb and click. Look first at the address where it came from. This will save you time from visiting sites you've already been to, give you an idea of what kind of site is passing out the information, or let you know if the blurb is a distraction to get you somewhere where you really don't want to go.

9. Handle the e-mail just like you do the snail mail. Sort through it over the trash can. File what needs to be filed immediately (invoices from online purchases), answer what needs to be answered and immediately dispose of the spam and mark "block sender" immediately. If you're in e-mail groups, and they start to pile up unread, hit "Select All" and "Delete". The topics of discussion that you missed will come around again someday. Keep your e-mail box clean and tidy.

10. Put your computer near the main part of your house so that it's another workstation for you and your kids. My computer is just off the kitchen, ten steps from my stove. I can hear everything that is going on in the main part of the house, and I am able to monitor the children's activities.

11. When you sit down at the computer, prioritize your time. Check your bank balance and balance your checkbook first. Sort your e-mail and do the most important items first. Then visit your favorite sites in order of importance to you. Do your important research tasks before "fun time". If the research to be done is not very important, then save it for Office Day and schedule time for it.

12. If you use a PDA: Update your calendar, shopping lists, To Do lists, and then hot-sync before leaving the computer.

13. Before getting up from your chair, straighten your computer area. File any papers that you printed. Put your pens and papers away. Push your chair in. If it's Office Day, allow extra time for clean up (because you probably have more things out), then dust your computer, peripherals, and desk. Pick up things that have fallen on the floor. Call your children to pick up things that they dropped while visiting you. Put your drink in the sink or dishwasher. Empty the trash basket.

Take these ideas, make a list of your own, and then tape it above your computer. Start implementing them into your daily life. Make your computer time one more routine in your life to improve efficiency and productivity rather than a distraction that takes you away from more important priorities.

Planning Menus

Every week on Office Day, look at your menu plan and write changes. Look at your recipe books and add new recipes to your menu plan. Write your grocery list in an organized way so that you can move through the store faster. If a holiday or hospitality event is coming up, plan your menu, the grocery lists, and the order of events that need to happen for the recipes you are going to use.

Planning Chores

Take the time on Office Day to adjust your chore charts. If the seasons are changing and there is new outdoor work, then make a plan for it. If you are having a hospitality event, plan the work to be done for it.

A popular idea that I love and use is a chore list for each room of the house. Each room has particular work that needs to be done in order to make it look neat and clean. Make a Daily Chore List, Weekly Chore List, and Quarterly Chore List for each one. Start the list with the obvious, such as straightening the room. If it's a playroom or bedroom that can have a lot of clutter on the floor, divide the clutter up also, such as: dolls, stuffed animals, tractors, and trucks. Number the chores so that the cleaning moves from top to bottom and left to right. Take a picture of what the clean room looks like and attach that to the chore list. Put it in a page protector, and place it in each room. When it comes time to train a child to clean a room, the chore list and picture for the room is the guide. Create these chore lists on Office Day.

School Planning

On Office Day, plan for what you want each child to learn over the next school year.

Here's a bit of my own experience and counsel on this front.

A few years ago, after being pulled this way and that by every homeschool catalog, great web site, book I read, magazine review, and the praise of other moms of a certain curriculum, I decided to make my own Scope and Sequence.

A Scope and Sequence is, as you probably know, a chart of what subjects are studied each year. Many textbook providers offer a Scope and Sequence as a guide to their curriculum. I took this idea and made my own for our family. My goal was to chart out a direction for my family's education rather than being blown about by the wind.

The purpose of the Scope and Sequence is to serve as a guide for your homeschooling vision. Whether you call it a "Scope and Sequence" or something else, it is important that you establish goals for training your children, both academically and otherwise. As you endeavor to do this, talk to your husband and make sure that whatever educational priorities you outline for your children are in keeping with what he wants them to learn. Your children's training is of no small consequence, and you want to be on the same page with your husband as to what your goals should be as you plan. Once you have prayed over this and come to conclusions on what your vision is, it's time to move ahead.

Gather all of your favorite homeschooling how-to books, catalogs, and book lists, a 3-ring binder, page protectors, a pencil, and sticky notes. Put it all in a tote that you can grab whenever you work on this project. You could:

- Work on this a bit every day while the children do schoolwork.

- Work on this once a week on Office Day.

- Set aside a day and tackle it all at once.

- Work on it in the evening with your husband after your children go to bed.

Start by figuring out how old each child will be in each year of the future. This helps to see things in a different way and gives you an idea of how many children you will have of "school age" each year. This can be an intimidating look into the future, and you must remember that God will bless you with strength and wisdom for each year!

List the upcoming years in a column on the left. Make a column for each child, listing each name at the top. In each box of the chart, write down the child's "grade" for each year. Along the way, things will be more flexible in regards to what "grade" a child is in his subjects. This exercise is simply to give you a picture of the future and help you plan for it.

Once this exercise is done, take your papers and write at the top of each a grade. This is not to lock your children in at certain grades; it is simply a guide in planning what to study when. If you prefer to put an age instead of a grade at the top of your papers, then do so. Each child is different and will develop at a different pace.

Starting with your "preschool" page, write down what subjects you would like the children to do. How much time do you want them to spend doing certain activities during the day? If you or an older sibling is going to sit down with them and teach the alphabet, write down how much time per day to devote to this. If you want them to have a "music" time, what specifically do you want them to listen to and for what period of time? What will they do with their hands while they listen? Play dough, blocks, puzzles, coloring? What literature do you want read to your preschooler? Do you want a "boxed" curriculum for your preschooler? Will you implement a Montessori approach?

Now do this for each "grade", using your favorite books and catalogs to help you choose curriculum. As the years go by, the lists of subjects to study will grow, and once you have readers, you will want to add a Book List of literature that you want a particular aged child to read. My Scope and Sequence has a list of subjects and curriculum on the left page with a book list on the right.

Once things are penciled in, and out, and you have things the way you think they should be, enter your Scope and Sequence into your word processor, save it, print it out, and put it in page protectors.

This is a huge project, and it will take time. I did most of it at the end of my fifth child's pregnancy when I was sitting around a lot anyway.

Keep in mind that all your children are different. Some children will take off reading and will read the book list for a year in two months' time. Never fear: There are plenty of good books out there! Another child might not read well until they are ten. You will have to work with various learning styles and learn each child's "bent".

A Scope and Sequence is a guide to assist you, not a book of curriculum commandments. Do not be legalistic with it. Its purpose is to give direction to your school plans, not to tie your down.

Making your own personal family Scope and Sequence helps tailor education to your particular family. It's important to ask: What are your family's strengths, weaknesses, ministries, gifts, setting, goals, and so on? The Scope and Sequence helps plan the how and why of these particular variances.

Using a Scope and Sequence also helps in planning what to order when and in budgeting for future expenses. It will save you money. It will help hold back impulse buys. When you see something that you know is on your list and the price is right, you can buy it with confidence.

The biggest advantage for doing this is that it keeps you from waffling and wavering between curriculums. When you hear about a new curriculum, you can look back to your Scope and Sequence and evaluate, "Is this better than what I already planned?" "How much better?" "Is this a good second choice?" Keep sticky notes and a pen in the binder pocket for this very reason. Use them to jot down notes and ideas.

When another successful homeschool family nearly convinces you and your husband of switching to a video curriculum because you just had a baby, you can go back to your Scope and Sequence and think about it. Is this really necessary? Is the Scope and Sequence working? Would it cause more disruption to switch (children get accustomed to a curriculum and when switching can become confused)?

When you read about the newest math curriculum and are tempted to switch to it, you can look at the Scope and Sequence and say, "What I'm using is fine. We have no problems with it. It costs less. I have one child done with the series with no problems, and the other children have no problems with it."

Take a deep breath and let the temptation go. When a new science curriculum comes out that is much more thorough and Bible-based than what you had originally planned for high school, then you can put sticky notes for a new plan on your high school pages.

Years down the road, you might have so many sticky notes that it is time to rewrite the Scope and Sequence. That's okay; it's a guide for your personal family's education. As you and your family grow and change and better curriculum becomes available, your guide will change. But having this guide is a reference point for evaluating and making changes. It will help keep you from being a "curriculum junkie".

Children's Meetings

Make an appointment with each child to review their schoolwork. When you have a lot of children, it is pretty easy for one or more of them to fly under the radar and get away with things. It is also easy for someone to look like they are getting along fine in a subject when they really don't understand the concept and are doing things wrong.

It is wise to keep on top of this day-to-day while our children are working, but let's be realistic: There are a lot of children to stay on top of! By taking one day a week to have a meeting with each child and their schoolwork, you can avoid long-term problems going unnoticed.

An appointment won't take very long for the small children. Give them lots of praise, stickers, hugs, kisses, and promise to tell Dad about the great job they are doing. Explain what needs to be explained, and be sure to keep an eye on problem areas day-to-day until they are resolved.

A meeting with the older children will take longer, and if there is a problem to rectify, it might take a lot longer to explain the concept and work through the problems with them. You might need to stop and continue the meeting later during "free time" or in the evening with Dad.

It is wise to use a part of the time when you meet for prayer. Keep a notebook for these meetings with your children and record their progress, along with prayers you prayed with them.

Do this while the other children are sitting at the table, working on their schoolwork. Hold the one-on-one meeting in another room, if possible.

The Bill Paying System

As a very busy mom and home manager, you need to keep things as efficient as possible. An easy way to add time to your life is to simplify your bill paying system. Online banking is a great way to streamline your finances and keep track of your balance. Next Town Day, stop at your bank and set up your account so that you can access it online. Every Office Day, you should look at your account online, reconcile it with your checkbook, look ahead at upcoming expenses, and know where your money is and where it is going.

Managing Your Family's Fixed Expenses

Take a notebook page and write down "Fixed Expenses" at the top. These are all of your monthly expenses that don't vary much from month to month.

Collect your bill statements and take a good look at them. Put the Fixed Expenses in the order of when they are due in a column on the left side. For instance, if your mortgage is due the first of every month, then that goes at the top; the phone bill is due the 15th, so it goes in the middle; the electric bill is due around the 22nd, so put that towards the bottom of the page; and the bank service fee comes out at the end of the month, so put that at the bottom. Don't forget monthly expenses for things such as piano lessons.

While you're writing the bills down, also write the day they are due and the amount. This will help you know where and when the money is going. It will also help give you a focus in looking at ways you can reduce expenses. If your husband is not aware of what your household costs are, then show this to him.

One very handy thing that you can do for Fixed Expenses is to have them electronically withdrawn. Many businesses do this now. Set this up to save you time and stamps. Mark on your Fixed Expense paper the bills that you have set up for electronic withdrawal so that you don't send off a payment for something on top of an electronic withdrawal. Yes, I have done that!

Next, check to see if your bank does automatic payments. Use this for those businesses that do not offer electronic withdrawals. Automatic payments through the bank are another very handy thing for us busy moms. The bank prints the check and mails it on the date that you specify. This can be changed at your discretion with online banking. One important tip: Be sure to check your bill statements to confirm that they are truly being paid when you scheduled them.

If illness strikes and puts you, the Chief Financial Officer, out of commission, the major bills that keeps the lights on will continue being paid!

How to Plan for Variable Expenses

Variables Expenses are of course those that change from month to month, such as gas, food, clothing, cleaning and paper products, entertainment, etc.

How much do you spend per month on Variable Expenses? Look at past banking statements and your checkbook register to learn where this money goes and how much you spend in each category. These numbers must be kept within what is in your checking account, or you will overdraw.

Write the categories for Variable Expenses and the average money needed for them on your notebook page. On Town Day, you will know that you have x amount of dollars to fill the big van with gas, x amount of dollars to spend at the grocery store, x amount of dollars to spend at the super-store, etc. Some people find it helpful to carry this amount in cash to help control their spending.

Make it a habit to look ahead for anything that you need to save money for. For instance, next week you have plans to go out to eat at a new restaurant with friends. If you don't look ahead and plan to save back money for the dinner date, you might accidentally blow it all when you're at the super-store on Town Day. By looking ahead, you can plan to only withdraw exactly what you need at the super-store, thus saving money for your special dinner date.

How often does your family receive income? If it happens on fixed days, then write this in the column of your notebook paper on the day of the month that it happens. This will help you see how the paychecks are weighted. It might be that most of your bills come due towards the end of the month, which is why you seem to go through the second paycheck so fast compared to the first. If this is the case, then you are going to have to be more careful with not spending so much the first part of the month and saving it for the Variable Expenses that occur in the second half.

If you are paid biweekly, then the pay date is constantly moving, and you will have to gauge your spending accordingly. In the biweekly scenario, you will find it helpful to take another paper and write down the date of every paycheck for the next year. Then, figure out how much cash flow you will have for each pay period. Subtract all the Fixed Expenses from each pay period. There will be two months of the year that there are three paycheck months that look like a bonus. However, there are also two pay periods that have very small cash flows compared to the rest, leaving little for the Variable Expenses. When you write it all down, it becomes much more obvious how the money comes and goes and why you need to be very careful about spending.

Keep this list of Fixed Expenses and Variable Expenses in your Bill Drawer, and look at it every Office Day when you pay bills and plan spending.

To give you breathing room in your checking account, keep an extra month's pay there and, in the current month, spend what was deposited the previous month. When you follow this approach, the money coming this month will be for next month's expenses.

Read more about this method and buy software to help you do this at You Need A Budget (www.youneedabudget.com). I highly recommend this software. In reality, budgeting is goal setting with your money, and using this software helps you manage things so that you can meet your expense projections. You work with the future, not the past, as with other money software options.

There are four principles that the creator promotes and incorporates into the You Need a Budget software:

1. Stop Living Paycheck to Paycheck
2. Give Every Dollar a Job
3. Prepare for Rain
4. Roll With the Punches

The Bill Drawer

"Everything has a place, everything in its place."

The bills should have a place to be until they are paid or filed. The first thing you need to do to achieve this goal is to choose a desk drawer and empty it. Nothing in this drawer is as important as keeping your bills in one place. A paper pile or more than one paper pile sitting around the house is unacceptable. This is how payments are missed or late, and important papers are lost.

You must be very disciplined about this drawer. It's a habit like anything else. You cannot allow junk mail to accumulate there. The only things that belong in the drawer are bills, and the tools used to pay the bills. Every day when you sort through the mail, take the bills straight to this drawer. Remember— bills only! Other papers that need attention should be filed elsewhere.

The tools you will want in your Bill Drawer are envelopes, stamps, address labels, and a calculator. Two other tools you will keep there are your list of Fixed Expenses, your plan for Variable Expenses, and your Short Term Savings Plan.

Do not let your children meddle in the Bill Drawer. Do not keep anything they would want or need there. You do not want them messing around in the drawer. Make it clear to them that it is full of mom and dad's very important papers. You might consider keeping stamps in your purse or in a high place because, in your four-year-old's eyes, stamps can be very pretty when stuck all over an art project on the wall.

An alternative to the Bill Drawer is the Bill Bag. In the past, I have kept a tote bag with all of the bill drawer items and a manila folder for the bills. Instead of putting all of the bills into the Bill Drawer, I put them into the Bill Bag. I would grab this bag on our way out the door to piano lessons. While the children were at lessons, the rest of us shopped at the grocery store, visited the library or park, and then we waited in the van until the piano kids were done. While we waited, the children listened to a story on CD or looked at library books, and I paid bills using my Bill Bag. This worked fine for a couple of years.

When the mail comes, sort it immediately. Do this over the trash can and junk the junk mail.

If there are important papers that need to be filed, put these in a file basket on your desk. Ideally, you would file these papers in their proper place right away (try to do this!), but filing can take some time. The reality often is that while you are sorting the mail, some sort of crisis erupts. Remember, you are the mother of a large family, and life can be quite unpredictable. So put these in the File basket, and on Office Day, file these papers away. Do not let this File grow into a huge disastrous mess. Write down on your Office Day routine to do the filing that needs to be done. It will be so helpful for you to have everything in its proper place!

Put the newspapers, magazines, and catalogs in a basket or on a table beside the chair where they will be read. It should be the weekly chore of the person who cleans that particular room to clean out the old newspapers and magazines. Write this down on the chore list for the room.

Paper management is just another area of life that we need to deliberately have a place for things and keep things in their place. It's a habit to work on. You already have habits with your paper system; you just need to replace the bad habits with good ones. It might even help you to take a paper and write down what your current paper habits are. This will help you see what needs to change. Remember, creating new habits requires thought, but soon it will become ingrained, and you won't have to do the extra mental work. Your bill system and paper management will just happen automatically!

How to Plan for Short-Term Savings Goals

Take a fresh notebook page and write Savings Plan at the top. Next, get your family calendar from last year and look at all the activities that your family did that cost money. Make a list of the months of the year in a column on the left-hand side. Using your old calendar to help jog your memory, write down the yearly recurring activities beside each month in the column and the expected cost associated with each one of them.

For example, our homeschool convention is in June, but there is an early payment discount plus hotel booking, so I write beside April, "Homeschool Convention". This is a reminder for me to save up for this event. A short list of other Short Term Savings I need to think about are:

- January—seed order
- March—TeenPact
- April—Brooke's Birthday
- May—graduation gifts, landscape plants
- June—Big Birthday Bash
- July—4-H Fair
- August—State Fair, Family Camp
- Fall—winter shoes, Christmas gifts

Look ahead and plan for when you will need to hold back money for these events. Otherwise, you will be surprised with the extra financial demands the week they occur and may run into a money-pinch.

This is also a helpful practice to follow in order to have money set aside for future good deals that can be reasonably anticipated. Some businesses run various specials on things throughout the year. By anticipating this, you will have money when these specials occur. Your daughter's birthday might not be for another six months, but when the special on the doll happens, you will have the money to get her birthday gift because you were planning for the special sale.

If you have months where you have no big expenses due, plan to use these times to buy those things that aren't on a time frame, such as books and curriculum, home projects, magazine subscriptions, clothes shopping (even for the next season), etc. Write relevant items that fit this category down on your page so that you remember to save for and purchase them at the appropriate time.

Keep this Short Term Savings list in your Bill Drawer. Every Office Day, look at this list and think about how you can plan and save for these upcoming expenses. Home managing is about more than cooking and cleaning; it also involves managing savings and expenses.

Planning for Vacation

Many times things you want to do that involve money never happen because you haven't given your finances the thought required to do them. Yet if we go through the brainstorming process, plan, and save, we can often do things that we previously thought were financially out of reach.

Let's say that your family wants to take a trip to a big celebration event. In doing some research, you determine that it will cost your large family $1,652 for the week at your destination. In addition, it will take you two days to get there and back in your big van, requiring $400 for gas. Add one hotel night, two rooms for your large family: $250. Don't forget the hotel night when you come home: another $250.

Plus food: Eat breakfast at home the first day's travel, pack a lunch, healthy snack food and water for eating in the big van on the way, eat a decent supper out for $75; or eat off the $1 menu at Burger King for $25, because everybody wants two of the measly burgers. Second day: Eat breakfast at the hotel's free continental buffet, lunch at McDonald's $1 menu, $25; and a decent supper somewhere, $75. On the way home, you have two $1 menu lunches for $50, and two decent suppers that total $150. Total food for the trip to and from the event: $375.

Your Grand Total for the trip is $2,727, plus or minus. You have six months until the vacation event, and you have no money in your vacation savings account, so you will have to save $454 a month for six months. Let's say there's no way that you can save $454 a month. Then maybe next year you can make it work.

Don't stop with the thought; do the math. Next year is 18 months away. Let's add 10% to the cost, because you will probably have some children jump into the next age group that costs more. Your children might be hungrier next year, gas prices might go up, etc. So let's plan on $3,000 divided by 18 months: that's $166 dollars a month to save.

Can you do it? Maybe you need to reevaluate things. How badly do you really want to go to this event? How badly do you just want a vacation, and you don't care where? Maybe your husband thinks that this event will be an extra, wonderful blessing for your family, and that other things that you normally spend money on will take a back seat, and you will go this year. Perhaps you can sell something and use the money for the trip.

To plan for a vacation: Pick a goal, do a bit of research and math, and then save the money back for it. Have it automatically transferred every pay date into a savings account. If you're doing online banking, this will take a minute or so to get that automatic transfer set up. If it automatically comes out, you won't miss it. You will mentally see it as another Fixed Expense coming out, just like all of your other bills.

Use this same system for anything you want to save up for: a home, your next vehicle, an emergency account, tiling the bathroom floor, a patio, etc. Do your research, set a date, figure the monthly amount, and set up an automatic transfer to make it easier.

Home Business Management

She considers a field and buys it; with the fruit of her hands she plants a vineyard. —Proverbs 31:16

Industrious moms are great at generating ideas on how we can help our husbands bring in more income. This is not a bad thing in itself. Where it can go wrong, and often does, is when the wife becomes a helpmate to a man not her husband and when the work and relationships at home are neglected.

In my own life, there was time in the past that our home life became neglected when I pursued a home business that took me outside of the home on the occasional evening. When my husband traveled for his work, this meant that I had to get a baby sitter; and when he was home, he wanted me to be home with him. The result of this business pursuit was that I was neglecting my relationship with my children (missing those precious bedtime rituals) and neglecting the few hours I had with my hard-working husband.

J.R. Miller puts the misstep I made into perspective with this powerful quote that underscores the wife's sacred mission in the home, a mission that must remain inviolate:

> *Home is the true wife's kingdom. There, first of all places, she must be strong and beautiful. She may touch life outside in many ways, if she can do it without slighting the duties that are hers within her own doors. But if any calls for her service must be declined, they should not be the duties of her home. These are hers, and no other one's. Very largely does the wife hold in her hands, as a sacred trust, the happiness and the highest good of the hearts that nestle there. —J.R. Miller,* Secrets of a Happy Home Life

Some of us seem to be born entrepreneurs, and I count myself in that number. I love to read entrepreneurial stories, and I constantly see needs that aren't being met: "Somebody should make a business for that!"

I like to do the research on a business idea and to analyze the cash flow requirements involved. One of my sisters-in-law and I used to get together and work out cash flows on rental properties we found in the real estate ads. One market I saw not having its needs met were large families. It seemed like I was always searching in all sorts of odd places for products to meet the needs we were coming to realize as our family grew and grew. I developed the idea that we as a family could start a business to meet the needs of other large families. My brain went into overdrive, and I had pages of product ideas.

Everyone in my family was very agreeable, even coming up with further ideas, ways, and means to help this business happen. Yet the reality of the business was not as fun. The reality was that my husband already had a job that kept him very busy. In addition to that, he and our sons crop farm and have a beef cow herd. I was counting on my oldest sons to help with shipping and inventory management for this new business venture. The reality was that they had enough on their plate already with schoolwork and farm chores to do.

The biggest challenge in this business venture was that nobody in our family had a passion for it once the rubber met the road. My husband and oldest sons love the farm life and all the components of it. They love animal and plant genetics; they love to create and build with wood and steel; they love to plant and harvest; they love to buy and sell cattle, tractors, corn, and beans; they love calving season— yet they weren't that wild about shipping boxes.

What eventually happened was that I, the mom, was doing all the work from idea hatching and research (my favorite) to shipping, and everything in between. God saw fit to end the business when

I was on strict bed rest in a hospitable bed for two weeks, and then pumped milk for our NICU baby every two hours for three months after, living two hours away from home. "Business? What business?"

My heart is about family and home. God didn't create me to be provider, but to be a help-meet to my husband and a manager of our home.

Over and over, I hear of homeschool moms who want Dad home from his job. A family living and working together is ideal. Where we err is in not working on Dad's idea based on his interests and passions, but focusing instead on our own great desire to bring him home. As home managers, we need to bring our home business ideas not only under our husband's authority but also under his unique talents, interests, and passions. We are his helpmate; he is not ours. Lauri Bluedorn put it this way:

> *There are lots and lots of homeschool mothers who are super organized, highly motivated, go-getter-take-charge type of women—that's probably one reason they started homeschooling in the first place. If they weren't homeschooling they would be starting a million dollar business! I think homeschooling families starting home businesses is a great idea, especially if Dad is an integral part of it and the children are included in a meaningful way in the adventure—not as only hired workers but developing and using their gifts and talents. The trouble seems to come when the home business becomes a "Mom only" thing—Dad isn't particularly interested and the kids watch from a distance. Mom desperately wants it to work and puts her all into it, staying up late at night and spending every spare minute on it. This doesn't seem to be compatible with homeschooling. —Lauri Bluedorn, TriviumPursuit.com*

Lauri is right. When mom's focus isn't on home, her family suffers. Some moms even quit homeschooling because the home business begins to take on a life of its own, and the children's education becomes neglected. Don't fall into this trap! Be careful and diligent to keep priorities in line with the Scriptures.

Magazines, Crafts, and Recipes

Instead of filing articles and recipes, put them into three-ring binders. Articles that are filed are rarely seen again.

This is another project that doesn't need to be done all at once. Start now with anything you clip from this day forward. Use a binder for each season, and fill it with page protectors. The reason you want one for each season is that we live our lives seasonally. We make things with strawberries and rhubarb in June, decorate for Independence Day in June and July, make pumpkin pie in the fall, and paper snowflakes when the snow flies. Magazines have certain themes for each month that have to do with holidays, produce that is in season, and seasonal crafts and garden projects. Keep in mind that the articles and recipes will come around again in a year or two.

Start with seasonal binders, and if you would like to be more specific, then make one for each month. If you have time, make them pretty by using scrapbooking paper behind your cut articles and recipes. Do this regularly with your magazine subscriptions, and pull out only the projects you want to do, and toss the rest of the magazine in the trash. When your binders get full, purge them. Do not keep making binders for the rest of your life! Only keep what you have real intentions of doing.

Phone Center

Keep near your phone a basket or drawer with pens, pencils, notepaper, tape, and sticky notes.

On the wall near your phone, keep a list of frequently called numbers. Remember to add your husband's work phone and your family's cell phone numbers for the children and baby sitters.

Daily Tasks for the Home Office Manager

Open the mail over the trash, immediately disposing of the junk mail. Handle paper once.

Bills go into the Bill Drawer. Always open a bill in case it needs immediate attention.

Magazines and newspapers go to predetermined spots—the table by your husband's chair or your chair or a special basket. Purge these spots on Cleaning Day.

Take newsletters, invitations, etc. with dates of events straight to the calendar and write down their dates immediately. Then put the details into your Pending File.

Place catalogs that you order from with your magazines and newspapers, and toss catalogs you don't order from into the trash.

File statements and important papers immediately or put them in the Action File and file them on Office Day.

Schedule time every day for this chore—don't let it pile up!

CHAPTER 22
Town Day

She is like the ships of the merchant; she brings her food from afar. —Proverbs 31:14

The purpose of Town Day is to knock out your errands. Why establish a day for this? For some of us the answer is clear: We live so far away from town, that to run in for every little thing would drive us into poverty. We would no longer be homeschooling, but vehicle schooling.

For those who live conveniently close to all stores, I would still strongly suggest that you establish a Town Day in your family life for the same reason we country folk do—efficiency. You will save time and money by disciplining yourself to doing your errands on one day.

Keep track of the time you spend running here and there for this and that. It takes effort to dress, shoe, buckle in, grab the purse and diaper bag, just for a few things at the store. Work on being more efficient with your time, using the time and money you save for greater purposes. Schedule appointments, lessons, and outside-the-house activities for Town Day as much as possible.

Home is the best place to be for the stability of the children, for productive homeschooling, and for the care of the home. It is very easy to get involved in many good activities; I know all too well! But when we do that, we end up substituting the best with the good or even the mediocre. Sometimes we run around to various activities as a way of escaping our home responsibilities. Out of sight—out of mind. When we are busy going here and there, busy doing this and that activity, everyone tends to get tired and irritable, the laundry piles up, the quality of the food we eat goes down, and relationships suffer. And for what? What is worth all this?

When it comes to activities outside the home, I would encourage you to talk to your husband about what priorities beyond the home that he wants your family involved with, and then plan these into your life as carefully as possible.

You should plan your errands carefully to make the most of your time. Following are my step-by-step suggestions on how to do this effectively—starting with your routine the day before through the end of errand day itself.

The Day Before

- Balance the checkbook.

- Make your menu plan and shopping lists. Put your lists in your purse.

- Pack the diaper bag.

- If you have items to take back to town, put them in the vehicle.

- If you have stops to make after the grocery store, then put an ice chest in for your cold items.

Plan your route to be as efficient as possible. If you will need to eat in town, work that into your plan.

If you have a lot of little children, you need to be extra diligent about how you plan your day. Miserable children make for a miserable day. Do not stress them more than they can handle. If they are even slightly ill, take that into account in how you plan your day.

The Night Before

Lay out town clothes and shoes for everyone. Put everyone to bed at a decent time, if not earlier than usual.

Know what your supper plan is for Town Day, and do the prep work for it.

Know what your lunch plan is, and either pack a lunch, get it ready to eat when you get home, or decide where you plan to eat out.

The Morning Of

Load the crockpot so you do not have to worry about making supper that night. Leave immediately after the breakfast table chores are done so that you can be home as soon as possible for the little ones to get their naps. Require everyone to use the toilet before leaving.

If it's raining, don't go, or cut out most of your stops. Fighting the rain is usually not worth the effort, and it can be very stressful on everyone. Simply reschedule your appointments for another day.

Hints for Being Efficient

In scheduling your day, add in extra time for changing somebody's complete outfit at the last minute, for losing one of the toddler's shoes, and for hitting every red light.

Plan your stops so that you do not have to back track. Do the most necessary stops first; if the little children begin to meltdown, you can cut your losses and head for home.

Do not give the children anything except water to drink unless you like to go into the restroom of every store you visit. Take along a drink cooler of water and paper cups or water bottles. I like to keep a case of water bottles in our van.

Park your vehicle by a cart corral so that you can immediately put your little children in a cart and push them into the store.

If you have a little baby, time your trip so that he won't be starving hungry half-way through the store. Keep an eye on the clock, and don't dawdle.

Stores typically have low-volume traffic in the early mornings which makes it much more easy to move through then. In the late afternoon and towards the end of the week, they tend to be very busy which can give an instantaneous headache. Do your best to plan the brunt of your shopping when the stores are more navigable.

Store Rules for Children

Go over the Store Rules before you leave the vehicle, and review them again between each stop:

- When you get out of the vehicle, do not rub your coat against the cars and get dirty.

- When you get out of the vehicle, be careful not to door-ding the next car.

- In the parking lot, hold hands with your "buddy" (an assigned sibling) and stay together.

- Do not run around in the parking lot unless you want the most severe of consequences!

- Walk in age order behind Mom, with the oldest taking up the rear to make sure we do not lose anyone. Do not get out of line (a trouble maker or two might have to hold on to the cart).

- No crawling on the floor.

- No wrestling in stores.

- No yelling or screaming.

- No asking for things.

- No hiding in the clothes.

- No fits.

- Do not touch the price tabs in the grocery store. If you move price tabs, the next person will not know what the item costs.

> ### Apply the Golden Rule...
>
> ...to your children when you're out and about on Town Day. Remember that they are people too, not a burden to be carried about. They like to explore the world around them. Even the grocery store is an adventure in new sights. Take them out and show them the wonders of this "new to them" world. Delight in it with them. Make it fun not drudgery. Do your thinking beforehand through planning, not while you are going up and down the aisles.

- Do not touch items in the stores unless we are buying it. Would you like to buy something that smelled like a French fry?

- Do not touch each other unless you are holding hands.

- Smile!

- Don't talk to strangers, and don't go anywhere without Mom!

I do reward for good behavior. Disobedience is dealt with at home. I know that there are those that say to leave the store and go home with the unruly child. We live too far from town for that. Having well-behaved children starts at home. If they are obedient at home, they will be obedient in public. If I am concerned about a child's obedience, I have found that laying out clear expectations and their consequences and then following up with those consequences will usually prevent further infractions. If a child seems to want to "test", I will not neglect to give discipline for the first infraction of the day while we are still at home. This prevents them from further testing. Sometimes I need to bend over and have some words of instruction with a child in a store. This is an opportunity for ministry not only to our child, but also to those that might observe. As Christians, we are to be a witness to those around us.

I have found that the way the shopping goes is largely dependent on my preparation for the day and my attitude. I try to make it fun, and we take time to smell the fresh strawberries in the produce section and even window shop a bit. If you want your children to behave in public, you need to take them out in public and learn how to do it.

On especially good days, we will stop for ice cream on the way home. The children get accustomed to the stores and routines of your Town Day. They learn to help and anticipate your needs and the needs of their siblings. Children are a blessing! They will see things on the shelves that you need to buy and remind you of them. Believe it or not, you will come to rely on them and their memory jogs when you are shopping! They are like extra brains and right hands for you.

In the Store

Put the baby into your baby carrier or the shopping cart's seat (clean it first with a baby wipe). Put the toddlers into the back of the cart and require them to sit. It is nicer to sit on a coat or a package of toilet paper, paper towels, or diapers. If you need many items at the store, then have your biggest child push another cart. Or you can push one and pull the other. Some grocery stores have carts that are like a car in the front. Two children can fit in there—fasten the seat belt and teach them to keep their arms inside!—and the toddler can ride in the seat while you have the littlest in the front carrier.

Some stores will pull your items for you, and you will only need to pick them up when you're done shopping. Call around to your local stores to find out which ones offer this option.

Eating Out or Not

Drive-through eating costs a lot of money, often leaves the children still hungry, and is extremely unhealthy—not to mention the fact that the smell of drive through food in the vehicle can be nauseating! Given these facts, try to eat at home or pack along sandwiches (get them ready the night before), whenever possible. It is a treat to stop at a park for a picnic!

When You Get Home

When you arrive home from running errands, put the little ones down for a nap first. Have the older children unload the bags and put away refrigerator items while you feed the baby. Then let everyone go to Quiet Time. They need a break from running around, and so do you! After a big Town Day at our house, it is often commented, "I lost a day of my life!"

Wash the salad veggies. Cut up the dry stuff and toss. This will keep for several days if you don't add tomatoes, mushrooms, cucumbers, and other moist items. Cut those at each meal. Put your older children in charge of salad prep.

During Afternoon Choretime, have the children distribute the shopping items to their proper places.

Recovery

If it was a very rough day in town(and I know you know what I mean), thank the Lord you put food into the crockpot. The bare minimum is to get the cold items put away, and then everyone goes to their Quiet Time place until supper is ready. The chores can wait until tomorrow. Rest restores the sanity as nothing else does.

The next day, balance the checkbook again. Keeping on top of this small chore keeps the finances under control.

Homeschooling on Town Day

If your Town Day only involves a short trip, then you can do your daily schedule when you are at home. If you're gone into town in the morning, do your normal schedule after lunch. If you're home in the morning, then don't change your schedule until an hour before you leave, when you're getting ready.

When you are out, listen to educational audios whenever it is appropriate. There are so many great audios available to learn from. Driving is the perfect time for them, because the children are buckled in and are a captive audience. My children love it so much that they hate to stop the audios and go into a store!

If you are going to spend an extended time in a waiting room, pack their workbook type things and have them work while they wait.

When they get home from a big Town Day, the children are often very tired. This is a good time to pull out an educational video and let them relax in front of it for a time. Then send them outside to run awhile.

Do not forget that learning to be gracious to those around us is an important lesson to master.. We need to make it a point to be pleasant to other people, to smile, and to look others in the eye when we speak to them. When they ask us those big family or homeschooling questions, we should smile and answer graciously, even if the question is rude. We are to be a light on a hill and that means we should think of others more highly than ourselves. If we see somebody that needs help, we should help them. We should hold the door for others. Town Day is an opportunity for ministry to our communities!

Good Deals for Large Families

In the early days of large family living, before you have to start doubling, tripling, quadrupling, and buying cookbooks with restaurant-size recipes, it will be beneficial to follow the standard money-saving ideas like reading all the ads, shopping for the best deals at all the stores, keeping a price book, clipping coupons, and playing the coupon game.

At some point, however, if your family grows to be large, the effort it takes to do all those things will generally not be worth the time involved in the broader scheme of things.

There comes a time when you will simply want a pantry full of bulk goods that allows you to make virtually anything, and when you cross this threshold, your shopping habits will change dramatically. The convenience of bulk will outweigh the inconvenience of running out to get small things.

When you reach this point, it's important to learn to substitute food items creatively. For example: Out of cornstarch? Use arrowroot powder instead. Out of arrowroot powder? Use flour as a substitute. Is minute tapioca a better choice? In other words, creativity becomes an important rule to get you by when it's impractical to make a trip to the store.

If you have a well-stocked pantry, you have lots of creative leeway. Buying in bulk is not always less expensive, but it saves you time. Your workload as mom to a big brood is huge, and looking at the big picture, it is better to spend precious time building relationships than itemizing a price book.

Stocking a pantry for a large family does not mean buying more boxes of Uncle Ben's; it means a 25-pound bag of brown basmati rice. Stick it in the deep freeze for a day to kill any bugs, and you'll be set to go for awhile. It doesn't mean five extra jars of spaghetti sauce; it's a garden of Roma tomatoes that you freeze or can to make spaghetti sauce from scratch (it's not hard).

You don't need to learn this method all at once. One step at a time, one food at a time is fine, just as with any other new thing you're seeking to master.

- Ask around your community to learn about any food co-ops. If there aren't any, then start one. Create a group, contact wholesalers, divide the labor, and stock up your pantry.

- Buy in bulk from your local grocery store. Ask the management about ordering a case of an item for a discount. You both win with this scenario: you get a discount, and they are selling more product and might get a further discount from their supplier.

- Shop at a food service store. These are the type of stores that supply restaurants and institutions.

- Shop at warehouse stores such as Sam's Club and Costco, especially for paper goods.

- Garden and buy produce from a farmer's market or a CSA (Community Supported Agriculture) farm.

- Shop at bulk food stores.

- Buy meat by the whole beef, pork, etc. Get it cut how you want it, and store it in your deep freeze.

Storing bulk food will cause you to be creative if your kitchen is in small quarters. Look around and reevaluate what is truly necessary. Look inside your cupboards and closets and think how you can group and arrange items more efficiently, like with like. Remove nonessential items and put them into storage. One thing we did to add more needed storage space was to put shelves in a coat closet near the kitchen. We also have shelves in the basement for extra food. Five-gallon food grade buckets are the most common way to store large quantities of things. Also: Be sure that your storage containers are mouse-proof!

Our hands are God's and can fitly be used only in doing his work. Our feet are God's and may be employed only in walking in his ways and running his errands. Our lips are God's and should speak only words which honor him and bless others. Our hearts are God's and must not be profaned by thoughts and affections which are not pure.
—*J.R. Miller,* Being Christians on Weekdays

CHAPTER 23
Cleaning Day

The woman who makes a sweet, beautiful home, filling it with love and prayer and purity, is doing something better than anything else her hands could find to do beneath the skies.
—*J.R. Miller,* Secrets of a Happy Home Life

Pick Up the Mess!

Cleaning is a task that is easy to do if all the stuff that your family leaves laying around is picked up. Those of you who have had a house cleaner know what I mean. A house cleaner comes and whips through the house, and it's spick-and-span. She's like a magic fairy. How does she do it? I'll tell you how: She has the easy part, the actual cleaning. You and the children did the hard part of putting away everything that you left lying around since the last time she came. The actual cleaning part is not that hard. It is everything that has to happen in order to clean that is hard. Put simply: Your stuff is in the way.

Flat surfaces are magnets for people to lay stuff down on. Catch people at it, catch yourself at it, and stop the bad habit. Instead, put things where they belong. "A place for everything, and everything in it's place." Say it over and over and over to yourself and to your family. Make fold-up signs on every level surface for three weeks to help train them to stop laying things down where they don't belong. When things are constantly put in their proper place, then the house is not messy.

This is another reason why Afternoon Chore Time is so important. Do a daily pick up of every room and clear all flat surfaces. Do it to catch everything that those still in training (toddlers) leave lying around. If everyone works on a room, the load is shared, and the pickup time will be finished much more quickly.

If you don't have enough big kids to help, then it is essential to your peace of mind to limit the stuff that can be carried about. Here are some practical ideas to help you control needless clutter:

- A locked cupboard for games, puzzles, and art supplies. Keep the key out of reach, and get activities out only at designated times of the day. When the children are done, help them put the activity away. Keep the key out of reach.

- Limit the amount of toys your children have. Do a massive de-clutter. Focus on quality and imaginative toys.

- Rotate the toys by the week, month, season. Keep the rest boxed. Out of sight and mind.

- Every month, sort the toys, puzzles, games, art supplies. Keep the number limited.

- Designate specific places for things. Make sure everyone knows where certain things belong and what it should look like when they are clean and straightened. Take a picture of the spot so the "cleaner" knows what it should look like.

Help Me, Please!

If you're a mom with a lot of littles and no big kids, or you are having a difficult time keeping up with the cleaning for some other reason, then, by all means, don't be reluctant to get some cleaning help. Managing the home is a biblical duty of wives and mothers, and sometimes that managing involves managing others who are helping you. I do want to caution you to not buy into the world's philosophy that you have more important things to do than clean, and so you need a full time housekeeper. But there are seasons in life where you just need some help. I recommend that you look first for a young lady who would like an opportunity to serve. Perhaps she would like to trade helping in exchange for the experience of being around lots of Littles and learn from watching you throughout the day. Trading services for goods or bartering is a wonderful way to meet needs without using money. If you find that you need to hire out some of the housecleaning work, try hiring a younger person to help after their schoolwork is done. And then some professional services will let you pick and choose what you want help with. Maybe you want two hours of help, or perhaps you just need the kitchen and bathrooms really scrubbed once a month. Be creative and don't hesitate to ask for help!

Fitting it in the Day

IN THE MORNING

Instead of making the beds, strip them and take the sheets straight to the washer. Do the nappers' bedding first, and remake those beds before lunch. That way, as soon as lunch is over and the Littles are clean, they can go straight to their nap times.

AFTERNOON CHORE TIME

First, put the baby/toddler in the play pen, and get the preschoolers involved in an activity that will occupy them for one hour, or send them with their buddy to help and learn how to clean. Which one you do will definitely depend on the preschooler and the older buddy's unique personality and personal work ethic. Matching him up with a buddy can be a great thing or not, depending on the maturity level of the children involved.

Then, you and the older children do your regular room chores just like you always do during Afternoon Chore Time, but today add Dusting and Vacuuming for each room. It shouldn't be that much time added to each room's regular chores.

Another way to do it, depending on each family's dynamics, is for the children to team up and straighten rooms as a group, with one child being the Duster and another child being the Vacuumer.

Remake the beds with the clean sheets.

Reward the children with a break and a treat. Then do the Deep Cleaning work.

Keeping Up with the Work

Playing "beat the clock" is a fun game for the children. We love challenges, and it is fun to beat old records. An older and wiser mom at my church told me once how she did a re-training with her boys in "how to clean a toilet". They had their toilet-cleaning lessons, and then raced each other to see who could clean the toilet the fastest. What speed-cleaning does is teach the children not to procrastinate. When they know that a certain task takes a certain amount of time, they will do it and move on! Eye-balling a task for a long period, dragging our feet, and grumbling through it is allowing a poor work ethic to develop. Teach your children to stay on top of their work by doing it thoroughly and quickly.

The good thing about systems is that they don't require a lot of thought once you understand and master them. You and your team can just go to work and knock out what needs to be done without a lot of deliberation. The tasks and methods are in place; the workers just need to show up and do the job.

By contrast: Without a system, a plan, or a simple chore chart, nobody gets much done because they don't know what they are supposed to be doing. If the team is told to do something, but do not know how to do it, imagine the frustration that occurs! Without systems, without children who have been trained and are being trained, the house work will be hard. It will lose its joy and be depressing. As a an overwhelmed mother, you might look around for pity. You might be tempted to escape from reality and hide with a good book, go shopping, or, worse yet, to send your children off on the bus!

A good system and willing workers promote a good attitude in everyone. It's a good feeling to look at a house wreck and know that it will all be put back together with a little time and elbow grease.

CHAPTER 24
Deep Cleaning

By mutual forbearance, gentleness, confidence and love; by deeds of kindness, delicate attention, and graceful demeanor seek to transfer as much of the purity, love, and sunshine of your Father's House above as you can, to your Father's house below.
—*Octavius Winslow,* Our Father's House

Dig In!

In times past, people did Spring Cleaning and Fall Cleaning. Cheryl Mendelson tells us in her encyclopedic book on keeping house, *Home Comforts*:

> *The custom of a seasonal "housecleaning" in the spring arose because after two seasons of heating and lighting with wood, oil, gas, kerosene, and candles, the condition of the house made it essential.*

We no longer have to clean the grime that our foremothers did, but we still need to dig in deep on a regular basis in order to keep things clean that are in, under, and behind the furnishings of our homes. It is preferable for the deep cleaning to be regularly kept up so that we don't have to upset our home for a week. A little bit here and a little bit there goes a long way in getting deep cleaning work done so that it won't become a behemoth that overwhelms us.

Here's the course of action I recommend; divide your home into key areas. I call them "Focus Areas" because we are good at what we focus on, and I want to focus on an extra-good cleaning on a regular basis. Each home is going to have a different arrangement of Focus Areas, depending on the structure of the home and the lifestyle of the family.

In my home, I have each Focus Area written on a specific week of each month on our wall calendar. We do deep cleaning work for each Focus Area and then extra things that are situation-specific to that area.

WEEK 1

Dining Room/Schoolroom/Bookshelves

Devote some time this week to going on a book hunt throughout the house and returning all books to their proper place.

WEEK 2

Bathrooms

It doesn't take long for a large family to make a bathroom gross. If you keep the bathroom work assigned to certain children to clean daily, then they shouldn't be too bad. However, once a month, clean all the corners, cracks, and crevices. De-clutter the cabinets and drawers, and organize all the ponytail holders, barrettes, headbands, bows, ribbons, etc.

Mudroom/Backdoor Entry

The entries that you use most frequently need special focus. They can get cluttered and dirty quickly! Assign a family member to do daily maintenance on this area during Afternoon Chore Time.

Scrub the walls once a month. If everyone takes a wet rag for fifteen minutes, it will be done in no time. If you involve the kids in the cleaning, they will be more apt to catch themselves and notice when a sibling puts their grubby mitts on the wall! During a Project Week, paint this area with a high-gloss paint. This will make cleaning the walls much easier.

WEEK 3

Bedrooms

This should be an easy week if you have your children work on cleaning bedroom areas as part of their chores throughout the month. Have them spend a few minutes every day picking up as part of their Morning and Evening Routine. Then have them spend one 15-minute period per week working on a Bedroom Management Focus Area. If you follow this approach, keeping the bedrooms clean will be a cinch.

WEEK 4

Living Room and Family Room

Vacuum the dust out of the furniture. Don't forget to clean in couches and chairs, under tables, behind furniture, and under curtains where those cobwebs tend to hide.

WEEK 5

Playroom/Toys/Games/Crafts

This week is devoted to de-cluttering and organizing efficient systems in key areas of your home.

When Do I Do This?

There are two ways to go about Deep Cleaning in your week. You and your children can do a small part each day, or you can devote a larger segment of time on Cleaning Day, or you can do both. Do what works best for your home and family situation. As the weeks go by and the house becomes better managed and more consistently clean, Deep Cleaning will become easier and easier, which means that it will take less time to do. Hooray!

The following is a listing of how we have Deep Cleaning chores divided up by day of the week. Sometimes we need to mix up the tasks so that they fit better with other things that are going on with that day of the week.

Maybe you will only schedule these things on two other days, plus Cleaning Day. For instance, we don't do window washing on Town Day. Our Town Day might change year-to-year, depending on what day of the week we schedule to do music lessons. Often we don't do Deep Cleaning on Kitchen Day, especially if we have a lot of kitchen projects going on. We do the Deep Cleaning tasks during Afternoon Chore Time. When everyone works together, it goes fast.

If you don't have a lot of big kids to help divide the work with yet, then just do your best at pecking away at it. Use our family's Deep Cleaning schedule to brainstorm and devise a Deep Cleaning schedule that works best for your home.

Monday

Decluttering and cleaning are ongoing processes. The less you have, the less you have to take care of. "You don't own your stuff, your stuff owns you," as the saying goes. Take care of all the clutter in the Focus Area. This includes clutter in drawers and cupboards. Evaluate everything in the area:

- Is it useful?
- Is it needed?
- Is it loved?
- Is it beautiful?
- Does it promote your family values?
- Do you have more of this item than necessary?
- Is it taking up needed space?
- Do other people need this item more than you do?
- Does it create problems in your house?

If you have a lot of clutter, just work on it for ten or fifteen minutes in one area of your home, and then stop until you come around to this area of the house again next month. In the meantime, do not add more clutter to this Focus Area! Load the clutter up in boxes. Take the boxes to the vehicle to drop off at charity on Town Day. Declutter!

Tuesday

Catch cobwebs (elementary age kids can do this). Kill the spiders! Dust lights and ceiling fans and replace light bulbs (a job for your tall boys). Dust base boards (a good job for preschoolers). Assign tasks to the children, and race the clock!

Wednesday

Straighten a drawer or cupboard (elementary age kids can do this). If it goes fast, do another one. Stop after fifteen minutes.

Thursday

Wash windows and curtains, as necessary (everybody divide and conquer). Wash area rugs. Wipe grime from light switches (a preschooler's job).

Friday

Vacuum in the corners and around the edges in the furniture and under the furniture. This counts as an exercise workout for today! If there are Deep Cleaning tasks that you didn't get done earlier in the week, do them today.

Saturday

Putter and pretty! This is the fun day! Look around and think about how to add a little something special to the room, but be sure that you aren't adding clutter that will increase the work load. There's a fine line here. Does the Focus Area need a new furniture arrangement? Should you start shopping for something that will fit a certain wall area? Write it down and put it in your wallet to remind you when you're out shopping. A simple vase of garden flowers or a bowl of fruit will add a dash of pizzazz to a room.

Do not feel that you must get every single task done; you will be cleaning in the same Focus Area of the house next month. Your home will slowly become de-cluttered and more clean as each month goes by. In focusing on one area of the house at a time, you are less likely to be distracted and running around cleaning a bit here and a bit there. This approach also creates a great sense of satisfaction to see an area of the house clean and well-managed.

Window Cleaning

Do not be intimidated by window cleaning. Clean windows will brighten and cheer your day! A Focus Area might have one window or eight. Some windows, due to location, don't get that dirty, and a once-a-year cleaning is fine for them. Other windows (like the ones on my front porch) need to be washed once a month during fly season.

With the windows for each Focus Area, think about these things:

- How dirty are they?

- How much help do I have?

- How easy are the windows to clean?

- Do I need to hire a professional to help?

Create a system for window cleaning. If you have children who are old enough to be helpful, then give them each a task. Time it, and see how long it takes you to clean one window. Then you will be better able to judge how much window cleaning will fit in a day.

I have lived in old houses and know full well the trials of trying to clean the worst window situations possible. When we built our house several years ago, new windows were one of the things I was most excited about. I would go to the new house and lift them up and down and open them and imagine how easy it would be to clean these windows. They are a blessing from God! But I should have been just as thankful for the old windows simply because I had them! How many pioneer women were so excited to just get a single pane of glass to let light into their dugout during the winter? God forgive me for my discontent.

Here's my window washing system.

Son #1 washes the outside window with a bucket of soapy water and then sprays the cleaner on and wipes with newspaper. This step isn't necessarily done during cold weather.

Son #2 washes the screens, either with a hose and rag or a bucket of soapy water for the really dirty screens, or in the bathtub, during cold weather.

Daughters #1 and 2 clean the grime in the window frame first with a vacuum and then with a rag and their own buckets of soapy water.

I give directions and clean the inside windows and the outside part of the bottom pane that folds into the house. If I'm hugely pregnant or postpartum, then the children also do this part.

If we're washing upstairs windows, Son #1 also goes out on the roof and cleans out the gutters. He enjoys this task. It's the danger part. He's male; need I say more? I think he's been doing the gutter cleaning since he was eleven.

When we are all working together, window cleaning goes very fast. I have some windows that don't get that dirty, and I just employ one child to do the screen, and I do the rest with just the window cleaner—no soapy buckets necessary. These kind of windows take less than ten minutes for me to do.

If we do a lot of Deep Cleaning in one day, then we work on it for an hour and stop. What we don't get done in that Focus Area of the house in one month, we work on the next month. Like anything else, if the cleaning is kept up with, the windows don't get that dirty and they're fast and easy to clean. If you allow them to go uncleaned for two years, it will be a huge chore and take a lot more time.

CHAPTER 25
Gardening Day

The LORD God took the man and put him in the garden of Eden to work it and keep it.
—Genesis 2:15

The Outdoor Life

Gardening Day is the scheduled day that we focus on outdoor work. It doesn't mean that we don't do things like sweep the porch or water plants on other days, but by focusing on the outdoor areas of the home one day every week, we keep things nicely kept and groomed.

On Gardening Day, I assign each child specific tasks for the day. These tasks are things that need done weekly during certain seasons. If it's a big job, we all work together. In the days when my older children were small, my husband and I did the majority of the work while the children tagged along or played in the yard. By assigning tasks, you are ensuring that the job gets done, and you are building responsibility in your children.

Take a look around your outdoor areas, and make a list of things that need to be done to help keep it tidy and attractive. Think about hospitality and making it easy and pleasant for guests to approach your front door, or to conveniently sit on the front porch, or in another outdoor eating area, for iced tea.

Here is a basic list of tasks our family does on Gardening Day:

- Pick up trash and toys from the yard.
- Mow.
- Weed.
- Water plants.
- Sweep the porch and sidewalk (shovel snow in the winter).
- Sweep the deck.
- Straighten the garage.
- Sweep the garage.
- Clean the vehicles.

During the outdoor living season, you should give serious thought to making your landscape hospitable. Do you have an outdoor sitting or eating area? Think about folks' yards that you admire, and jot down ideas that you would like to incorporate into your landscape. It can be as simple as two chairs and a drink table placed beside the sandbox for you and a friend to sit at while your children play. Do you have a front porch? Then put a couple of chairs there for evenings so that you can enjoy listening to the night sounds. When you look at your yard, start thinking of it in terms of hospitality.

My personal favorite part of gardening is growing flowers and food. It is not complicated. Seeds are life in suspension. It is a beautiful thing! Add soil, water, and sun, and amazing things happen.

If you are intimidated by what it takes to garden, then start with plants from the garden center rather than seeds. Flowers will beautify your landscape and vegetables are nearly free organic food! Even if you just learn to grow one vegetable, you will save money and help out the health of your family.

My sister-in-law likes to save money by growing onions. She uses them every day, and finds them easy to grow. When she has to buy them in the spring because her supply is used up, she is shocked by the prices.

I am a fan of growing my own salad greens. I am still learning, and one of my life goals is to learn to grow greens all year long. I know it can be done, and every year I get a little smarter about extending the season.

Another thing I love to grow is tomatoes. There is nothing like the flavor of a fresh tomato from the garden! My mouth starts watering just thinking about it. BLT sandwiches with fresh tomatoes! Yummy! It is fun to snack on sun-warmed cherry tomatoes as you walk through the garden. Delicious!

My children frequently get their snacks from the garden. Asparagus spears in early spring, strawberries, lettuce, green onions, peas, green beans, carrots, raspberries and more are all eaten fresh right off the plant throughout the growing season.

Selling your beautiful flowers and vegetables is a wonderful experience for everyone involved. The

Farmer's Markets are so fun! It is good to get to know new people; it is educational for the children to learn business skills; and it is satisfying to know that others are enjoying food that you and your family worked hard to produce. We have had several fun years taking our garden fare to local markets. I highly recommend pursuing this activity as a family.

Gardening is an extension of the home life, and managing the outdoor work is part of the whole picture. Nearly free organic food, a bouquet for your table, a spot for you and your daughters to have an outdoor tea party—all these things make our lives more beautiful. Plan a day to focus on the tasks that make them happen.

Build houses and live in them; plant gardens and eat their produce. —Jeremiah 29:5

Gardening 101

You can have a green thumb! A key component is going to your garden frequently and keeping the weeds down. This is great exercise and will save you money from buying exercise equipment and incurring gym fees. It will also help you keep an eye on how ripe your crop is, or if it could use some water.

If you are a beginning gardener, I do not recommend going all out and growing the one-acre market garden with every conceivable vegetable. Tuck that idea away for when you and your children are more proficient gardeners. It's a great idea, but not one for beginners.

From experience, I also know that if you are pregnant and due at the end of summer, do not grow a big garden. Unless, of course, you think five-foot-tall weeds are a thing of beauty. If you are going through the first trimester of pregnancy at the beginning of the gardening year, it also wise to forego a garden.

If it is the middle of a pregnancy and you're feeling great, go for it, just keep it in moderation. Maybe grow a tomato plant in your flower garden, but that's all. But no market gardening. If you have a fresh baby, you will not feel up to a large garden. Take it easy and plan a weekly excursion to the Farmer's Market instead. You will be getting better prices and a far higher quality than from shipped-in produce. You can get to know the grower and gain tips from him on how to prepare the produce you buy for eating, as well as how to grow it for yourself.

If you have big kids that are obedient and know a little bit about gardening, you can rely on them to be the gardeners, and you can direct from your lawn chair in the shade. Choose cool times of the day to work, and be their cheerleader.

If you feel healthy and wonderful, and you want to start growing food for your family this year, here's what I suggest: First, decide what your family's favorite vegetable is. Study how to grow it in a gardening book, and then make it a family project. You might decide that your family's favorite vegetable looks too touchy, so choose another one to start with. My point with the favorite vegetable strategy is that you will be committed to it, will look forward to the harvest, and the children will have fun in the process.

Another easy beginning strategy is the Salad Garden. Salad vegetables tend to be very easy to grow.

If children grow their own salad, they will also be more liable to start eating salads, if they don't already. Salad gardens can be tucked into existing flower beds around the house, eliminating the need to till up a separate garden plot.

Salsa Gardens also have easy vegetables to grow. You don't need to put in the super hot peppers, although you may. If you do, beware that they should not be touched without rubber gloves! Take this into consideration if you have a very curious toddler.

Once you have decided which vegetables you want to grow, then decide how much of each vegetable you want to raise. That will determine how big of a garden plot you need. If you are planning a garden on the large side, you will need to get your garden plot tilled. Look in the local paper or ask around for somebody who does this for hire. If your soil is poor, you will need to take steps to enrich it. The how-to of this is well-covered in gardening books. Typically adding manure will give you a great start towards good gardening soil. Another very helpful source of information is your State or County Extension Service. They are there to help people farm and garden and have lots of information that your tax dollars pay for. They will tell you what you need to know or where to find the information you're looking for. They might also know of somebody who will till your garden or provide you with a source of manure. Look in the government pages of your phone book.

Once you have your vegetables planned, your plot tilled, and the soil adequately enriched, it's time to plant the seeds or plants that you purchased at the local nursery. For easy beginning gardening, buy the plants at the nursery rather than start by seed (tomatoes, peppers, cabbage, broccoli, herbs, etc.). For some vegetables, this isn't an option, such as beans or peas. Thankfully, these are easy to start from seed anyway.

Try to minimize disappointments during your first year of gardening. Follow the directions that come with the seed or plant. It might seem a little silly to plant a little itty-bitty seed or plant so far away from the next one, but you will experience one of the beauties of God's creations and that is how a plant can grow in front of your eyes. Don't blink! When the asparagus comes up in the spring, it grows an inch per hour at 70 degrees!

Seeds that provide nearly instant gratification are radishes, lettuce, and beans. Vines such as cucumbers, squash, and pumpkins are also easy to grow. You can buy these as plants, but growing them from seed usually works out just as well. Cucumbers, peas and runner beans will grow up a fence, though a fence is not necessary. They will also spread all over the ground in a big green tangle, up and over nearby plants. You can call it a ground cover, and it will help prevent weeds from taking over the garden. If you want beans to climb, buy the pole beans not the bush beans.

A fun thing for children is to plant a teepee garden. "Plant" bamboo stakes in a circle, fastening them at the top with twine. At the base of each pole, plant a couple of bean seeds. Scarlet Runner Beans have red flowers that are pretty for this project. Children like to hide and play in the teepee.

The easiest garden plan of all—ideal for beginners or for years when you are short on help and/ or incapacitated in one way or another—is to plant vegetables among the plants and bushes in the established beds around your house. Tuck a tomato plant here, a cucumber there, or a line of lettuce behind a row of flowers, and you will succeed at growing nearly free organic food with ease.

Gardening with the Children

I would encourage you to share the things you are learning in the gardening books with your children. Every time you go out and putter around in the yard, take them with you and tell them what you are doing.

Little children like to garden, and their sharp eyes will probably be better than yours at distinguishing between which seedlings are weeds and which are the plant you are seeking to grow. They are wonders at spotting bugs too!

Gardening with toddlers, however, is not always fun and can be a real challenge. They tend to walk on the baby plants and will often tear them out with their hands. They can be utter and complete destroyers of the work you've done. Toddlers should only be in the garden with complete supervision. If you take your eyes off of them, they can cause serious damage to young, tender plants!

This being said, you should take your toddler to the garden on a regular basis and talk to them about the plants. Teach them to respect what you are growing, and they will eventually learn. Soon the plants will be so huge that the toddler can't do much damage to them. In the meantime, keep your toddler in a playpen outside where he can see you (with special toys only for this time), assign him to an older sibling, or do the gardening during nap time.

Babies are much easier to garden with than a toddler. They take more naps, so it's easier to slip outside and garden then. They don't need to be trained in contentedness for the playpen. My sister-in-law kept an old swing beside her garden for her baby. A stroller or playpen under a tree is also good for little ones. They love to watch moving leaves. You may also need to get a bug net to protect them from bites.

When you are working in the garden, your other children should be at your side, helping with various tasks. They can dig holes for seedlings, water, weed, find pests, carry a harvest basket, and more. Praise them for all their help, talk to them, answer their questions, and ask them questions.

Gardening is a huge learning opportunity, and there are so many helpful books out there that can assist you in your effort. One book that we use all the time when gardening is *Rodale's Color Guide to Garden Insects* by Anna Carr. In this book we can find nearly every bug we see outside in all of its life stages. It explains how to control the insect naturally if it's a pest. Children are fascinated by watching insects.

Older children appreciate the business opportunities that a garden can present. Children that don't yet have a driver's license are able to produce something, get paid for it, and have a social opportunity with the community through market gardening. Farmer's Markets are something the whole family can contribute to and enjoy together.

Gardening is also an opportunity for ministry through giving your excess produce away. Take your bounty to church, your neighbors, retirement homes, and more.

Gardening is a very healthy endeavor for children in so many ways!

CHAPTER 26
The Lord's Day

If you turn back your foot from the Sabbath, from doing your pleasure on my holy day, and call the Sabbath a delight and the holy day of the LORD honorable; if you honor it, not going your own ways, or seeking your own pleasure, or talking idly; then you shall take delight in the LORD, and I will make you ride on the heights of the earth; I will feed you with the heritage of Jacob your father, for the mouth of the LORD has spoken. —Isaiah 58:13-14

Get Me to the Church on Time

Our family takes seriously God's directive to rest and honor Him one day each week, and yet Sunday has been the most challenging day to effectively organize for our family for many years. It seems that as soon as we get it figured out, we have a baby and start a new learning curve.

Part of repairing the problem is first identifying it. There are two things that I think are at the root. One is that six days of the week, we have a completely different Morning Routine; and second, we go to bed with the thought in mind that tomorrow we are going to rest and relax. What I have learned is to treat Sunday morning just like any other day of the week when it comes to getting up on time—do not sleep in!

As the mom of the family, get up and get yourself ready first. Know what you are going to wear—and know that it fits—the night before. Get completely ready except for putting on your church dress (you don't want the baby to have a blow out on you).

Have a simple breakfast planned, or make one ahead on Saturday (breakfast casserole). Get the children up and sitting at the table early. If they have a filling breakfast (protein), they will be happier kids throughout the morning.

Lay out the children's clothes the day before, including their tights, socks, and shoes. Make it a task on Laundry Day to wash and get the Sunday clothes ready. Keep them in a separate place (Laundry Room, your closet) so that a small child doesn't lose a part of their Sunday clothes during the week.

Pack the diaper bag on Saturday (always keep the diaper bag packed but re-check on Saturday). Also on Saturday, put the Bibles in a spot where they are easy to grab while going out the door, or go a step further and put them in the van.

Track how long it realistically takes for your family to get-out-the-door during the week on Town Day. On your Sunday morning routine, allow time for the lost shoe and spit-up mess. Know that your get-out-the-door routine will take longer on Sunday, and plan for it. I suspect that it takes longer because the children are excited that Dad is home, and also because Dad is part of the get-out-the-door routine.

Be sure that everyone uses the restroom before leaving the house.

Know how long it takes for you to feed the baby, and plan this into your Sunday morning routine. Burp him well so that he will not spit up all over his really cute Sunday clothes or on you.

Inspect everyone before they get in the van. Too many times we have arrived at church only to discover that some small person is not wearing shoes.

When it comes to honoring the Lord's Day, don't give up, but persevere!

CHAPTER 27
Tea Party Day

Sharing tea with children is just one more tangible way of offering the gift of our time and our attention, sharing ourselves and passing on what we've learned.
—*Emilie Barnes,* If Teacups Could Talk

Building Relationships

After three-and-half months away from my family when Matthew was born, I simply wanted to be with my family. It was not in me to get caught up in the tyranny of the urgent. My previous life had come to a screeching halt, and everything laid bare for me to see with a clear eye the truly important things.

Without a doubt, the most important things in life are the relationships we have with those closest to us, the ones under our noses—our children who can at times get just as busy as we are with their own little projects and play ideas or with books, sports, and friends. They are the "least of these" (Matthew 25:45). They are the nearest "neighbor" (Galatians 5:14). They are the children we are to be teaching to love God (Deuteronomy 6).

Our primary efforts must be invested in relationships with our children. One way to do this is by hosting Tea Parties with your family. This is one thing that my children, boys included, have always enjoyed doing. Over the years, we have had many with grandmas, aunts, cousins, friends, or just with ourselves. We did not do them regularly, though. Some years, we only had a couple of tea parties.

Everyone loves a tea party because, for that hour, we stop what we are doing, sit still, eat yummy food, drink good tea, talk, and laugh.

When I came home with Matthew, that is one thing I decided that we were going to do every single week, and what a joy it has been! Everybody looks forward to Tea Party Day! It is one of the highlights of our week. We plan it for late in the afternoon, and Matt joins us when he gets home. Our Tea Party then transitions into a light supper of soup and story time after the Table Chores are done.

Tea Parties have been very profitable and have helped bond our family together, and I highly recommend taking the time and effort to have them regularly in your family. Your Tea Parties might not look like ours; the important thing is to take the time to build relationships through this delightful and relaxing activity.

Make it Easy

I've made a two-page spread in my Home Management Book of Tea Party Recipes so that we can flip it open, divide the tasks, and do it quickly. We have learned how long it takes the kettle to boil, so we know when to put it on for 4 o'clock tea. We know how long it takes to make scones, mini-quiches, biscotti, and more, so that we can plan backwards and know when to start. Some weeks we go all out; some weeks we just make scones. By making this two-page spread of the tea party recipes, a no-effort soup recipe, and learning when to start the production in our day, we are making something easy that looks hard.

After lunch, we quickly do all of our work so that we can start on our Tea Party production. The faster we get done with the work, the more fun we get to have making the things for the tea party! We always use the pretty china tea cups, saucers, and pretty plates. It requires hand washing, and some have broken, but the pretty is part of what makes it so charming. It is sad when things break, but that is life. We can't get upset about things like that. What good is to just look at pretty things? That's no fun! It is wonderful to look closely at the pretty designs, to feel the china, and to use our hands in a very careful way which provides our children with an opportunity to learn how they should take care of things.

Fun and Games

Everyone at our tea party must make some effort to arrive at the table looking "proper". Good manners are required! The girls have improved at ironing and folding napkins. The men folk keep us laughing at their antics! We talk politics and current events when they're around, but when it's just us girls, we read and discuss a chapter from Raising Maidens of Virtue by Stacy McDonald. Another family we know has been having tea parties once a week over lunch and working through a similar book for girls.

Tea Parties offer a special opportunity for us to bond with our children. I recommend that you plan such times of enjoyment with your family.

CHAPTER 28
Morning and Evening Routines

And rising very early in the morning, while it was still dark, he departed and went out to a desolate place, and there he prayed. —Mark 1:35

Joy Comes with the Morning

If you have ever been camping or slept outdoors, you know the joy that all of nature expresses at the morning. Before the dawn has even broken, the birds begin their morning songs. As dawn nears, the sound of wildlife becomes louder and more fervent. Then, when the sun begins its rise into the quickly lightening blue, all of creation seems to burst into glory. The sky puts on a show of color from the palest yellow-pink to lavender as the last shades of midnight blue disappear to the west.

This is a revelation from God to us every morning. The mornings are a gift of still, calm, beauty, and majesty. We can see the sun rising over the horizon and get a glimpse of an idea of the glory of God. As the weather and seasons change, so do the sounds and the sights, revealing even more all the facets of order in His character. To receive this gift of common grace, all you have to do is be there.

When camping, you have no choice in the matter. There are no thick walls and windows to block out God's wake-up call. In the everyday reality of life, however, you have to deliberately choose to get up, go outside, and praise God for His gift of another glorious day. Spending those dawn moments with God and your husband can give real inspiration and energy for the day ahead. Memories of the glorious morning linger as the daylight hours progress, spurring creativity and motivation to foster the same kind of morning the following day. Momentum builds, and soon the days when you can't have that beautiful early-light time together become a disappointment. Starting the day with God and your husband is a great way to build strength and vigor so that you can, in turn, be a blessing to others.

When life has us feeling beat up, pressed down, and anxious, we sometimes wake up cursing the day. We have to choose to rejoice and be glad in it. We need to replace the groan with praise, "This is the day that the LORD has made; let us rejoice and be glad in it" (Psalm 118:24).

Then, after we choose to rejoice and be glad in it, we must commit our works to the Lord.

> *The plans of the heart belong to man, but the answer of the tongue is from the LORD. All the ways of a man are pure in his own eyes, but the LORD weighs the spirit. Commit your work to the LORD, and your plans will be established. —Proverbs 16:1-3*

Yes, it may be a "bad" day, but if we cultivate an attitude centered on bringing glory to God and doing our work heartily as unto the Lord, that bad day will be looked at with supernatural eyes. The interruptions and things that go wrong—the pressures that build and even explode around us—are serving some purpose that we may never know the reason for. Some moments you just have to pray, "Your will be done," and there are some days that we will have to pray this prayer unceasingly. When we seek God's will first and do His will joyfully, we can make it from dawn to dusk and beyond with His strength.

When planning your morning, your first priority is for your husband to have a good start to his day. Do some thinking and ask your husband what you can do to make the morning more of a joy for him. If he says something like, "Whatever makes you happy makes me happy," take a step back and consider your past. Your husband may sincerely mean this, or he may have begun this line of thinking because he became tired of your complaining and grumbling and "why bother" attitude years ago. Perhaps he simply found it easier to keep you happy by giving you your way rather than hoping you would bless him by giving him his way.

This is a sobering thought to contemplate, but it is necessary. It may be that you have contributed to his disengaged attitude through wrong attitudes of your own, and if so, these need to be recognized and repented of. In fact, you might have to do some hard thinking about the expectations that you both brought into your marriage. Both of you may have come into marriage with unbiblical ideas of how the husband-wife relationship should function.

Here's something to consider: If you had asked your husband when you were first married, "How would you like to spend the little bit of morning we have together," what would he have said then? Time has gone by, and you have both matured, children have come along, and work schedules have changed. Now think about the morning time, and ask him sincerely the same question again. When he has given you an honest answer or you have made some educated guessing, plan for your morning time together as wisely as you can.

Pleasant mornings and good starts are largely dependent on our attitudes. If you are having to hurry and scurry to catch up on what you didn't get ready the day before, your stress will likely spill over to our children and cause them to be on edge. If you are yelling, "Move it! Move it!" like a drill sergeant, then you're picking and tearing at the relationships with our children. Proverbs 31:26 tells us that the woman of virtue "opens her mouth with wisdom, and the teaching of kindness is on her tongue." This should be your goal: to start off your mornings teaching your children wisdom and speaking to them and your husband with kindness.

Here's what I have learned: When we are prepared, then we have no fear and are calm. When we are calm inside with surety as mothers, we speak with calmness to our children. On the other hand, if the children wake to no direction at all, they learn to be wasteful with their time. When our children wake to a plan and a calm and kind mother, then they in turn have pleasant mornings.

Children thrive on order; it gives them security. They want to know the plan for the day. They want to know what to expect when they get up. They are healthy in a home of order, peace, and security. As home manager, this is your duty to facilitate. Planning and preparation help build a happy heart in yourself which overflows to your children.

A Good Morning Starts the Evening Before

I am convinced that a good morning experience for the whole family starts with the preparations that have been made the previous evening. Proverbs 31:18 tells us that the lamp does not go out at night for the hard-working wife of virtue. From what I understand, this means that she filled up her lamp with oil so that it wouldn't go out. She prepared ahead. We can gather that she was good at preparing ahead from this verse and from other verses in Proverbs 31. Let's take her example and do the same!

Think about all the things that need to be done in your home in the morning for your husband, for your children, and your home. Write every little event down and start working backwards. A lot of tasks are dependent on other tasks. For example, you can't lay out clean clothes to wear if the laundry is not caught up.

Work on these ideas the day before in order to prepare for the morning:

- Gather laundry and sort so that you can toss a load in, first thing in the morning. If you're sure it won't get stinky over night, start a load in the washer.

- Prep the kitchen for breakfast. Who wants to wake up to a dirty kitchen? It is so much more pleasant for you and your family to walk into a clean and pleasant kitchen, coffee brewing (load and set it on a timer), breakfast ready to cook. One of the children can be assigned to set the breakfast table.

- Check your calendar. Do not be surprised in the morning! Know when you go to sleep what the agenda is for the following day. If you need to leave right away in the morning, then get the bags and needed things ready the night before, even going as far as putting them in the van.

- Lay out your clothes every evening for the appropriate activity scheduled the following day. If it is Cleaning Day, lay out clothes that are comfortable for cleaning. If it is Kitchen Day, choose short or ¾ sleeves. Even if you're not leaving the house, dress in a way that is self-respecting and will bring glory to your Father and your husband.

- Put your bedside lamps on timers to help you and your family go to sleep and wake up at appropriate times. You must get adequate sleep, yet you do not need to be lazy. Light or lack thereof helps the eyes and brain to shut down and to come on again in the morning.

- Before the light goes off and you go to sleep, make sure that you have done a bit to straighten your bedroom and bathroom, that you have read a Psalm and have it in your brain to sleep on, and that you have prayed. Give thanks to God for the day that has passed. Thank Him for the day to come and make your requests to your Heavenly Father; pray the Lord's Prayer.

Do not be anxious about anything, but in everything by prayer and supplication with thanksgiving let your requests be made known to God. —Philippians 4:6

The next morning when the light comes on and the alarm goes off, do not ignore them. You are prepared. You have a plan. Get up and get started on your day. If you need help with a plan, write it all out on a note card and lay it on your bedside table the night before. Then pick it up and "do the next thing".

Here are some ideas for a Morning Routine:

- Stretch.

- Read a Psalm.

- Make your bed.

- Straighten your bedroom and bathroom.

- Get dressed and ready for the day.

- Drink water.

- Start a load of laundry.

- Make breakfast for your husband, and read the Bible with him.

- Emilie Barnes teaches us to ask our husbands: "Is there anything I can do for you today?"

- Drink your morning coffee on the deck, and watch the sun come up.

- Exercise.

- Read a Psalm and a Proverb to your children while they eat breakfast.

- Go over the plan for the day with your children and pray about it.

- Do food prep for lunch and supper while your children do the Table Chores.

- Take 5 minutes to check up on their bedroom and bathroom chores: "Inspect what you expect."

Use these ideas as a springboard for what works best for you, your husband, and your family.

Be Specific

Work on putting your routine in the most efficient order. A portion of mine looks like this:

- Thank God for the morning.

- Wash face; put in contacts .

- Put on deodorant.

- Brush teeth.

- Moisturize.

- Enhance natural beauty (mascara, etc.).

At times, I have woken up late, gone straight to the kitchen in my robe, drank coffee, fed the troops breakfast, and started supper. In the process, I have cut up an onion and then gone back to my bathroom to do the bathroom routine.

Do you see a problem with this picture? Have you ever tried to put in contacts after cutting up an onion? It will ruin your day. My thought was, "I'll get back to my bathroom when these hungry kids are fed first."

The lesson is this: Discipline yourself to get up before you are rushed and do your Morning Routine in the most efficient order—contacts before onions!

As home manager, you are responsible to see that you are helping your husband, serving healthy food to your family, and setting the tone for the day. These are big responsibilities, and when they are met, you will see big changes in your life! Of course there are seasons (new baby, illness, etc.) when it is very hard to meet these responsibilities, but don't give up. It's okay for a season to call out to our husbands from the depths of the blankets, "Can I do anything for you today?" Just keep in mind that this isn't the picture we want to give him to start off the day every day. He wants care, and he wants to know that his family is having productive days. Keep pressing on, and soon you will have great mornings and days again. Commit these things to the Lord.

We plan, prepare, and work on our attitudes not for our own glory, but because the woman who fears the Lord and lives according to His will brings glory to God. She is a light shining on a hill and salt to the earth. She has joy like a fountain. She is not bitter but is a sweet fragrance to her family, home, and community.

Put yesterday behind you and get started today by planning for tomorrow. Do the necessary prep work today to make tomorrow a success, and start each day out with joy!

Weeping may tarry for the night, but joy comes with the morning. —Psalm 30:5

My voice shalt thou hear in the morning, O LORD; in the morning will I direct my prayer unto thee, and will look up. —Psalm 5:3, KJV

CHAPTER 29
Meal Time Routines

A homemaker largely determines the general atmosphere in the home—whether it is tense,
full of hostility and bitter feelings, or warm, loving, helpful, and cooperative.
—*Ella May Miller,* Happiness is Homemaking

Streamline and Save Time

Meal times can be the most hectic point of the day for a large family. It can be a challenge getting everyone to the table at the appointed time. Keeping everyone seated is another challenge. The sheer amount of food it requires to feed the clan can also be overwhelming. And then clean up time—a big family makes a big mess!

Here are some practical ideas I've found to help master meal team routines.

Table chores should be done immediately after a meal. There are several reasons for doing the table chores right after you finish eating, besides the germ factor. First of all, it just looks yucky to walk into a kitchen half way through the afternoon and see all the lunch dishes, table scraps, crumbs, and petrified gunk on the table. What an ugly picture that can lend itself to an ugly attitude! Second, when the table is clean, you can use it for other projects. If it is still dirty, you might be tempted to not do that craft or game that you were intending to do with the children. Third, it is easier to clean when the food is not dried hard as a rock to the dishes and table. Fourth, and most importantly, prompt action teaches your children discipline. Remember that we are teaching all the time, through our actions and inactions. Discipline yourself and your children to do the work immediately.

My current problem at lunchtime is keeping the children from running off to their next activity instead of waiting for the other members of the family to finish eating. The children think they will come back to do their chores, but in reality, someone else ends up doing them, usually their mother. We are working on staying at the table and having polite conversation while waiting for the rest of the family to finish their food.

The ultimate goal is to train your children to work attentively, cheerfully, and promptly. Proverbs has plenty to say about laziness. As a parent, it is your duty to train this out of your children. We are born with a sin nature; nobody taught us to be lazy. If we had poor examples that encouraged us in our sin nature, we cannot use this as an excuse. We are to press on towards the goal that Christ has called us to. This is part of our sanctification. We have been blessed with children to disciple, and part of discipling is training them to exemplify the qualities of a mature Christian. It is a relentless parenting task which involves real work, yet we are to do all our work—including child training— "heartily as unto the Lord."

Table Chores include the following, though your household may vary a bit:

- Set table.

- Fill water glasses.

- Scrape dishes.

- Carry to sink or dishwasher.

- Load dishwasher.

- Collect trash from table, put cloth napkins in laundry.

- Put food away.

- Wipe table, chairs, high chair.

- Sweep under table.

- Wash dishes.

- Dry dishes.

- Put clean dishes away, unload dishwasher.

- Wipe counters.

Assign these chores to your children. If you have a lot of children, there is more work but also more help to do the work. Set up your work to be done efficiently in your kitchen. If you find that two people are tripping over each other trying to do their job, maybe those two jobs need to be combined and made for one person.

Use the timer and race it while doing kitchen chores. Try to get it all done in 10 minutes or less. When you knock out these chores promptly, the children realize that the reward of doing work quickly is that they can then move on to other pursuits. They do not have to spend prolonged time in the kitchen. They can then go outside, read, or play until the next thing on the schedule. Work every day at getting it done more quickly and cheerfully.

As soon as Table Chore time begins, the person assigned dishwasher duty should go to the sink and fill it with hot, soapy water and begin cleaning the dishes. Everyone else should follow suit and work quickly. You might want to reward your children with a treat occasionally for being diligent or working cheerfully. Always reward them verbally, encouraging them as you see improvement. When the kitchen and table are clean, have them admire their work and point out to them how pleasant it is to live in a clean home.

If your children are doing all the work, what are you doing? You are helping the little ones, being the cheerleader, looking at what needs done for the next meal, putting little ones to a nap, switching laundry loads. You're doing the next thing—cheerfully, of course, as unto the Lord!

If you don't have enough big kids yet to be of real help, then you will have to do more of the work. Include your little ones in the work, and cheerfully train them. Soon they will be helping more and even doing it all. Preschoolers can do nearly all of the Table Chores, especially when you use light-weight dishes, small glasses, a small water pitcher, and store your table dishes low. They can be taught to wipe the table and sweep the floor. They can unload and load the dishwasher. They can wash dishes.

Do not expect their work to be of the same quality as an adult or an older child, but do allow them to do this work. Do not expect one preschooler to do the Table Chores after a meal for eleven people. Spread the Table Chores between the children. Give them ample praise, hugs and kisses. Brag about their good work to Dad.

Washing the Dishes

Dishes should be done at every meal, regardless if there are two or twenty. Dirty things lying around the kitchen promotes messiness and germ spreading. When you keep up with the dishes, other things in the house tend to stay kept up.

Preparing the next meal is a joy if you are walking into a clean kitchen. If it is a dirty mess, you do not feel like making anything. Creativity dies on the vine. A dirty kitchen is depressing. If you keep up with this one thing, it will make your family's life much more pleasant.

Choose which side of the sink you will keep your dish rack. This will depend on the layout of your kitchen and whether you are right or left-handed. Put all of your dirty dishes on the opposite side of the sink from the dish rack. Clean the counter around your dish rack, as you do not want to contaminate your clean dishes.

Scrape and rinse the dirty dishes, and place them in the order that you will wash them. Cleanest to dirtiest: glasses first, then serving dishes, then plates, then silverware, then cooking pots and pans.

Fill one sink with hot soapy water and the second sink with hot rinse water. The water should be as hot as you or your child can stand it. If you don't have many dishes to do, then do not waste water on filling the sinks; use a dish pan or a large mixing bowl instead. Also, running the water constantly for dish washing or rinsing is unnecessary and wasteful.

To wash, you will need a dishcloth, a scraper, a bottle brush for glasses, and a scruffy. Wash the dishes and put them into the rinse water. Have your dishwashing apprentice (this is the person you are training to wash dishes) pull the dishes out of the rinse water and onto the drying rack. Then have him dry them with a fresh, floursack-style drying cloth. The advantage of this kind of towel is that it does not leave lint on the dishes.

When the towel gets wet, the apprentice should get a fresh towel. Lay the wet one over a rack to dry, and once it is dry, put it where you keep your dirty laundry to keep the germs on it at bay.

Your apprentice should put away the dishes as he dries them. If the dishwashing sink gets too dirty, you will need to refill it with hot soapy water. If the rinse sink gets too soapy, you will need to refill it.

When you are done with the dishes, take your dishcloth and wipe the counters, the stove, and lastly the sink. At this point, the apprentice should have everything put away. Wash the dish rack and drainer, and place them in the cupboard underneath the sink. Then scrub the faucet and the crevices around the sink. Next, clean the drain, and wipe the sink itself. Finally, take your last dish-drying towel and dry the sink.

Stand back with your apprentice and admire a job well done! This is true beauty, a necessary work done with excellence. Take time to appreciate it, and pat each other on the back. The next time you walk into the kitchen to prepare the next meal, you will be so much more cheerful and ready to do the work with a good attitude.

I wrote out every little detail I could think of in the process to give you a full picture of all the steps involved. When you are actually doing it, you might have to focus on the details quite a bit until you practice making it a regular routine. This system is efficient, and once you have it down, you will whiz through it and have a beautiful kitchen!

If your children are too little to help and you have plenty of other work to do alone, let the dishes air dry. Lay a clean towel over the dish rack full of dishes for a more neat appearance in your kitchen.

If you have a dishwasher, use it for all the small things. Large things such as mixing bowls, pots, and pans take up too much room; a lot of these things can be washed while you are preparing the meal. Wash those items in the sink after every meal. During the day, train your family to put their dirty dishes into the dishwasher. This means it must be empty. Assign one or two of your children the task of emptying the dishwasher as soon as it is done running, whether this is one time a day or three. Assign this task per meal, per day, per week, or as sometimes happens at our house, "If you complain, you will keep the job until you can do it without complaining."

I like to post Scripture verses that I'm memorizing above my sink. I got this idea from my mother-in-law who does this. A close friend of my family told me once that she and her daughter had many precious dish-washing sessions, memorizing scripture posted above the sink. What a wonderful memory to have!

Do not sigh while you are washing the dishes. Do not have a pity party, and do not teach your children to act this way, because they will learn from your example. If you work cheerfully and use the time well, you will teach them to enjoy their work too!

The Dinner Hour

Mealtimes offer a unique opportunity for fellowship because the family is gathered together in one place for a common purpose. How do you redeem this time around the table in your home?

I would encourage you to make the most of dinner time in particular by creating an event of it. Don't allow it to be just throwing food down the hatch. Enjoy the time, enjoy the food, and enjoy your fellowship together as a family. On a regular basis, set a lovely table for your main meal of the day. Put the food in serving dishes rather than the pot they were cooked in. Keep a vase of flowers or a candle on your table. In doing those things, you are teaching your children to appreciate art and beauty as well as the communion God has with us as part of the spiritual household of faith.

A prayer should precede the food. We need to be thankful for the daily bread God has given us!

Eat slowly and engage your family in edifying conversation. When Dad is there, this is something he should take the lead in. Discuss the day's events in the home as well as world events. Have your children give personal reports to Dad about progress on projects they've been working on, along with interesting episodes that have transpired throughout the day.

Don't let children wander off during dinner time when they are done eating. Not only is this rude and unmannerly, but by leaving the table when dinner is still in progress, they are going to miss out on important family conversations. If they have need or desire to depart, they should ask the head of the table whether or not they may be excused.

When your children leave the family table is a matter of discretion. If you are planning a long evening at dinner, sometimes a young child who hasn't had a nap will need to be put to bed early for their wellbeing as well as for the good of the time you have left together with the rest of the family. This said, children need to learn patience and learn to stretch their typically-short attention spans. Your time at the table is one of the best opportunities you have during the day to teach your children discipline and attentiveness, so do your best to make the most of it.

CHAPTER 30
Table Time

A happy Christian home is a tiny circle of heaven on earth. In it our children learn of God's eternal truths and values; they learn of His claims on their lives.
—*Ella May Miller,* Happiness is Homemaking

Studying God's Word

It is important that we show our family that God's Word is at the foundation of education. Toward this end, I would encourage you to gather together your children every morning after breakfast and chores are finished and read the Bible together. If you have lots of little children, you can sit on the floor for this. For a slightly older crowd that uses pencils and paper, the table usually works best. However you choose to organize your Bible study, the point is that you demonstrate to your children that you "Seek first the kingdom of God." This time is separate from the family worship time, which hopefully your husband leads. Family worship is dealt with in another chapter. This Bible time reinforces family worship and begins your lessons for the day by reminding your children that the "fear of the Lord is the beginning of wisdom."

While the Bible should be the essential component of your study, here are a list of a few ideas of ways you can use your time: read the Bible (non-negotiable); read a children's devotional; work on Scripture memorization; review catechism questions and answers; go through a Bible study curriculum; sing together.

It is wise to teach your children to always check what they read against God's Word. When they learn something new in a story, go to the passage in the Bible that teaches this lesson so that they will learn to reason directly from the Scriptures. Teach them how to use Strong's Concordance and Nave's Topical Bible God's word more fully by studying through topics and have the ability to locate verses as they do research. These steps will help your children to be discerning Christians whose thinking is rooted in God's Word.

After studying the Bible, work through the rest of your family's school curriculum. Their minds are generally sharpest first thing in the morning, especially after a good breakfast. Use this time wisely by working on the subjects that require concentration, such as math, phonics, and language arts.

Catechizing Your Children

A catechism is a question-answer method of teaching that is an efficient way to inculcate in your children the foundational truths found in the Scripture.

There have been some great catechisms written over the centuries to teach essential Bible doctrine which I would encourage you to avail yourselves of as a parent.

Choose the catechism which most closely aligns with your family and church's teaching. The Puritans and early American forefathers learned The Shorter Catechism which is based on The Westminster Confession of Faith (1643). The Heidelberg Catechism, adopted by the Synod of Dort in 1618-1619, is also another excellent one to consider.

Catechisms do not replace the Bible, of course. What they do is put all of Scripture into context with the whole and teach elemental truths. They encourage further study in God's Word as you learn the scripture proofs for the various questions and answers.

Learning a catechism takes your children beyond drinking the milk of the gospel and onto the meat of wonder, beauty and depth of who God is and what His plan is for His people. A catechism acts as a filter for all teachings. When our children have that filter instilled in them in their youth, they will be strong and well-equipped to expose false teaching for the rest of their lives.

I saw this played out first hand several years ago. I have two sisters-in-law who were taught the Heidelberg Catechism as children. After a church service one Sunday, I had raised eyebrows and red flags about something being taught while they were able to pinpoint what the false teacher said and why it was wrong. I was floored by how well they responded and I was convicted to teach a catechism to my children so that they could be this discerning when exposed to wrong teaching. There is strength of character and sound mind when a person can hear untruth and stand against it with confidence.

This is what we want for our children: To know the Lord's truths as found in the Bible and be very familiar with the Scriptures that prove those truths. Teaching this discipline is integral to raising a godly seed. When your children know what they believe and why they believe it, they will have strength and peace within and be equipped to help rebuild a godly culture.

All your children shall be taught by the Lord, and great shall be the peace of your children.
—Isaiah 54:13

There are many resources available to use in catechizing your children. There are devotional books, songs, curriculum, and cartoon books which teach the major confessional catechisms. Yet if you are not inclined to invest in additional resources, the catechism itself works great as you simply sit around the table ask the questions and have your answer children them, looking up the Scriptures that support each point.

If Christ's parting commission to the church is "to make disciples" (Matt. 28:19), she cannot fail to begin by catechizing her own children. To do less is to neglect our own household, which Paul says, makes us worse than an infidel (1 Tim. 5:8). If we as parents would be faithful to our calling as the primary teachers of our children, then catechizing should be a priority in our homes. —Donald Van Dyken, Rediscovering Catechism

CHAPTER 31
15 Minutes of Phonics

In the beginning was the Word, and the Word was with God, and the Word was God.
—John 1:1

Teach Me to Read!

When a child can read, they can fly. The world is wide open, and they can learn just about anything. To see the light bulbs turn on in reading skills is one of the great joys of parenting. Their faces light up with delight when they read books for the first time. The teaching process to get to that point can be arduous, but when they finally get it and are to the point of reading proficiently, it is heart-warming to observe.

If some of your children are a bit slower in learning than others in your family, relax. This is normal. Children's brains develop at different paces. Boys are often late in learning to read, for example.

Children also have different learning styles. Some are better auditory learners while others learn better visually. Do your best to discern these differences in your children and adjust how you teach them to read accordingly.

Read to your little children, moving your finger under the words. Have your older children read to the little children. If you're worried that your older child who doesn't read yet is going to lag behind, then have him listen to audio books.

Every morning, when their minds are sharp, sit down with your non-readers and do a phonics lesson. Slowly but surely (barring a learning disability), the phonics will sink in, one concept at a time. Some children will want to fly through it! I have seen each of my reading children get stuck at a concept and it seems as though their brain had to catch up developmentally, but once they did, they would fly along again—so don't be discouraged!

Once your children understand the phonics concepts and can correctly sound out words, continue to practice the rules and word examples with them. Repetition helps them remember the rules, and soon they will become ingrained in their thinking and flow naturally for your children. They will be sight reading instead of sounding words out and will fly through books. Practice makes perfect!

Teaching reading doesn't take lots of time; you just need to do it. Consistency will take you a long way toward success. Just spend fifteen minutes every day on it. Make it part of your early-morning schedule, and the results will come. And keep the TV off. They can't read if they're watching television!

Make reading fun and interesting by keeping good classic books around that provoke imagination. Keep the conversation going by asking them about what they are reading. Have them give you oral book reports. Encourage them in their interests by getting them books that explore their topics of delight.

Like everybody else, your children will want to talk about what they are interested in. And they can get very excited about their passions at times, so much so that their words race out faster than they can organize their thoughts. Talking is communicating, so just as you guide your children's reading habits, guide their conversations so that they learn to express themselves well.

CHAPTER 32
Quiet Time

And he said to them, "Come away by yourselves to a desolate place and rest a while." For many were coming and going, and they had no leisure even to eat. —Mark 6:31

Rest for the Weary

Everybody in the house appreciates a Quiet Time. It sooths us. It tames the wild out of little children. If the weather is good, have the little children run around outside for awhile after lunch to get the last bit of energy out. Then lay them down for Quiet Hour.

If they are starting to grow out of the need for sleep, give them a stack of books to quietly read. Each child has different sleep needs. I have children who took naps until they were six. I have one who stayed awake to all hours of the night wandering around the house, playing alone if she had a nap during the day!

Older children appreciate the quiet for reading or intense subjects. They are often the children who want to be sure that we have Quiet Hour!

The littlest children and babies need to sleep! If they don't sleep during the day, then they are grumpy in the evening, which is their time with Dad. It's a sad thing if their only time with Dad is a grumpy time, so be sure they get a nap in the afternoon.

Toddlers often need to be taught to hold their hands together when they go to sleep. This acts like swaddling does for little babies. When they hold their hands together, the rest of their body holds still, and they are able to relax and go to sleep.

Be sure to put Quiet Time for the whole house in your schedule after The Noon Hour.

CHAPTER 33
Read Aloud Time

. . . to make known to the children of man your mighty deeds, and the glorious splendor of your kingdom. —Psalm 145:12

Tell Me the Story

Read Aloud Time is a wonderful time of day in the life of a mom and her children. Through books, you can travel together through time all over the world on all sorts of adventures. With all that learning, you can take the rest of the afternoon to look at maps, make projects, and do more reading. Yes, this is fun!

Everybody wants to sit by Mom and the book, so we take turns. Each child is assigned a day at our house for this. On that day, the child gets to sit by Mom during Read Aloud Time and to help Mom in the kitchen and run out to get the mail. It's a day with special privileges.

Depending on your family dynamics, you may want to do Read Aloud Time during Quiet Hour. What I find is that if I read right after lunch, I tend to fall asleep. It doesn't matter how neat and exciting the story is, I start to fade. . . . and then somebody shakes my arm, "Mom! Mom! Mom!"

Sometimes they get ruffled at me and, at other times, they pull funny tricks on me. Eventually I fall over on the couch and sleep for awhile, and the kids move on to other things. It works much better if we have Quiet Hour first. I don't normally nap during Quiet Hour, but if I don't have to read aloud in that first hour after lunch, we have a more fruitful Read Aloud Time later.

CHAPTER 34
Afternoon Chore Time

And the men did the work faithfully. —2 Chronicles 34:12

Consistently Clean

The key thing to keep your home consistently clean is to have a consistent chore time. This does not mean that you and your family clean and then sit around twiddling your thumbs so that the house doesn't get dirty. You can still be creative and make messes; the children can still play with play dough and Legos—you simply need a system for everyone to help get things cleaned up and back into place. The key thing to keeping your home consistently clean is a consistent chore time. Every work day of the week do the work of tidying your home.

Work is not discouraging unless we let it become discouraging. Work is simply the process needed to get to an end point. In this case, I mean a clean house, the goal of every homemaker.

When a large family lives in a home twenty-four hours a day, seven days a week, things get dirty, messes are made, clutter is left lying around, and small children create chaos. Yes, it will be a mess. That's a fact. But don't let it discourage you, just get to work! Make housework a habit that happens without a great deal of thought, and it will become much easier to do. Soon you'll learn to fly through most of your tasks, and then there will be more time to do things that create more work.

Now smile! You want a clean house; you want to do fun things that give you pleasure—these things are living, and living is work. Work is fun, if you make it fun; and work is a joy, because it is serving the Lord.

Keep Work and Rest in Perspective

Rest is what God has given to us for our physical bodies on the seventh day. Rest is not something that you do during the daylight hours unless you are ill, are postpartum, or are taking a nap with your babies. Remember that God set up the universe this way before Adam's Fall. Working six days and resting on the seventh was something He called "good" in the beginning, not a curse, though the curse he placed on the ground when Adam sinned now makes work harder for us.

> *Six days you shall labor, and do all your work, but the seventh day is a Sabbath to the LORD your God. On it you shall not do any work, you, or your son, or your daughter, your male servant, or your female servant, or your livestock, or the sojourner who is within your gates. For in six days the LORD made heaven and earth, the sea, and all that is in them, and rested on the seventh day. Therefore the LORD blessed the Sabbath day and made it holy. —Exodus 20:9-11*

Balance

While cleaning is an important task we should approach with focus and vigor, it can become an obsession that is destructive to our families. Clean is not the only goal of the home keeper. The home keeper also wants her family to live with love, comfort, and happiness. These are intangibles that have more to do with atmosphere and attitude. The pulse of your children's hearts are more important than excess dirt on the floor. While you need to conquer the dirt monster, don't do it at the expense of your children. Demonstrate to your family that you care more about them personally than you do about keeping the house in perfect order all of the time. And show them that it's because you care about them that you want to keep a tidy home.

This being said, it is hard to create the atmosphere and attitude of love, comfort, and happiness in our homes if they are pig pens. Have you ever watched pigs or seen their pen? Pigs root around with their noses, turning over anything and everything in order to find something to eat. This process is very destructive to the place they are kept. They eat anything and everything. Pigs wallow and move their bodies around in the dirt in order to create a bed. When it rains into their wallow, it becomes a mud bath where they take residence until cold weather comes. And when they pile on top of each other, they routinely suffocate the pigs at the bottom of the pig pile. This is not a happy site or a model we should emulate!

Think of the word images that come from the lifestyle of pigs: "pig pen," "wallow like a pig," "pig pile," "boar's nest." Imagine a family doing the same thing: rummaging through cupboards looking for food and then wallowing about, doing nothing productive but sleeping in their mess. It is our sin nature to be lazy, and we must renounce our fleshly habits.

> *How long will you lie there, O sluggard? When will you arise from your sleep? A little sleep, a little slumber, a little folding of the hands to rest, and poverty will come upon you like a robber, and want like an armed man. —Proverbs 6:9-11*

Daily Duty

*For the grace of God has appeared, bringing salvation for all people, training us to renounce ungodliness and worldly passions, and to live **self-controlled**, upright, and godly lives in the present age, waiting for our blessed hope, the appearing of the glory of our great God and Savior Jesus Christ, who gave himself for us to redeem us from all lawlessness and to purify for himself a people for his own possession who are zealous for good works.*
—Titus 2:11-14 (emphasis mine)

Keeping your home tidy and clean is as simple as keeping a daily chore time. It is important to my husband that the house be tidy in order for him to have a relaxing evening, so we hold Afternoon Chore Time every day. This is the time of day when we restore order. We put away the schoolbooks and projects that we were working on. If it's a large project that we will come back to the next day, we tuck it away in a safe place and straighten up as much as possible around the project. We make the mood one that Dad can come into and relax and enjoy his family. We have food cooking that tantalizes the senses for an enjoyable family suppertime. We put on calming music that sets the mood for the evening.

All these things are done in the hour or two before Dad arrives home. We are setting a place for the king of the castle.

The Procedure

"An ounce of prevention is worth a pound of cure." —Benjamin Franklin

At a set time every day, say "Afternoon Chore Time! Let's pick up and clean before Daddy gets home!" Children love to please their dad. If you keep them focused with encouraging words and do the work quickly, they will grow to love the satisfaction of looking at a pleasing room and showing it off to Dad when he walks in the door. Don't be a drill sergeant; be an encourager. Say things like you would want to hear from your mom. Sing while you work; make your work in preparation for Dad's arrival fun!

Tell the children to quickly put away whatever projects they are working on. While you are instructing them, light a candle (high out of reach of the littlest climbers), and put on music. This helps signal to the children that evening is coming, and it is time to prepare for it.

Assign each person a room to straighten and clean. If you have no big children yet, you will need to do the straightening and cleaning alone. Bring your children along with you to do these chores. This is training for them. They might be a hindrance now, but in this training, they are learning the work and will be soon training their younger brothers and sisters how to do it. Make a list of Daily Chores for each room and laminate it or put it in a sleeve protector to be kept in that room.

As you go to each room, refer to the chart. Show it to the children so that they will know that there is a list of work for the room. Take a photo of the room when it is picture perfect so that the children know what the room should look like when they are done, and attach the photo to the Daily Chore sheet.

Work quickly and efficiently. Pull a basket or wagon around to collect toys with and send the children on little missions to put the toys away. Give a trash bag to a child, and send him around to be the trash collector. Hand out feather dusters and/or dust cloths, and teach them to dust. By quickly dusting every day, the rooms do not get caked with dirt. Feather dusters are great fun for children, and a quality feather duster does an excellent job.

Teach your children to put things away when they are done with them. This works if you are with them; remember to teach them while you work. It is when you become busy with another thing in another room that they will drop the object and move on. If you remind them while you are tidying up, they will learn the value of the habit and eventually do it on their own. When things are picked up on a regular basis, there is generally far less to put away during Afternoon Chore Time.

If you have big children that can work well at room cleaning, then have them work alone or with a little buddy. Assign them to teach a little child how to clean their assigned room. Train them to be an encouraging teacher.

If there is a need for speed, then set the little ones up with an activity that will keep them busy for the clean up time. There are some children and some ages of little ones that are simply more distracting to the assigned room cleaner than they are helpful. For instance, toddlers seem to delight in following a room cleaner around and undoing what was just done which causes the room cleaner to be working in a never-ending cycle of frustration. Put these children at an activity at the table, in a pack-n-play with special toys only for this time of day, or in a high chair with a snack or with crayons and paper.

Assign a day of the week for a certain activity to be done while the rest of the crew cleans. For example: Monday—play dough; Tuesday—washing dishes (water play); Wednesday—chunky puzzles; Thursday—coloring; Friday—finger paint. Not all of these will work for all children and situations, but come up with your own list of activities for the particular child who is not able to clean or be a good little buddy yet.

Have the children choose their favorite room to be the one they are responsible for cleaning. This adds ownership to it for them, because they care more about what their favorite room looks like. If there is disagreement about who gets what room, then have the children draw straws. Keep the same rooms for a long stretch of time (3-4 months), so that the children will get really good at that room's particular chores. This teaches them to do their work with excellence. By changing room assignments frequently, nobody gets really proficient at doing a particular room. It is also easier to let tasks slide by for the next room-keeper to do next week. In addition, keeping a room assignment for long periods makes it easier for the home manager by not re-training new room-keepers every week.

After the Room Chores are done for the main rooms of the house, then the children are to do their Bedroom Chores. After the Bedroom Chores, do the Deep Cleaning chore for the day. Sometimes it's a big chore; sometimes it's miniscule. It all depends on the Focus Area of the house and the chore for the day.

If a chore doesn't get done one day, it's okay. You can do it next time it comes around in the housecleaning schedule. The system is your tool; you are not it's slave.

After the tidying is done, go to your bedroom and bath and spend five minutes freshening up. You want a picture of loveliness for your beloved when he comes in the door. Then put on a fresh apron, and start the supper work with your Assistant Chefs.

Once the house is clean, have the children do Sit Time. Assign them a chair and give them a stack of books to look at. If they can read, then they can have Reading Time. If the children have had enough reading time in the day, then you can have them play a game that is easy to set up and tear down before supper, such as checkers, pick-up-sticks, Uno, Skip-bo, etc.

At our house, after the Afternoon Choretime, the big kids go outside to do their Animal Chores. Sometimes they are done by the time Dad comes home, and sometimes the older children do outside chores with Dad. Each home is going to be a little different; the goal though is to have as much of the work done as possible before Dad comes home from work, so that everyone can have a relaxing and pleasant evening enjoying each other.

What time you start doing chores is also going to vary with your home, the ages of your children, the size of the messes they make with their projects, what time your husband comes home from work, and other variables. If Afternoon Chore Time is a new thing for your house, expect to have a period of fine tuning to iron out these sorts of details.

When we do daily chores in every room of the house, the house always looks clean and is never more than ten minutes from looking picture perfect. If we skip Afternoon Choretime for a couple of days or a week, then our house looks like a pig pen and will take an extended period of time to straighten and clean. Having a system for doing the regular maintenance chores helps the house seemingly run by itself and keeps it beautiful.

CHAPTER 35
Bathroom Management

. . . and having a reputation for good works: if she has brought up children, has shown hospitality, has washed the feet of the saints, has cared for the afflicted, and has devoted herself to every good work. —1 Timothy 5:10

I'm sure you know by now that the bathrooms in the home of a large family can get disgusting very quickly. It's simply a volume factor: The more people that use something, the more quickly the clean factor expires. The large family must therefore learn some bathroom management techniques in order to keep things under control.

Here's a simple and effective rule to cut down on bathroom uncleanliness: Every time you are in the bathroom, do something to clean it.

Teach this rule to everyone in your home. Even start teaching it to the toddler you are potty training. You'll be surprised at the results!

This is a habit that each person should develop and carry all through life. Just doing one thing to improve the room does a lot to keeping it clean. Put a little sign up on your mirrors as a reminder of this.

Shower Control

When you are in the shower, wipe down a wall with an old bath scruffy that you keep in there just for cleaning. It only takes a couple of minutes. For a tub/shower, do one wall and the tub on odd days and the two end walls on even days. You do not need a special cleaner, just agitation. If you have hard water, use CLR or a similar product once in awhile. There are good products available to put on the shower walls to keep them clean, but if you keep up with wiping it every time you're in it, the build up shouldn't get too bad. Train your family to do the same with their showers.

Daily Duties

The main users should be the chief cleaners. Our girls, for example, sleep on the second floor, so the second floor bath is their responsibility. On a daily basis, boys should clean any toilet that is used by boys. This will train them to aim correctly. Make it easy for the children to clean by keeping a bucket of cleaning supplies and paper towels under every bathroom sink. Cleaning supplies do not need to be toxic. A dish soap and vinegar solution kills germs and is safe. If you have hard water that creates build up, then tackle the heavy duty cleaning when the Deep Cleaning Focus Area for bathrooms comes around.

In each bathroom, post a list of Daily Chores:

- Wash the sinks and counters.
- Wipe toilet from top to bottom.
- Sweep floor.
- Spray floor around toilet and wipe.

If you want, go a step further and post the names of the children beside a chore for each day. Do these chores during Afternoon Chore Time.

Multi-Task

While you are in the bathroom watching little bathers, clean it. Rather than browsing a magazine, spruce things up. Get the corners and crevices that the children miss; wash the window. Wipe the cupboard doors, and straighten a drawer. It doesn't take long to do a couple of these tasks. You can have the whole bathroom clean tip-top while your little ones are playing with the rubber ducky.

Little Bathers

Little children love water play, but they aren't that wild about water in the face. What I have found helpful is to let toddlers play while showering to get accustomed to water dripping in their face. They don't seem to notice if they are playing. The second thing I've found helpful is to keep the water low in the tub and show them how to do the back float. If they can feel the tub under their back, it is not as scary. Gradually increase the amount of water as their confidence builds. Playtime in the bathtub gives toddlers confidence in the water. Always stay in the room during their bath, of course, and take the opportunity to clean. While shampooing, teach them to hold a dry washcloth on their face. This keeps the water from getting in their eyes, and the washcloth doesn't get soaked until the shampoo is rinsed out of their hair.

Finger and toe nails should be inspected during the bath and should be clipped as needed afterwards. Soft nails are easier to clip.

Saturday nights are always "bath night" at our house. In the winter, we also do baths on Wednesday nights. The babies and toddlers often get a bath after a diaper blow out. In the summer, the little children get a bath or shower every evening before supper.

Conditioner and a tangle-free spray are essential for painless hair-combing. I have five girls, and it seems like each girl has a different hair texture and thickness. Each one also has a preference for the type of brush or comb used on her hair.

Cradle cap seems to disappear with oil and scalp stimulation. I think it is also helpful to stay on top of probiotics because I have read that it can be caused by a yeast overgrowth in the baby. Probiotics are healthful in many other ways besides helping with cradle cap, so why not take them? When I was in the NICU, the nurses used a soft brush when washing babies' scalps. It was the same type as a mushroom cleaning brush or corn silk remover brush that you will find in a kitchen store.

Another baby cleaning trick I learned in the NICU is to swaddle the naked baby and gently put him in the warm water. The baby feels more secure with his limbs close to his body, and the blanket keeps the water from shocking his senses. It also makes it easier to hold onto the baby during his bath. Uncover each part of the body as you wash him, and then recover as you move on. Wash his face with pure water and the rest of his body with a very mild soap. A baby doesn't need a bath every day; it dries out his skin. Do wash the parts that get dirty: his face, ears, neck, hands. And, of course, clean his bottom with each diaper change. As soon as you're done, unwrap him from the swaddle and immediately lift him up, out, and into a towel to reswaddle him.

Before you bathe your baby, get completely set up. If you can, do the bath in a warm room. If you don't have a heat light in the bathroom, do your baby's bath after somebody has taken a steamy shower. Lay out clean clothes, diaper, clean swaddling blankets to warm him up quickly, and towels to wrap him up in as soon as you remove him from the water. I like to give my babies a massage with coconut oil after a bath because it is so good for their skin. Baby finger and toe nails are easiest to do when the baby is sleeping!

CHAPTER 36
Bedroom Management

Bedroom Stuff

Simplify bedrooms to the bare minimum for easier cleaning. Do you and your children really want to spend your time taking care of "stuff"? When there is too much in the room, it gets spread around, trampled on, and lost, and can become a supreme nuisance. With fewer things, the stuff is enjoyed more and usually better cared for. Put simply: It's easier to manage a few things than a lot of things.

The overabundance of stuff infringes on better things to do with our lives. It takes time to pick things up and put them away, to wash, to fix, to sort, organize and store stuff. Why do we need so much stuff? If the things you have are not helping in some way, they're a hindrance and a liability.

The answer to this over-accumulation: Purge out the unnecessary! Get rid of your extra things. Stuff sometimes looks helpful, but if it saps time from better activities, then get rid of it.

Bless others with your extra stuff. Hold things with a light hand, because they are not yours in the first place. They belong to God. Materialism in our current culture is a constant battle to fight. When we redirect our purpose in life to serving others, then we replace materialism—a preoccupation with material things—with a life lived for God.

Closets

Closet space for a large family's clothes is at a premium. Here are some practical steps to deal with the space shortage.

First, eliminate anything you don't need. Your children do not need a lot of clothes, if you are staying caught up with the laundry. They do not need any more clothes than they can wear in a week's time in any given season of the year.

Second, organize your children's clothes so that little children can carry a small basket or wash tub of laundry to their drawers and put them away. If there is no room in the drawers for their clothes, then you may need to cut the amount again.

Another option is to keep some of your children's clothes on shelves or rods in the laundry room. Currently, this is what my boys do.

If you have built-in closets, put a dowel rod low enough for the children to reach their hanging clothes. Otherwise, they will climb, and that is liable to be destructive.

For a few years, I had hanging shelves in my girls' closets, one shelf for each day of the week. When they started to shove things in, I knew we had too many clothes again. Usually somebody grew and had things passed to them without cleaning out the clothing that was too small. The shelves also enabled me to see who was short of clothing. Now they have grown, and we have moved to hanging all of the big girl's clothes and storing the little girls' clothes in drawers placed at the bottom of the closet.

Shoe organizers work well over the door for storing socks, tights, hair bows, and more. Be sure to store articles within their reach so that the children don't tear it down trying to get their things.

Beds

Bunk beds and lofts are essential for saving space. Whenever you need space in your home, look around the edges of the rooms and go up with storage. If you have high ceilings, you can even do triple bunks. Trundle beds also save space.

Many times large families will have to build in order to get the custom beds that fits a specific rooms' bed needs. Bunk beds are not hard to build. Our oldest son built all of the beds we needed, and he is self-taught at construction. If you want them to be pretty, use hard wood and stain the finished product. We chose to paint the frames in our girls' room a baby blue. The boys have a John Deere theme in their room, and the bunks are painted green. I have seen cute bunks with white bead board on the ends. The girls' bunks have shelves built in around the head of each bed.

Cleaning

There are two key things to keeping bedrooms clean. One is to train the children to pick up every night before they hop in bed and every morning when they get up. The second is to dust and vacuum every week on an assigned day.

If they keep their rooms picked up as a daily habit, then cleaning is easy, just like it is elsewhere in the house. The key is that your children need to be trained to pick up after themselves and that happens when you "inspect what you expect". While you pick up your bedroom, instruct them to pick up theirs and then check their work. When they see you keeping your room in order, they will be more liable to keep their room in order also.

Every week on Cleaning Day, wash the sheets, vacuum, and dust the bedrooms.

It's not hard if the bedrooms are kept orderly every day. Divide the bedroom into Focus Areas, and each week of the month, assign a fifteen-minute period on Cleaning Day to clean that area. Make a chart for this, and post it on the bedroom door.

Week 1: Closet.

Week 2: Under the Bed.

Week 3: Shelves and Dresser Tops.

Week 4: Ceiling Lights, Cobwebs, Light Switches.

If these chores are done consistently, they do not grow to be big, day-long tasks. Use the timer and do the work with the children. "The speed of the leader is the speed of the pack"—they will match their effort to yours.

CHAPTER 37
The Children's Hour

The Children's Hour by Henry Wadsworth Longfellow.

> *Between the dark and the daylight,*
> *When the night is beginning to lower,*
> *Comes a pause in the day's occupations,*
> *That is known as the Children's Hour.*
>
> *I hear in the chamber above me*
> *The patter of little feet,*
> *The sound of a door that is opened,*
> *And voices soft and sweet.*
>
> *From my study I see in the lamplight,*
> *Descending the broad hall stair,*
> *Grave Alice, and laughing Allegra,*
> *And Edith with golden hair.*

A whisper, and then a silence:
Yet I know by their merry eyes
They are plotting and planning together
To take me by surprise.

A sudden rush from the stairway,
A sudden raid from the hall!
By three doors left unguarded
They enter my castle wall!

They climb up into my turret
O'er the arms and back of my chair;
If I try to escape, they surround me;
They seem to be everywhere.

They almost devour me with kisses,
Their arms about me entwine,
Till I think of the Bishop of Bingen
In his Mouse-Tower on the Rhine!

Do you think, o blue-eyed banditti,
Because you have scaled the wall,
Such an old mustache as I am
Is not a match for you all!

I have you fast in my fortress,
And will not let you depart,
But put you down into the dungeon
In the round-tower of my heart.

And there will I keep you forever,
Yes, forever and a day,
Till the walls shall crumble to ruin,
And moulder in dust away!

A Pause in the Day's Occupations

What happens in your home "between the dark and daylight"? What is going on "when the night is beginning to lower"? Pause for a moment and put a picture of it together in your mind's eye. Typically, this is when the work is done and the family welcomes Dad home, and the time is spent together as a family.

As home managers, it is our job to see that this time of the day falls together nicely with a restful retreat from the world, happy hearts, comfort food, and time well spent. Those things are the goal to aim for. It will look different in each home. We all have unique family personalities. The bottom line is that we are to glorify God with our evenings.

How do you set the tone of the home? It starts with your attitude. How do you react to things? Put good things in, and good things will come out.

> But the fruit of the Spirit is love, joy, peace, patience, kindness, goodness, faithfulness, gentleness, self-control; against such things there is no law. And those who belong to Christ Jesus have crucified the flesh with its passions and desires. —Galatians 5:22-24

Work on setting the tone for the evening in the late afternoon by putting on refreshing music. Put a memory verse card above your sink, and review it while you put supper together. Pray over the supper, and ask God's blessings on the evening as a family. If someone has trouble eating something on the menu, pray about it. If there are relationship problems in your home, pray about those during this time as you prepare your heart for the upcoming Children's Hour.

Respond to the needs of the children with the law of kindness on your tongue. Easy for me to say, but not so easy for me to do some days. It takes self-discipline and relying on the Holy Spirit that lives within. Help your children be prepared for the evening by getting their chores done by a certain time. If they are piddling and bickering, then stop everything and call a meeting. Explain to them what the family's goals are for the evening—happy hearts, a restful retreat, comfort food, and a good time had by all. You might need to paint a picture of what this looks like in your home for the children. Then, go to work making it happen.

What does your husband like to do when he arrives home? Does he like to rest in his chair to unwind, or does he want to be in the yard playing ball? Each dad is different; help the dad in your home find the haven of respite from his daily work.

Do you have supper early or late in your home? There is no right or wrong answer; however, it is important to have structure and regular meals for small children. Those two things go a long way towards content and peaceable children. If your husband likes to have supper late, then you will need to have a substantial snack in the late afternoon for the children. Plan for this. Add it to your schedule and grocery list. Plan a peaceable suppertime routine to promote a pleasant evening.

How The Children's Hour is spent will depend on each family's priorities. Some spend it in front of the television. Don't let the blinking blue light rob your family any more! Better choices are reading aloud, playing games, talking, playing musical instruments together, singing, breathing the fresh air on the deck, and watching the sun set. Each family needs to decide what works best for them.

We do things differently throughout the year with the changing seasons, the weather, the amount of farm chores to do with Dad, and so on. Sometimes we have The Children's Hour before supper, sometimes after. Things we do in our family are read a book aloud, board games, softball games in the back yard, sit in the backyard and talk, play badminton, play piano and guitar, review catechism questions, play in the sandbox, read the Bible, show off bike tricks for the family, wrestle on the floor, and Dad's very creative stories about Ricky the Skunk and Tommy the Raccoon.

What The Children's Hour is not: separate activities for every member of the family, outside-the-home meetings and activities (especially on an every night basis), parents in one room doing something while children do their own thing or sit in front of the TV, everybody with a nose in their own book, or family members gathered around the other blue blinking light (the computer).

Family time means interacting with each other. Every night will not go perfectly and be a beautiful picture of The Children's Hour. The idea is to have a goal to aim for: "If you aim for nothing, you'll hit it every time." The Christian family is one that loves each other, takes care of each other, and is the salt of the earth and a light to the world. It is hard to build relationships with each other if we aren't doing anything together.

I would encourage you to take make the most of The Children's Hour to build healthy, God-glorifying relationships together as a family.

> *Let the children come to me, and do not hinder them, for to such belongs the kingdom of God. —Luke 18:16*

CHAPTER 38
Family Worship

Your wife will be like a fruitful vine within your house; your children will be like olive shoots around your table. —Psalm 128:3

I inherited a book from my grandparent's bookshelf many years ago called *How to Build a Happy Home* by B. Charles Hostetter. It is a gem! The back cover shows Mr. Hostetter's happy-looking family with eight children, ages 18 to 5 weeks. From my vantage point, the most valuable part of the book is the last chapter title, "Making Family Worship Meaningful," which includes this powerful quote:

> *Do you have family worship in your home? Many homes do not, but not because they don't believe in the practice. They are too busy; it doesn't fit into their program. But to me that is not a justifiable excuse, except for a few times that are exceptions. It may seem that there is not time for some of these most important things in life; we have to take time for them. They may not easily fit into our schedules, but we have to make them fit. As parents it becomes our duty to put first things first. We dare not let the good become the enemy of the best.*
>
> *Many parents would be a lot happier today if they had sacrificed a little profit and had had family worship instead. Now their children have grown up and are gone and oh, the heartache they have caused! The fertile period to mold the character of their children is gone. Oh, yes, they have money in their old age, but how gladly they would exchange it*

for Christian, parent-honoring children! But they can't; their best opportunities for child training are gone forever, and neither money, tears, nor high position can change the picture. Remember, you must take time for family worship in the home. You may have to sacrifice something else, but it will be worth it.

Mr. Hostetter goes on to write about making family worship a happy time and giving it thought and preparation. He encourages families to conduct it at a time most convenient for all, but he counsels that mornings, when our minds are clearest, is the best time to have it. He suggests singing, taking turns reading Scriptures or reading in unison, and each person praying. To add variety to worship, he notes that you can spend the time in singing or praying only, memorizing Scripture together, making the children responsible for a worship time, dramatizing a Bible story, and planning service projects.

I don't know whether or not my grandparents practiced Family Worship their whole married life, but I clearly remember that after Grandma cleared the breakfast dishes, we took turns reading a passage of Scripture, followed by Grandpa praying. At home, while we ate breakfast, my mom would read a devotional story to us, and as the bus came down the road, Dad would gather us by the door and pray with us. Mr. Hostetter summarizes his perspective on morning devotions this way: "Give Christ first place in your lives and homes, and you will know the greatest secret for building a happy home."

My husband leaves early in the morning, so after doing chores, I read Psalms and Proverbs at the breakfast table when the children get up (unless it is a new baby season). What's true in Hostetter's counsel is that when we read scriptures in the morning when our minds are clearest, it sets the tone for the day. Due to the importance of this, our children are also required to do the Bible portion of their schoolwork first.

In the evening, my husband—the creative story-teller—makes up a character lesson story about Ricky the Skunk and Tommy the Raccoon. I'm not sure how the stories started, but it was when our big boys were little. Then we pray together as a family. This family worship time, centered around the leadership of Dad, is critical to the family. Do whatever you can to encourage and facilitate this.

How wonderful that Jesus is in the midst of us when we are praying as a family! As I can see in my own heritage, God is faithful to families that honor Him.

For where two or three are gathered in my name, there am I among them. —Matthew 18:20

CHAPTER 39
Home Crafts

She seeks wool and flax, and works with willing hands. —Proverbs 31:13

She puts her hands to the distaff, and her hands hold the spindle. —Proverbs 31:19

She makes bed coverings for herself; her clothing is fine linen and purple. —Proverbs 31:22

She makes linen garments and sells them; she delivers sashes to the merchant. —Proverbs 31:24

Crafts are an expression of art and creativity. Crafts are fun, promote creativity, and may even turn into a home business. By working at various crafts, we make gifts, learn skills in many artistic areas, and crafts keep our families occupied on rainy days. Scrapbooking our pictures leaves a historical record and legacy of our families.

The more people we have in the family, the more varied the individual artistic interests can be! I am finding this out as my girls grow older. We are doing more crafty things, and the projects are becoming larger. It is definitely something they enjoy doing and want to do more of. This has directed more thought into how to accommodate opportunities for growth and development in their artistic endeavors.

Boys, of course, are also creative. As your children grow, their interests will evolve and develop. Watch for their unique interests, and cultivate them by allowing them space, time, and materials for them. Our oldest son has spent his gift money and earnings on shop tools since he was ten. He goes to auctions to get tools for a good price. Our second son has an eye for detail, and has always enjoyed photography.

Location, Location, Location

As wonderful as they are, crafts can be messy and take up a lot of space. They require storage of an assortment of tools and materials. This has required us to carve out a space for crafting. In our home we call it "The Sewing Room." It is our place for all crafting endeavors, though sewing predominates.

In the past, we used the unfinished part of the basement for arts and crafts before we turned it into a Laundry Room. Then we rearranged our house by moving all the girls into one bedroom and using a previous bedroom for a Sewing Room. Then we did more rearranging. We tore out a wall between two bedrooms in the basement, and now we have a bigger Sewing Room. Think creatively for making room for the creative projects. In our case, it was more efficient to move the girls into one room for sleeping. That is all their bedroom is used for anyway. Their toys are in the Playroom, and their craft projects are in the Sewing Room. Their clothes are in the bedroom closet. Update: At time of this printing, we've moved all the girls' clothes into the Laundry Room.

What about "alone time" for children? What is the alone time used for? Think about the child that is seeking alone time. Is it a need for quiet reading or study? Is it a self-centered escape? If the child needs alone time to calm their spirit in a healthy way, then help that child carve out a niche somewhere in the home to have that quiet time. It doesn't need to be a bedroom. It can be workshop, a reading chair, or a bubble bath. Let's dispense with the culture's idea of how things should be done.

When Inspiration Strikes

Our latest endeavor for drawing took place every Thursday afternoon before our Tea Party. At other times, we have held art class every day during nap time for a couple of months. Often we take an afternoon for working on various projects in the Sewing Room. Sometimes a child or two are excused from school for the day so that they can work on a project all day long.

Once in awhile, we will cancel school for a week while we diligently work on sewing projects. During these weeks, we try to prepare ahead with freezer meals or an easy crockpot menu plan, extra cleaning ahead of time, and specific activities planned for the little children.

Because we have a Sewing Room, it works well for us to leave our projects in limbo there and schedule a time period in the day to come back to them. This did not work well when we did our projects at the dining room table. The effort to get out a big project kept us from doing them. The Sewing Room has allowed us the freedom to work on projects a bit every day, and because of that, we get more accomplished.

Little Children

We have special things for the little children to do only while we are in our Sewing Room. They are not to take these activities and toys to other places in the house, and they are not allowed to be in the Sewing Room unless Mom or a big girl is there to supervise. These activities are:

- A jar of buttons and a muffin tin to sort buttons into.

- Yarn to thread buttons onto.

- Sewing cards of various difficulties.

- Very simple children's crafts (things they can do on their own or with a small child to instruct).

Pursue creative and meaningful home crafts with your children, and watch as their artistic gifts come to light and bless others!

> *Art in various forms expresses and gives opportunity to others to share in, and respond to, things which would otherwise remain vague, empty yearnings. Art satisfies and fulfils something in the person creating and in those responding.*
> —*Edith Schaeffer,* The Hidden Art of Homemaking

CHAPTER 40
Homeschooling the Large Family

Your Purpose in Homeschooling

When our oldest was a baby, I gleaned a lot of baby wisdom from another mom at church who had five children. Her children were sweet, pleasant, well-mannered, intelligent, and homeschooled.

We watched and admired those children. As the years went by, they had more babies, and we had more babies. My questions to this mom changed to stubborn toddler questions, and then the prospect of school began to loom on the horizon for our oldest child. I could not bear the thought of putting my sweet tender boy on the school bus to learn what he already knew. We live far enough from town that it would be an hour ride both ways. Two hours on the school bus!

I remember my experience on the school bus all too well, so I started asking my mentor questions about homeschooling, and she started handing me materials to read. It didn't take long for my husband and I to decide to homeschool due to several philosophical reasons beyond simply having our son avoid two hours a day on the school bus.

Our goal as Christians is to raise up a Godly seed for future generations; to teach them to "fear God and keep His commandments" (Ecclesiastes 12:13) that they might be used as "the repairer of the breach"(Isaiah 58:12) in response to a culture that has, to a great extent, destroyed the Christian foundations that once made our nation strong. Our purpose for homeschooling should not simply be to save our child a bus trip and to have fun with them. The most important lessons to be learned are when we walk with our children and proactively teach them how God wants us to live.

Know Your Child

Each child is unique. Part of the beauty of homeschooling is that we get to know each one of our children and can tailor a curriculum to meet each child's individual learning needs. We learn to know our children by living and working with them, through building relationships with them.

As the years go by, our children grow and mature, and our teaching styles must change and grow with them—another beauty of homeschooling! As teachers, it is our privilege to know our children and help them with their unique needs. A method that works for one child might not work as well with another. We need to be sensitive to this fact.

Teaching Your Children to be Self-Taught

As a mom with a hundred different hats to wear, you cannot teach all your children like it is done in the world's idea of the typical "classroom". You need to let go of this idea.

One of your goals in training your children is to teach them to teach themselves. If your children learn how to teach themselves, they will be set for life. Anything they get curious about they will be able to learn. Education is not as simple as stuffing their heads full of facts; it is giving them the ability to learn new things and to develop thinking skills, tools they will use for their whole lives.

Anything that requires you to read a script to your children in order to teach it must be strictly evaluated. Is this exercise really necessary for your child to learn the subject at hand? Is it necessary that he learn it right now with this method, or can it wait until he is able to read and comprehend it better another way? Is there a product out there that teaches the same thing directly to the student, apart from cumbersome teacher aids?

Every home is different and will have different needs. I'm sure there is a time and place for a scripted lesson. That said, this should not be the norm for the large family. This takes time away from other things that are more important. There are other ways for a lesson to be presented rather than you standing there reading a script. The parent as teacher should primarily be an aid to self-teaching, not a script reader.

Any child that can read well should be able to pick up a book, read directions, and learn. Once a child can read for comprehension, they can fly. They can self-teach if you encourage them in it. Spend your time with younger children reading good books and exploring, not giving a scripted lesson.

When starting a child off on a new book, look the whole thing over with him. Read through the contents, the introduction, the index and glossary. Teach him that every time he picks up a new book, he should familiarize himself with it before he reads it.

About the age 12 or 13, our children read *How to Read a Book* by Mortimer Adler, and read through it again every year until they "graduate". They also reference *The Elements of Style* by E.B. White when they are doing any writing. If you haven't invested in these titles and read them yet, do so. It's worthwhile teacher education.

If you think your child is an auditory learner, and that is why he needs you to read his lessons to him, then get more audio books and related curriculum. Singnlearn.com has a huge selection for every subject. Audio learning is also a great way to do double duty on Town Day, while mopping, and other cleaning work.

If your child seems to need constant help and has constant questions, evaluate whether this is really necessary, or if he just has a lazy habit. When he comes to you for help, ask first, "Did you read the directions?" "Did you go back and read them again?" If it's language arts or spelling, ask him, "Did you read the rule?" "Did you go back and read the rule again?"

When you are satisfied that he truly doesn't understand what he's reading, then help him. If he is stumbling because of a word, teach him to do his schoolwork and reading with a dictionary in hand and to look up words that he's unfamiliar with. Keep dictionaries laying around so that learning can happen on the run.

Self-teaching is a ball that you start rolling when the children are little, and your job is to keep the ball rolling. Encourage your children to make a project or write a news report about whatever it is they are learning. When they are producing something that is an outgrowth of an interest, they care about spelling and grammar and handwriting. These things must be taught as well, but in the simplest and most pain-free way possible. Do not use a sledgehammer (endless workbook pages) to reinforce these skills. Use a project instead that they are already interested in and care about.

Steps Toward Working Independently

AIM FOR SELF-TEACHING CURRICULUM

Evaluate the things that you are using that are causing the most teacher-work, and ask if it's worth it, or if there is possibly another available option that can do the same thing in a better way.

Reference books are essential for self-teaching. These can typically be picked up free at library book sales, or for a song at thrift stores. Sometimes you need to fork out the big bucks and get something like Webster's 1828 Dictionary (used every day at our house). Use these reference tools with them, and teach them how to use them. I have seen curriculum for teaching how to use a reference book—how silly! You don't need a curriculum for teaching how to use a reference book. Just do it. If you don't know how, you will find instructions at the front of the book that explains it to you.

Reference books are an important and highly useful investment. Leave dictionaries and Bibles in key areas around your house for your family to use. Place them where people typically read. Watch where your children go when they are reading; that's where you will want to place reference books. Where do they write? Place a thesaurus at that location. Decorate your house with books!

EVALUATE YOUR TEACHING

Perhaps you have inadvertently encouraged your children to overly rely on you for their learning. If so, begin to self-consciously encourage them to be problem-solvers. When they request help, ask if they have read the directions, and if so, have read them again, and to do so out loud. Sometimes reading out loud helps with comprehension. Urge them to look up vocabulary words they don't know the definitions of in the dictionary. Ask them if they have studied the examples.

Train them to do this by keeping a chart and giving rewards and penalties. A friend of mine had great success with this approach. Her rewards were Lamplighter books, and the only way a child could earn a new book was through improving on the character traits that she was encouraging.

If you teach your children to read directions, they will soon be applying this discipline to everything. They will be cooking from scratch, putting things together for you, hooking up new appliances, building, and much more. Directions aren't just in schoolwork; they are part of life. Beyond formal education, we don't have teachers following us around in life, telling us how to do every little thing. We thus need to learn to be resourceful problem-solvers and teach our children to be the same.

Give your children access to the world around them and teach them to "see" it and wonder about it. This happens through active conversation between you and your children. It's important that you engage with them. Go lay on the sidewalk with them, watch ants build a hill, and talk about it. Ask questions about everything. Why is the sky blue? What is that bird doing? How is cheese made? Who invented taxes? Talking and listening—conversation is education. Children are naturally curious unless they have been brought up on a steady diet of TV, boring toys, and Kraft Dinner day after day, and it's important that you cultivate a sense of inquisitive wonder in them.

Make Lesson Plans

Create lesson plans that they can follow without your help. My children know that they are supposed to do two pages of math every day, no matter what, for example. I don't have to tell them to do it.

For an easy lesson plan to follow, just take a piece of paper and write the child's name at the top. Then write a column for each book that they are to work in or read and another column for how much they should do every day.

LET THEM THINK

Encourage your children that it's okay to sit and think about something and process it and try to figure it out themselves. This builds confidence in problem-solving and creative thinking. Tell them that the important thing is not what they get done but what they are learning.

TEACH THEM DILIGENCE

This might sound contradictory to the last point, but your children need to learn to work diligently. Teach them that when they get something done, to move right to the next thing. When they are all done with their schoolwork, then they can do whatever project/activity/toy it is that they love to do. "We work before we play!"

TEACH EACH OTHER

Your children can give each other spelling tests. This helps both parties learn spelling. Have the older children read aloud to the younger. This makes the older children better and more expressive readers. Older children can help younger ones with math concepts as well. Both the older and younger children benefit.

At the table, when schoolwork is being done, have buddies sit beside each other. The older ones can teach the younger ones and help them do things. A lot of times the older ones are teaching the younger ones without me encouraging them to do so. Over time, it has come naturally for them.

New Curriculum

Curriculum written for classroom use does not work well for learning to be a self-teacher. However it might still be used for self-teaching if it's not heavily teacher-oriented once the child learns the system of how it works. At first, they might need your help in breaking down lessons into daily pieces, learning how to do each piece, and then gradually breaking free from your intensive help to come to you only when they need help.

Using a curriculum to self-teach involves learning how to read the author's style of writing and presentation, learning new vocabulary, and developing new ways of thinking. When learning a new curriculum, encourage your child to be self-teaching by having them start by reading the introduction, contents, becoming familiar with the book by finding and perusing the glossary and index, and then looking at how the lessons are laid out.

Spend a week simply doing that. Then dive into the first lesson by doing a lot of thinking before beginning the lessons themselves. Following this approach, the first of a "new year" usually takes more time and energy from everyone, but then once the children learn the new curriculum, they can fly along in their new subjects with just a little bit of steering from you. This is also why you shouldn't throw out a new schedule you just created. It might not be working at first because everybody is taking so long learning new curriculums, but then things will fall into place, and it will work out.

While it's important to have a system with clear academic goals for your children to accomplish, you shouldn't be rigid. Break out of the box on occasion. Take your kids on a field trip on your own for the best learning instead of with a group. Read a history or science book. Plant a terrarium, hatch eggs, or make a timeline of a war. Talk about what you learned at supper. Make scrapbooks of your projects. Don't confine your homeschooling to a plan that stifles learning.

Accountability

I do not sit beside my children checking every single problem as it's done. I occasionally peer over shoulders and check, first, to see that they have done their work. Second, I ask the child if they understand what they are doing. Third, I check a few problems to know that they understand. I do that for each subject. I'm not sitting there checking every problem of every book that each child is working through.

My goal for them is understanding, and checking every problem isn't necessary to see that they understand. That doesn't mean that I never check every single problem of a page but, generally speaking, I do not, because it is not necessary.

When they are reading something, such as a history book, I will ask them sometime during the day to tell me what they have read in history. Then they narrate back to me what they read. I do this at meals, or when we're working in the kitchen, or just relaxing on the deck. I want them to be able to tell me names of people, time periods, and other interesting tid-bits. This opens up conversation among all of us. At our school appointment on Office Day, I will ask further questions.

I don't often require an older child to work completely through a grammar text. I'll pick out their problem areas and have them work through that part of the book that addresses their need. I have them self-check, and then at our appointment on Office Day, I will check to be sure they understand the areas I assigned them to learn.

Kitchen Window View or Teaching Art the Easy Way

As homeschooling moms, we buy a lot of books. It's a common joke that we are book-a-holics and bibliophiles. We browse book stores, collect catalogs, ogle old books, and de-cluttering books is probably one of the hardest of the de-cluttering jobs that we do.

I'm sure that in your library collection, you have art books, how-to books, and gardening books. I would also guess that most of you have taken your children to art shows, art museums, art lessons, and assigned them reading in art.

While these books and activities can be helpful, here is a practical suggestion to give your children some real life art. Take them to your kitchen window and ask them what they see. If they're shorter than you are, then you will want to get down on their level and look up. They usually have the best view: It's trees and sky. The taller they get, the more creative their choice of words describing it to you will be. Ask them and yourself, "What can we do to improve this view?" Write down their ideas, and make plans to put them into action.

Do you see how this is the most practical art you can do with your children? The window is your frame, and the content is something that you look at all the time. It changes with the weather and the seasons, so as the year goes by, you will want to add more to your notes and make plans to add interest to the view throughout the year.

A view from a window in your house is one of those common things that hold beauty and help us to understand God and His power, His creations, and the might of His hand. This is one way of taking dominion over the earth. He has given us this view of a little spot on this earth, and we can move things, build things, add to it, take away from it, and create order in it.

Inspiring ideas on how to "improve your view" might come from art books, gardening books, and building books. If you don't have these, then I would encourage you to acquire some; they're really inexpensive at second hand stores. There are landscape ideas online also. Learn how to divide your plants from these books and spread them around. If you and your boys don't know how to build things yet, start with a bird house or a bird feeder. Plant a cutting garden with your daughters, and create bouquets from it all season long. Once you and your children's creative juices start flowing, and you start improving your views, it will just build and build. Soon your Garden Days will be busy with projects, and your art frames will be works of great creativity—from the sky and tree tops down to the lawn and gardens.

By teaching your children to appreciate the window views, they will also start to see the toys and trash that they leave in the yard and be more diligent about picking them up. This works much better than any lecture. Their eyes begin to see more and more, and they will point out beauty to you that previously went unnoticed. The view from the window is art.

Preschoolers

Some years preschoolers aren't trouble at all and fit right in to the school plan for the older children. Other years, there seems to be rub in the mix. Personalities, ages, and other issues all play a role in what makes for a peaceful time and what is less than peaceful. The same children that are causing a problem now will peacefully coexist in a few months with another problem to replace the one that was solved.

One very helpful thing that I've done in the past was to train the little children to take one toy or activity at a time to their mat or spot on the table. I do this for the little one in the pack-n-play, for example. If the activity is an imaginative one, the child will do it for a long time. I remember a specific fifteen-month-old in the pack-n-play playing with only a can full of blocks for close to an hour. "One toy at a time" is teaching concentration. Any good activity will keep the child occupied with it for at least ten minutes. With a truly imaginative activity an older child will easily fill up an hour.

When the child is doing the activity, they are not to spread the mess all over the place. This is learning discipline and takes just a little encouragement. When the child is done with the activity, he puts it away before getting another one out. For the little one in the pack-n-play, I learned to keep an eye on her, and as soon as she started to tire of the activity, I switched it before she became unhappy. She usually settled right into playing with the "new" thing unless she was tired or hungry.

The children are not to distract each other or mess with another person's activity. They can play together cooperatively at another time of day. This is "school time".

If there is a time period during the day that you and the children need to work together and the preschoolers are not napping, then using mats and a pack-n-play and the one-activity-at-a-time strategy is a great way to teach the little ones at the same time. The hardest part is that you have to be there to help them learn the system (leaving to do the laundry doesn't work very well). Teach your older ones the method to help out during the training period.

Activities that work well are typically imaginative, self-correcting, and educational.

Sandpaper letters are an easy thing that you and the older children can make for the preschoolers. Simply take an alphabet stencil, trace it onto 220-grit sandpaper, cut out the letters, and glue them onto 3 x 5 cards. The preschooler can traces the sandpaper letters with his finger. In doing so, he will get to know the alphabet. By using his fingers on the sandpaper, it will help cement it into his brain. Do it with him for a while so he learns what directions his fingers should go in tracing the letters. You can do this same thing with numbers.

Activities to do at the table are puzzles of all sorts, peg boards, pattern blocks, Cuisenaire rods, and bead stringing. Pull together things that will help them learn classifying, sequencing, and matching. Put your activities together on a shelf or in a cupboard and get them out only for "school time". Wash tubs are a great size for holding activities, and they fit on shelves neatly and are inexpensive.

The Sh'ma

What is the most important thing for our children to learn? There is only one answer to that, and if it's not being covered in your home, then you need to start there. It's the Sh'ma, found in Deuteronomy 6:4-5:

Hear, O Israel: The Lord our God, the Lord is one. You shall love the Lord your God with all your heart and with all your soul and with all your might. And these words that I command you today shall be on your heart.

How do we teach the Sh'ma? We are to diligently talk to our children about the Sh'ma: "You shall teach [these words] diligently to your children...."

When are we to teach the Sh'ma? All the time—"when you sit in your house, and when you walk by the way, and when you lie down, and when you rise."

Surrendering the Homeschool to God

When you get overwhelmed, read Deuteronomy 6 and do the following exercise. We have found this to be a refreshing change which gets us back on the right track.

Gather all of your children around the table.

Pray for wisdom.

Open your Bible and pick a selection. Psalms and Proverbs are good choices for character applications.

Read it aloud and have your children copy it into a notebook. This is dictation that will sharpen their listening skills.

Check their dictation or have them check it.

Recopy it correctly in their best handwriting—they can look at the selection now.

This is their handwriting lesson. It will also help them learn how to write.

Copying the sentences of others is how many great writers learned the skill.

Have them copy each misspelled word from dictation five times. This is their spelling lesson.

Define the big words using the dictionary. This is their vocabulary lesson.

Do a grammar lesson with the selection, identifying each part of the sentence and diagramming it. Use one of your children's language arts books to figure it out.

Memorize the selection together and write it from memory. It should be easy by this point!

As a group, come up with project ideas built around this verse—drama, an act of service, a poster. Then write an essay on the selection or write a creative story about the verse in application. If there is a natural element in the verse, look it up in a science reference book. Look up the cross references, etc. Take the rest of your school day to work on these ideas.

Jesus answered, "The most important is, 'Hear, O Israel: The Lord our God, the Lord is one. And you shall love the Lord your God with all your heart and with all your soul and with all your mind and with all your strength.' The second is this: 'You shall love your neighbor as yourself.' There is no other commandment greater than these." —Mark 12:29-31

CHAPTER 41
Health and Wellness

She dresses herself with strength and makes her arms strong. —Proverbs 31:17

Evaluate your health. How do you feel? What is causing aches and pains? Do you wish you had more energy?

Sleep

Adequate sleep has a big impact on our health and mental clarity. It is very easy for us as mothers to short change ourselves on sleep. At different times we need different amounts of rest to be our best. I know that the more I get up with a baby, the earlier I need to get into bed.

What time do you want to be up in the morning? How much sleep do you need? How much time does the baby take during the night? How much time do you need in bed to unwind before falling asleep?

Figure out the total, and count backwards from your waking hour to learn when you need to go to bed. If you simply cannot get to bed early enough, then be sure to take the Quiet Hour seriously and get some rest then.

Water

Personally, I started feeling dramatically better when I started drinking water instead of soda, hot tea, iced tea, juice, kool-aid, hot cocoa, and coffee. There are too many detriments in those beverages that outweigh the good. Changing your beverages will go a long way towards improving your health. If you are nursing, then it is vital that you have a large glass of water each time you feed the baby. Water makes all of our body systems work better. It helps your brain function, muscles, joints, nerves, skin—everything!

Simply being hydrated improves our health. If you don't like the taste of your water, squeeze a lemon into your pitcher. The lemon is very good for your health also! Drink a tall glass of water first thing in the morning. Fill a pitcher and commit to drinking water regularly throughout the day.

Exercise

Exercise is another thing that gives you more energy. It seems a paradox that something that takes effort to do rewards with more energy, but it is true! I confess to being a warm weather exerciser. I love to get outside and walk or be active in the yard. Exercise does not just cause us to burn fat; it also builds all the muscles that hold our bones and joints in place. It builds bone strength and makes a healthy heart. We need to be mobile now if we're going to be able and fit grandparents who can help our children and grandchildren.

Have recess with your children—go play in the yard! Garden. Plant fruit trees. Hang out your laundry. Take your children on hikes. Make a habit of a daily walk, and take your children with you. Bike as a family. Read a book while you walk on the treadmill. Do an exercise video with your children; I really like T-Tapp videos (t-tapp.com).

Exercise is a habit that once you start doing becomes easier. You will come to love the way it energizes you. Look at your day's schedule, and find the ideal time to do it for this season. Ten minutes of walking or stretching is better than nothing. Do more if you can, but do something.

Having babies stretches out and can tear the muscles in the mid section, and it's not fun going around with a pooch. Exercises to repair this can be found at www.maternalfitness.com.

Supplements

I used to disdain supplements. I have always cooked from scratch and tried to serve balanced meals. I thought a person could get enough nutrients from this alone, but I discovered otherwise. I began to realize that I had better days when I took my doctor-prescribed prenatal vitamin.

Long story short: I have a daughter that is allergic to milk, and that caused me to do some reading on nutrition and learning some things about how much we really don't get in our diet. Now I sing the praises of taking a B complex. It keeps the hormone swings under control. I don't get weepy or short-tempered. Nor as tired or low in energy. Taking Cal-Mag-Zinc prevents me from having restless legs, leg cramps, and bone pain in my hands. Vitamin C decreased varicose veins and the itching and pain that accompanied them. Fish oil improved my skin.

I know that taking a multi-vitamin regularly makes me healthier overall.

If your health isn't quite up to par, or if you just wish you had some more energy, try searching out some information on what you need that you aren't getting through your diet.

CHAPTER 42
The Playroom

Toys!

Toys teach. Choose your toys with this in mind. Playing is externalizing what is going on internally. Children have an enormous capacity for creativity and are wildly imaginative. Provide your children with toys that encourage thoughtfulness.

An open-ended toy is one that can be played with for extended periods of time in different ways by each unique child. For example, a child might use blocks to build a fence for his farm animals one day, and the next day use the blocks to build a hill for a goat to climb on. The day after that, he might use the blocks to throw at a target. When de-cluttering toys, look at each one and ask if it is open-ended. Is the toy going to promote thinking skills, imagination, and creativity?

Even good thought-provoking toys can accumulate and overtake the home. I read recently that the average American child receives seventy new toys a year. I thought that we had an excessive toy problem—thank God that I don't have 630 new toys to manage every year! Keep the toys pared down to a number that is easily picked up and stored. Children do not need every new thing under the sun.

Have a place for the toys, and make it a practice to keep them put away when they aren't being played with. There are seasons when this is easy to keep on top of, and there are seasons when there are more important things to take care of. It is important for children to be self-disciplined in putting their things away. But when a mama of only Littles is laid out on the couch with pregnancy exhaustion, it is enough to keep the kitchen, bathrooms, and laundry clean.

There are many tips and tricks for managing toys in a large family, but I think the best one is to keep toy cupboards with locks. It is like having another adult in the house.

It is not a cruel thing to lock toys away. It is wise management. The toys are not all locked away at once. Locked doors are a method of managing which toys are available. Rotating toys keeps interest high and brains working in different ways with "new" toys.

I have one locked cupboard in the playroom for games, crafts, and some homeschooling materials. Two other locked cupboards hold toys. Each activity or toy is assigned a place on the shelves which are labeled so that anyone can put things away or look to see where to find something. Wash tubs and baskets hold things like Beany Babies, Legos, puppets, etc.

The locked cupboards have saved an immense amount of trouble. The kids that are old enough to responsibly get into the cupboards can reach the key, which is kept high. We avoid every single toy, craft, and game from being spread stem to stern. It is on our schedule once a month to restore order to the toy cupboards. By keeping on top of it, it doesn't get too out-of-sorts.

CHAPTER 43
Feast Night

Behold, what I have seen to be good and fitting is to eat and drink and find enjoyment in all the toil with which one toils under the sun the few days of his life that God has given him, for this is his lot. Everyone also to whom God has given wealth and possessions and power to enjoy them, and to accept his lot and rejoice in his toil—this is the gift of God.
—Ecclesiastes 5:18-19

Celebrate!

Life needs to be celebrated! God is good to us! We have beautiful lives around us to love and enjoy. Take the time to celebrate each other. Laugh and live joyfully! Gather your loved ones around regularly, and bless each other with good food, songs, and thanksgiving. Be grateful for every small and large thing in life and celebrate them! Count even trials as joy (James 1).

Plan a night every week or once a month to celebrate the goodness of God. Get out your good dishes, lay a table cloth on, make delicious food, light candles, dress up and celebrate! From the youngest to the oldest, everybody likes to have a good time. Love and laughter right many wrongs. We have hope and joy because we are children of God. Share this with your children.

Take the opportunity on Feast Night to praise and thank your children for their contributions to the family. Encourage them as they work on Christian character, and reward them for progress. Praise

God for your blessings. Take turns sharing what each is grateful for. Encourage each other to make goals and plot a path to reach the goals.

Serve a delicious and beautiful dessert. Share how God has been good to you. Teach your children that to fear God is to seek His wisdom, and God's wisdom is full of goodness. Yes, God is good to us. Live a life of joy!

> *Oh, taste and see that the Lord is good! Blessed is the man who takes refuge in him! Oh, fear the Lord, you his saints, for those who fear him have no lack! The young lions suffer want and hunger; but those who seek the Lord lack no good thing. —Psalm 34:8-10*

CHAPTER 44
Meal Planning

Of all the arts upon which the physical well-being of man, in his social state, is dependent, none has been more neglected than that of cookery, though none is more important, for it supplies the very fountain of life. The preparation of human food, so as to make it at once wholesome, nutritive, and agreeable to the palate, has hitherto been beset by imaginary difficulties and strong prejudices. —Mother's Cookbook, 1902

Enough Food for an Army

There are one thousand ninety-five meals a year that we as home managers are responsible for. As a new culture of godly homemaking is emerging, we are creating a new home environment, and a large part of this revolves around mealtime.

Gather your children and do some multiplying of your favorite recipes. Feel free to write in your recipe books—they are yours! Beside the ingredient amounts, write the multiple. Then write what pan to put the converted recipe into. You will have to use some trial and error with putting converted recipes into the pots, pans, crocks, and bowls that you own. Assign one of your older children to transfer all your favorite family recipes in the multiplied version to a new cookbook binder or card file, or add them into an online recipe system like www.allrecipes.com.

Keep your eye out for larger kitchen equipment. Since you will be using your equipment a lot more than the typical consumer, consider buying professional grade. Shop at a restaurant supply store for ideas.

For those one thousand ninety-five mealtimes that your family sits down together to enjoy, be encouraged that God will help you in your efforts. Talk to your husband about the mealtime culture at your house, and do your part to plan and pray about it. Ask God for wisdom, read the Scriptures daily, and He will teach you.

Food, presentation, etiquette, and conversation direction are responsibilities we need to take seriously as the matrons of our homes. We must give thought and plan for these times during the day. In planning meals, it is important to realize that these are times that the family is gathered together around the table sharing, talking, and enjoying each other and the food set before them. Speak to your husband about this and ask him what he would like to see happen in the mealtime culture of your home.

There are several things the home manager does to manage her kitchen. First, there is simply keeping it clean, and this is accomplished by establishing Table Chores and delegating them to the family. Second, there is the practice of keeping a weekly Kitchen Day. Third, is keeping things simple. Fourth, is organizing for efficiency. Managing the kitchen well makes everyone's time in the kitchen more productive and enjoyable. When the kitchen is well-kept, creativity flourishes.

One very important thing that the home manager needs to do well at managing is the meal plan and pantry organization.

There are several ways of planning meals; here are a few ways that other moms do it:

- Free and Paid Subscriptions to menu plans with grocery lists such as Menus 4 Moms (www.menus4moms.com) or Dinners In a Flash (www.dinnersinaflash.com).

- Planning around the sales flyers for your local stores.

- Planning around seasonal fruits and vegetables.

- Planning around what is available in your pantry and freezer during a money crunch or to pare down the excess.

- Planning around a specific recipe book or diet.

- Buying what looks good at the store and then trying to make something out of it upon arriving home—typically the most expensive way to menu plan.

> Mealtimes are a gathering time to converse, learn from each other, and enjoy each other from the littlest children to the older ones.
>
> What can you do to help make your mealtimes bring glory to God?

Menu planning saves you time and money, things we all can use more of. It blesses the Lord because we are being better stewards of His resources. Also, we are living according to the model of the Proverbs 31 who planned, prepared, and "brings her food from afar." Menu planning blesses your husband and family because when thought is given to meals, they are more apt to be delicious, healthy, and presented in a manner that shows love.

If you think about it, menu planning is always done. Food that is haphazardly gathered and slapped on the table is that way because the plan was poor. Your goal should be to have an excellent plan—a plan that blesses the Lord, your husband, and your family.

The Basic Menu Plan

It's important to have a Basic Menu Plan, and here's an outline for you to build upon. This will be the plan you use when you don't know what to make for dinner. It will be your easy reference tool. Your older children can use it when you're lying on the couch with morning sickness. Your husband can take the list and do the shopping when you're heavy with child and don't want to traipse through the grocery store with the brood in tow. You will make other more creative menu plans, but this one will be The Basic Menu Plan, the one you refer to in busy seasons and on bad days. These will be the meals that don't need a lot of thinking power to make because you know the recipes so well.

The first thing you want to do when making The Basic Menu Plan is to ask your husband what his favorite home-cooked meals are and how often he wants to eat those meals. Take a typical four-week calendar page, and write these meals down on appropriate days. If you know that you're going to be out of the home every Thursday evening, for example, then save that evening for a meal that can be eaten quickly. If you know that Wednesday evenings you are always home and the day is not hectic, plan your more detailed dinner for Wednesdays.

Homemade Pizza Nights are an event at our house. The little children like to get in on the dough making and roll bread sticks, which creates a big mess. We like veggie pizzas, and that means lots of cutting of veggies—more mess. After a few weeks of doing Homemade Pizza Night on our Cleaning Day, I decided that this was not an efficient arrangement. There was too much busy work going on and important cleaning work that was being neglected. Our kitchen isn't tucked away in a corner; it is Grand Central Station. We moved Homemade Pizza Night—the blizzard of flour and snowballs of dough—to Kitchen Day when we mop the floor. Homemade Pizza Night might work just fine for Cleaning Day at your house. My point is to think about these things while planning your menu.

After you have your husband's favorite meals planned on the calendar, ask your children for their favorite meals, and plan them on appropriate days. Look at what days are left in the calendar and plan healthy, inexpensive meals.

Plan crockpot meals for busy days such as Town Days and Cleaning Days. Plan your Lord's Day meals. Plan what your children will eat on your Date Night. Plan your Feast Night menus. When incorporating new foods to your diet, keep in mind that it often takes several meals before a new food is accepted by picky eaters. If you have older daughters, have them help you do this planning. They need to learn this skill before they're on their own and have to "sink or swim".

Planning is work. It might not feel or look like work when you are sitting down doing it, but planning is work, and it makes you a more efficient home manager and cook. With increased efficiency, you will have more time for other pursuits.

Once you have a month's worth of dinner menus, go through all the recipes, and write down the ingredients. These are the things you will need to keep on hand in your pantry and refrigerator. This is your Basic Grocery List. When you see things from your Basic List on sale, then stock up your pantry. This is part of how you save money with your menu plan. The other way is by learning which stores have the best prices for your Basic Grocery List. You will want to write down the typical price you pay beside each item on the list. Another way to save a lot is to look at your Basic Menu Plan and think about how many of these items you can grow yourself and freeze or can.

Keep your pantry organized by type of product so that you can check for recipe ingredients at a glance before Town Day. Keep like with like. Baking ingredients, salad dressing ingredients, canned goods, dry goods, and so forth should all be stored in the same places all the time so that any member of the family can go to the kitchen and create a recipe from The Basic Menu Plan without trouble.

Take a look at the recipes and their preparation needs. Write down the things that need to be done ahead and when. If the beef roast needs to marinate for three days, then write that task three days before the date it is to be served. If you need French Loaves for a specific meal, then plan when you will make them, and write it on the calendar. Do this for the needs of every meal.

Make three copies of the Basic Menu Plan and Basic Grocery List. Keep one copy at your desk where you will reference it on Office Day when you are planning your route for Town Day. Keep the second copy in your purse/diaper bag. When you are out and need your memory jogged, the Basic Menu Plan and Basic Grocery List will be handy. Hang the third copy inside a kitchen cupboard for easy access.

The Basic Lunch Menu

Do the same thing for the Basic Lunch Menu. This is a plan for the days when you do not have leftovers to serve. Choose healthy meals that you or a child can prepare in thirty minutes or less. Our lunches need to be efficient so that we can have time for the myriad of other things in our day. They need to be nutritious so we grow healthy children. They need to be inexpensive, because we are large families living on one income in a two-income society.

We need to create the ritual of eating lunch as a family. When I was a child, growing up on a farm, the big meal was always at noon and called Dinner. At meal times, we talked, joked, and teased each other. After dinner, my father then would lay down on the floor for a ten-minute nap, and if the day was a relaxed workday, we would get to play checkers with Dad. My husband, who also grew up on a farm, tells of his father and grandfather following a similar routine.

Family meals are an event. Conversation happens between parents and children, thoughts are expressed about current events, books being read, work that is happening, and interwoven throughout this is the calling of God on our lives. We need to explore the cultures of the world and of the past and find a way of creating mealtimes where real conversation happens and fathers and mothers are teaching their children the Sh'ma—to love the Lord your God with all your heart, with all your soul, with all your mind, and with all your strength (Deuteronomy 6).

Breakfast

The same could be said of breakfast for the homeschooling family. We as homeschoolers do not have to rush-rush in order to get our children on time to an early-morning school bus pickup, so we shouldn't be in a hurry and cut corners in how we approach breakfast. We have a mission, and that is our family's physical and spiritual health. We need to feed them nutritious food to fuel the brain for the activities of the day. Serving good food to them will require a plan and having the necessary supplies on hand.

Cold cereal and breakfast bars have little nutrition and do not fill the stomach well or feed the brain. We shouldn't feed our children junk just to fill them up. We should take responsibility to provide them with sensible and nutritious food for breakfast each day.

Everybody getting their own breakfast makes for a disorderly kitchen, breakfast-time, and an each-for-their-own attitude. It promotes selfishness and being me-centered. Plan ahead for what your family is going to eat for breakfast, and follow this plan. Some mornings, this may involve having one of your older children prepare the food or help you prepare it, but establish clear parameters for what food will be eaten and when.

When I visited my grandparents overnight as a child, every day after breakfast, each person was given a Bible and asked to read a verse from the passage that Grandpa directed us to. It didn't matter how well we could read, each person took a turn. After scripture reading, Grandpa prayed for the day, then Grandma wrote in her journal before we did breakfast chores. In my parent's home, my mother read a devotional to us while we ate breakfast, and Dad gathered us together at the door for a prayer over our day before getting on the bus.

As Christian families, we need to establish a culture for the breakfast meal where families start the day together as a team with scripture and prayer. When the day is started off with God from the littlest to the biggest children, the focus is completely different than the days that start off like a race. Even if it is a busy day, when the family focus is right early on, there is a steadying influence that carries throughout the day.

Snack Time

Depending on what time of day meals occur at your house, you will probably find that you also need at least one "snack time" in order to keep the motors running in your children. At our house, we eat breakfast around 7:30 or 8, lunch at noon, and supper anytime from 6:30 to 8.

The supper hour sounds crazy doesn't it? But we like to eat dinner with Dad. He works long hours some seasons, and then there are chores to do on the farm when he comes home from work. As you might suspect, we can't go from 12 to 8 without eating, so in the late afternoon, we have a snack.

Here is what we do and don't do concerning snacks.

Junk food is unhealthy and expensive, so we don't eat it, except for the occasional splurge on Oreos. Fruits and vegetables are a wonderful source of vitamins and minerals. Keep track of your fruit and vegetable consumption and try to get at least 5 servings a day into your family. In the summer, I send my children out to graze on what we have growing—peas, cherry tomatoes, grapes, raspberries, apples, pears, peaches, strawberries—which are nearly free and nearly organic food.

For those times when I need to buy fruit, I like to buy a different fruit for each day of the week, one for each member of our family. For example, if plums are a good price, then I buy nine for one day's snack. Bananas are popular with my family, so if they are a good price, I buy bunches big enough so that each person can have two. To determine if a price is good or not, you will need to know when different fruits are in season first. Usually that is when their prices are lowest, and they are at the best quality. Here is a short list to help you as you plan:

Fall: apples, grapes, pears, pomegranates.

Winter: pomegranates, citrus, kiwi.

Spring: strawberries, rhubarb.

Summer: apricots, blueberries, cherries, melons, peaches, plums, grapes.

Fruits are generally finger food. For the littlest children, you will need to cut some into bite-sized pieces. Be sure to cut apple pieces small for toddlers, and squirt some lemon juice over them to keep them from turning dark. Grapes need cut in half—they are one of the top choking hazards for children, along with hot dogs.

If you have children old enough to help (an older preschooler can do this easy job), then assign one to be Snack Lady or Snack Man for the day with the duty to prepare the fruit snack and do the clean up.

Do not let your children walk around the house with their snack. It makes the house dirty. They can sit at the table. It teaches them self-control to sit while eating and to keep their mess contained. Require them to wash their hands before and after snack time to prevent germs and to keep the house preserved from grubby mitts afterwards. With a bit of persistence on your part, this will soon be a habit.

Assign one of the children to wash the table afterwards; this can also be a preschooler's job. Keep a little bucket and sponge under the kitchen sink just for their use. Preschoolers love to help, so help them learn to be a productive part of the family. Buy your children fun cutting tools like a banana slicer, egg slicer for strawberries, and a crinkle cutter for carrots. These are inexpensive gadgets that make work fun.

Fresh vegetables are a healthy, inexpensive snack also. If you have them available for snacking on from the time your children are little, they will appreciate them. If you start late, you will simply need to be persistent in offering fresh vegetables and saying no to junk. As long as junk food is available, they will choose it over healthy alternatives. It's that simple. They might be hungry for a few days, preferring to eat nothing rather than the new healthy food you make available, but if you keep the good stuff in front of them, they will eventually eat it and learn to like it. Some children are more adventurous about food, and some are stubborn. I've found that it often takes several experiences with a new food before it is accepted. The key is to persevere!

If you garden, late summer and early fall, when fresh food is in greater abundance, is an easy time to get your family started with fresh vegetables for snacking. The children are used to seeing them and probably even like some of it. Get in the habit of having a vegetable tray in the refrigerator to pull out every afternoon. There are trays that you can buy that have a stay-cool bottom. Every afternoon, make it part of your routine to cut more vegetables to add to the tray or make a dip for the vegetables. Then set it out on the table and call the children. Baby carrots, green onions, and celery are affordable and easy to get all year round.

Seasonal vegetables good for snacking on:

Fall: broccoli, carrots, cauliflower, green onions, snow peas.

Winter: broccoli, cauliflower, radishes, snow peas.

Spring: asparagus, green onions, English peas, Sugar Snap peas, radishes.

Summer: cucumbers, Sugar Snap peas, peppers, summer squash, zucchini.

Here's a dip for Fresh Vegetables that our family enjoys:

Dip for Fresh Vegetables

8 oz. cream cheese or Chevre

3 T olive oil

3 T yogurt

Chopped fresh herbs (if using dry, cut amount to ¼):

2 T chives

2 T Italian Parsley

1 T cilantro

1 t mint

1 t thyme

½ t rosemary

Salt and pepper to taste. Blend. Keep refrigerated.

If you think that buying fresh fruits and vegetables is expensive, then I would encourage you to take a hard look at the alternatives that you are serving. Ask these questions: How is it contributing to the health of my child? Is it tearing down their immune system? Are there long-term consequences to growing up on this food? What is the benefit of serving this to my child? Serving for serving, is it really cheaper than offering something healthy?

Let's not forget about other foods you can keep handy, such as dried fruits and nuts. These are great to keep in the diaper bag or van. Be careful that the dried fruits you buy are not coated in sugar.

Sometimes children and moms need extra protein in the diet, and snacks can be a way of getting it. Protein really carries you to the next meal. I see a big difference when we have protein for breakfast vs. straight carbohydrates. I have found that a balance of protein and carbs is the best. The second best is complex carbs like oatmeal. And the worst is cold cereal which sends us all into melt-down at about 10am. If your family needs more protein to carry you through the day, boiled eggs (made more fun with an egg slicer) and cheese slices are easy protein snacks to prepare. Older children like beef or deer jerky—but you'll need to watch for detrimental additives on these snacks.

What would childhood be without cookies? Who doesn't get a little sappy sentimentalism going with the thought of chocolate chip cookies and a tall glass of cold milk? Yum! If you're going to make cookies, search out the healthiest recipes you can find. Avoid white flour, white sugar, margarine, and shortening. They are nasty for your health and, as a parent, you are responsible for the health of your children. It might take some experimenting and recipe-altering to find the right blend of healthy grains, sweeteners, and fat, but it can be done.

Be careful not to serve snacks too close to a meal time if you want your children to eat well. Your children's balance of appropriate snack consumption will vary. Consider their age, how much snack food is involved, and how close you are to the next meal in determining whether or not they will still have room for a regular meal following their snack. This point of deliberation illustrates another reason why snack food must be healthy. Consider the costs of getting filled up on junk and not eating a good meal. If your children are eating healthy snacks, then when they occasionally don't eat a lot during your regular meal time, they will be all right. They are still getting a well-balanced diet spread throughout the day.

Juice is like candy. Even though it might be 100% pure fruit juice, it takes a tremendous amount of fruit to get the juice to fill up that sippy cup. All the solids of the fruit that help digest the fruit sugars are removed.

Drinking the juice of fruit is like drinking sugar water. It will give the same highs and lows that candy does. It is far better to get fruit juice in the form that God made it—in the fruit itself. Instead of a cup of apple juice, serve a cut up apple and a cup of water. Instead of grape juice, cut a handful of grapes in half, and serve it with a cup of water. Instead of orange juice, serve orange segments with a cup of water. Instead of flavored milk, serve it white. It's the way God made it.

Read the label and ask yourself, "Do I really want my child to drink sugar, propylene glycol, alcohol, corn starch, carrageen, silicon dioxide vanillin, and Red #43 with their milk?" They do not need the shot of sugar or chemicals in their system. Hyper kids with sugar highs and lows are a detriment to your sanity and the peace of your family.

Serve your children healthy foods with lots of water, and watch their behavior become more moderated and your visits to the doctor decrease. If they are thirsty, give them water. Water is the easiest health food to serve. They won't die of thirst if you don't have juice and junk in your house. Do you have clean water and a glass? Then you're set to go. The children will figure this out pretty quickly, though they may be prone to whine at first. Any major change in their life takes about three days of adjustment. Just don't change too many things at once!

In saying all this, I am not suggesting that you should never enjoy a treat, but simply that there will be a price to pay if unhealthy food is a regular part of your children's diet. So choose wisely!

> *If you have found honey, eat only enough for you, lest you have your fill of it and vomit it.*
> *—Proverbs 25:16*

Saving Money at the Grocery Store

Processed and packaged food is expensive, and there's rarely a need to buy advertised food. Even the store brand knockoff of the name-brand processed foods is usually not cheap. You will be much further ahead financially by making your food from scratch, whenever possible.

Learn to buy only what you need and will use. Don't go to the grocery store if you are hungry, and do not take hungry children to the store with you. Shop with a list of the basic necessities, and stick to it. You don't need a treat. Stay within your boundaries. Limits promote creativity. You will be forced to think and do things in more creative ways when you aren't buying packaged food.

Buy store-brand canned and frozen vegetables. Store brand milk is generally the same milk as the locally processed milk label is.

Buy produce in season as a rule. Buy nutritionally rich food that is filling. Eggs are cheap protein. Potatoes are a highly-nutritious carb. Dry beans and brown rice are nutritionally superior and much more affordable than their processed counterparts. Buy meat on the bone, and use the bones to make a rich broth.

Buy dry goods in bulk. Generally they cost much less when bought by the 25 or 50-pound bag.

Watch sale fliers, and buy meat cuts when they are on sale, reduce portion sizes, and serve more vegetables. Better yet, buy meat by the side from a farmer. You will get a higher quality meat and a variety of cuts.

Make gourmet food with the ingredients you have and can afford. Save the specialized ingredient meals for an occasional feast that you serve with your best dishes.

Spices are an inexpensive way to jazz up any food.

Don't allow free access to your cupboards and refrigerator. Train your children when they are little to ask if they may have a snack. When you have a limited amount of fruit, give each person an assigned portion per day (one banana a day, for example).

Use cloth napkins instead of paper. Use wash cloths for napkins at everyday meals. They are great for mopping up spills and washing the baby's face after the meal.

Keep a box of rags under the sink to use instead of paper towels.

The number one thing you can do to slash your family's grocery bill is to garden. It is nearly free organic food! With a garden, you will have plenty of vegetables to eat, juice, and store for the rest of the year. In addition to cultivating a more traditional garden, plant fruit bushes and trees in your landscape. Grow your own herbs and spices. Get to know local gardeners, and learn what they plant and how they grow their produce with success.

CHAPTER 45
Project Day

...she laughs at the time to come. —Proverbs 31:25

Occasionally the need will arise to have a Project Day or a Project Week—a time when you really need to tear into a room and repaint, tear out the carpet, or something else hugely disruptive to the regular routine of home life. When doing projects of this magnitude, it is good to give thought to them and not do them on a whim.

Here are some lessons I've learned that you can apply the next time you have a big project to tackle.

A prefatory comment: Some find the idea of working with children impossible. This is a wrong perspective to have. Children do not need constant entertainment and play. They need to be learning from you. Even on big project days, they can and should be learning from you. With the right attitude from you, they will learn that work is satisfying and fun. You just need to plan carefully to make the process conducive to learning and fun.

Now let's cover the basics: food and sleep. These two things are very important to the happiness and well-being of your family. With this in mind, don't plan a project right after another big event; recover from the first event by getting plenty of rest, good food, and some down time. This will help the stress level for everyone in the family. Too much stress leads to grumpy, misbehaving children which can lead to a grumpy mom and dad. So plan the timing of your big project wisely!

Next, plan your food. It needs to be healthy for strength and stamina, but fast and easy to prepare. Going out to eat or pizza delivery do not fit the bill, especially if your project is more than a day long. That will also cut into the budget of your DIY project.

Make a list of your homemade quick meals. Then pin your list inside a kitchen cupboard for the next time you need a quick meal on a Project Day. Crockpot dinners that you can throw together in the morning are great. Keep a supply of paper service on hand for Project meals.

Finally, get to bed at a decent time the night before your project. You will have more energy and be able to think and move more quickly.

Also have your clothing planned, and do not forget the children's needs in this regard. Everybody should wear old clothes for when they unintentionally lean against the freshly painted door. Make sure that you have all of your clean laundry put away and your dirty laundry sorted and tucked away. You don't want to trip over it going to and fro.

Think about what your children are going to do while you work on your project. Is it something they can and should be involved with? If not, then you will want to plan something special for them that will keep them occupied while you're working. A new, open-ended activity is great for a Project Day.

If you suspect that your project is especially intriguing to them, then you will want to talk to them about it. Explain everything you are going to be doing related to the project, and make clear the things they can do to help you as well as what they absolutely cannot do. Then, give them a boundary, use tape to mark it, and tape some Xs on the floor for their assigned seats. Plan your consequences for disobedience.

It is also helpful to spend some special time with the little children at the beginning of the day, reading a story together or playing with them for ten minutes or so. Do this again after your lunch break. Make sure that they have access to food and drink during the day so that their needs are met without interrupting you.

A helpful tip: If you are interrupted while painting, have a plastic bag handy to put your paint brush into. This keeps it from drying out. If you are taking something apart, collect all the little pieces into a Ziploc bag, and put it out of reach of the children.

Plan the project shopping list carefully beforehand so that you aren't constantly running to get this and that. Collect your materials and tools at once and put them in safe spot high enough that the littlest ones won't carry fascinating things away. Move quickly and efficiently with your project. Plan your steps, and move things out of the way that will hinder you. A few minutes moving something could keep you from tripping, spilling, or wasting motion.

If your project is a short one, then do all the prep work you can before nap time. As soon as the children are laid down, do your project as fast as possible. Be ready for interruptions if they wake before you are finished. Quickly get them settled into their next activity, and then clean up.

If you are blessed with older children, they can be assigned to watch over little ones while you work on the project. It is still nice to plan something new and exciting for them to do together. One of your older children could plan an activity for the uninvolved to do while the rest work on the project. This is a good way to teach responsibility.

Sometimes it is helpful to have everyone out of the house for a day, except those that are working on the project. Call a friend and work out a trade. You will have her children for a day while she works on a project, and another day she will take yours. It is nice on these days to have a simple supper planned for both families.

Painting with children around is a challenge, but it can be done. If they have never painted before, they will want to do it very badly. I am a firm believer in teaching children to work while young and to enjoy their work. Give them something to paint. Put a fresh coat of paint on the dog house or stain the play equipment. Older children can do touch-up paint in the house with a small container of paint and small brush. I would highly recommend using latex paint, unless you want your children to look spotted for a couple of weeks and have people ask them what genetic disease your family has (yes, that happened to us).

For mechanical-oriented projects, keep your young boys close, as they will learn through watching. It seems that something in their brain causes them to understand these things easily. At a young age, they will be telling you how to do it!

Paper projects such as bookkeeping, filing, and tax prep are more easily done with silence. I have trouble concentrating on numbers when there's constant interruptions. Perhaps this doesn't bother you. One option is to do these projects during naps.

One important thing to keep in mind with projects is the clean up that needs to be done when the project is done. Sometimes I get so caught up in resting on my laurels of a wonderfully completed project that I don't notice that I've left tools out. Then the everyday life starts up again, people need to be fed and so on, and I find myself tripping over the same box of project materials for a week.

Make a rule for yourself and your house: "A job isn't done until the tools are put away." This applies to so many things we do around the house: making a meal, laundry chores, schoolwork, etc. Say the rule three times right now, and then go write it on a 3" x 5" card and post it in a prominent place!

A lot of times while doing a project, we have to tear apart the house to get to the thing that needs to be worked on. I'm thinking of our family room right now. I have a decorative painting project planned for it, but in order to do it, I will have to move furniture and take down curtains. I know already that I will also be mending tears in the upholstery, cleaning the curtains and blinds, and then the fly specks on the windows will bother me and I'll want to wash them again, and the list goes on.

Simply put: Projects can build on each other and take on a life of their own. Pretty soon, the daily routine is blown, we're eating take-out pizza, laundry is piling high, and everyone is irritable. Know when to stop and restore order. Know when to say, "I'll do _____ next month."

You do not need to put projects off forever; you can do them with children around. You simply need to plan carefully with them in mind. Think what a blessing it will be to them seeing you do projects, learning how to do these things together with you, and being instilled with a can-do attitude. In time, you will be handing over the tools, and they will be doing a project to benefit the whole family.

Remember this: "Many hands make light work!"

You shall teach them diligently to your children, and shall talk of them when you sit in your house, and when you walk by the way, and when you lie down, and when you rise. —Deuteronomy 6:7

CHAPTER 46
Pregnancy and Preparing for Baby

Feeling Your Best

When I look back on my pregnancies, the worst of them were when my diet pre-pregnancy and during pregnancy was poor. Not enough fresh food, way too much sugar, too much "bad" comfort food, no exercise, not enough water drinking, etc.—these factors lead to ill feelings, both physical and emotional.

If you are growing a baby and a placenta and are not eating well, then you will naturally become very drained. It will take huge effort to lift an arm or move a leg forward. I've been there. Last week, for example, we made cookies that had way too much sugar in them (even though I used Evaporated Cane Juice Sugar), and I ate way too many. I had the sugar spike and then a really bad crash. As a result, I was pretty much useless the rest of the afternoon.

The point is this: Rethink your diet. What you eat before pregnancy and in the early days when you're carrying a child really impacts how you feel. I know from experience and would encourage you to look at your diet and cut out the junk.

I have found that, during pregnancy, I need much more nutrition than prenatal vitamins provide. I am convinced that we especially need more B vitamins. Our modern diets are dreadfully short on B, and when we eat deficient foods such as white flour, white rice, and white sugar our bodies actually take from our bodies what is needed to digest those things.

Also learn to pay attention to your body. I have learned that my first trimester misery peaks at about 9 weeks and is almost over by 12 weeks. At 16 weeks, I'm feeling "normal" again. But everyone is different, and each pregnancy can also be different. Listen to your body and make appropriate responses. The first trimester is when your body is growing the placenta; it is an incredible organ! Good nutrition and sleep will go a long ways toward aiding your body in this tremendous task. Don't do things that will hinder yourself!

The following are tips that I have found helpful in general, but especially while pregnant. These recommendations are loosely based on Dr. Brewer's Blue Ribbon Baby diet, additional study, and on my personal experience.

- The #1 thing to do! Cut out all sugar, even "healthy" sugars. It is just simply draining. Eliminate corn syrup (which is dramatically worse than sugar), sucrose, glucose, maltose, dextrose, lactose, fructose, fruit concentrate, honey, barley malt, sucanat, cane juice sugar, brown sugar, turbinado sugar, etc. You will feel like a new person.

- Eliminate white flour and products made with white flour.

- Eat eggs for breakfast. Protein in the morning will make you feel much better and carry you further through the day. Eggs also provide brain food for the baby. As long as you are carrying and nursing the baby , eggs should be part of your daily diet.

- Protein helps with nausea, along with keeping your energy up. Spread protein throughout your day.

- Eat regular small snacks/meals of nuts, milk, pudding, custard, cheese, cottage cheese, yogurt, small portions of meat (red meat gives you other needed nutrients also), fish, hard boiled eggs (try deviled eggs), bacon, and beans (dips such as hummus), and more.

- Overeating makes things worse, especially for heartburn. Keep your meals small.

- Eat green, leafy vegetables for nutrients including folic acid.

- Baked potatoes are full of goodness and easy on a queasy stomach.

- Eat orange and yellow vegetables such as squash, carrots, and sweet potatoes.

- Whole grains give you fiber and B vitamins.

- Eat citrus and other fruits for nutrients including Vitamin C. Vitamin C keeps your immune system strong and helps with blood circulation. During pregnancy your blood volume increases dramatically, and Vitamin C contributes to strong healthy vessels.

- Drink water—lots of water. Being dehydrated exasperates every other health problem. I like to squeeze a lemon into a 2 quart pitcher, and drink it all day long. Water tasting bad is an indication of a nutrient deficiency, so pay attention to this!

- Sea salt is a good way to get micro-nutrients. It must not be white, or else it's not true sea salt.

- Take a really good prenatal or multi-vitamin with folic acid, a B complex, Cal-Mag-Zinc, and Vitamin C.

- Red Raspberry Leaf Tea helps to build a strong uterus.

- Walking, sunshine, and fresh air really help with nausea and feeling better over all. Keep moving even when you do not feel like it.

- Ginger in many forms helps with nausea, but sugar and corn syrup can counter-act so be careful about your method for getting ginger. Make a tea with fresh ginger root.

- Repair your intestinal system with probiotics, greens, and lemon water (it must be a real lemon—not bottled).

- When you are laid low with nausea, use a cool wet cloth on your face. It will help rejuvenate you a bit so that you can make the effort to do the most important things.

- Take a shower every day in the morning as soon as you are able. You will feel much better. Eat something first because the blood sugars are low in the morning and you may quickly feel faint standing in the shower. If you can, put on athletic shoes early in the day—it does something to your brain that gives a little bit extra umph to your energy.

- When cooking smells are intolerable, ask for help and have somebody cook a lot of meat ahead for you to put in the freezer. Have your husband grill, put the crockpot outside, cook double on good days, or eat cold food such as salads and sandwiches.

- If your supplements are making you feel bad, try a different brand. Try a buffered Vitamin C or a multi without iron.

Study nutrition for your and your baby's health so that you can be strong, both for your baby and for the rest of your family. All of these things will help, some a lot, some just a little, depending on your physical make up. We are all different. You might find further things that help your situation beyond what I have outlined here.

The key is to pay attention to your body all the time, not just when you are pregnant. Pay attention to your health status before you get pregnant and while you are nursing. It is important for the sake of your family!

The House and Kids

During the early days of pregnancy, and for some expecting moms who feel bad the whole way through, the house can really fall apart. Having big kids can help so much when you're in this position. They aren't perfect, my children don't do everything exactly the way I would like, but with each year, they get better at their work! In times of need, I have to relax my standards of order and cleanliness, knowing that things can be recovered later.

First of all, a person must realize that work cannot get done while sleeping. You cannot do both at the same time. The key is in accepting the fact that growing this baby must take precedence over the house. Frustration, worry, and anxiety do not help anything. "This too shall pass," must become the mantra. Take heart; you know how to whip things back into shape. You simply need to wait for the energy to come back and enable you. With systems in place, the work will slowly get done and things will be back up to par again.

The children, of course, should be doing their work as usual, but remember that they are children who won't always get it right. Thank God for our men who do their own personal best to help us during this time. A home cleaned by a man and children is not quite clean like a woman would clean but—but so what? Eventually your home will be clean again, according to a woman's cleaning standards. Slowly but surely, one room at a time, one laundry load at a time, the house will be back in its normal cleaning system.

It's all in the attitude: grumping, moaning, and crying about it will not help. Just accept life in the way it is at this moment, and deal with it in a godly manner. With systems in place that simply need their manager back in the managing role, it will be all right soon. Take notes so that when your daughters and daughters-in-law are at this point, you will know how to help. My mother has always been wonderful about having us all over for supper to take a load off of me at times, and my mother-in-law brings us great food as well as a gesture of encouragement.

When I only had little children, it helped to place limits on the house—closing rooms off and reducing the number of toys. I clearly remember laying on the couch, with everyone kept in the same room, simply waiting it out. I was available to calm squabbles before they escalated. I could read aloud occasionally, show interest in their delights, and give direction from the couch. Remember it's only for a season.

When you get that surge of energy, concentrate on the most important things. Bathrooms and the kitchen must be clean. Laundry should be kept up and floors clean. Each time that you get off the couch, do one thing. If you are able, give yourself a little routine to do every hour, or every two hours:

- Change laundry loads.

- One thing to keep the bathroom clean.

- One thing to keep the kitchen clean.

- Sweep or vacuum one area of the floor.

Use paper plates, plastic cups, and eating utensils for this season. Stock up on paper towels and napkins. Switch from cloth diapers to disposables.

Baby proof your house really well. Lock room doors and use baby gates or blockades of some sort to keep the children—and their subsequent mess—contained. Box up all things that are breakable or cause extra dusting (no knick-knacks).

Consider using video and audio curriculum to help you homeschool. Without question, have a whole house Quiet Hour. Put your little children in the bathtub to play (and get clean as an afterthought) while you sit with them and rest, read, and slowly clean the bathroom. In the room where you and the children "live", keep a basket for diapers and wipes, the telephone, paper and pen for you to jot notes on (the brain tends to go fuzzy during these longs days), sippy cups and easy snacks (dry, not anything wet or goopy) for the you and the children, and your water jug (with a lid).

If you have older children, keep them busy. They can be quite mischievous without Mom's eyes on them. They must be held accountable to Dad. With Dad's help, make a list of specific things they should do each day. They should be helping and contributing to the good of the family. Do not allow them to be aimless. "There's nothing worse than an unoccupied child."

Baby Countdown

When you first find out you are pregnant, you are in a race against the calendar. You need to be prepared for the days coming up when you will feel progressively worse. My worst days started at six weeks, peaked at nine weeks, and then gradually get better. The first trimester seems to be a lesson in endurance!

Before you get pregnant, keep your home prepared and take care of your health. When you discover you are expecting a child, start stocking up freezer food for the coming days of exhaustion and nausea.

In the second trimester when you are feeling great (the placenta is doing its job of nurturing the baby), prepare your house for the last trimester (when you are big and awkward) and the postpartum time (when you are busy with your baby).

- Hold a room-to-room de-cluttering and cleaning.

- Put your home management systems in order and get them running smoothly.

- Work with the older children toward independent chores and independent schooling.

- Revamp your Home Management Book, and teach your children how to use it.

- Work hard on character issues with the children, especially obedience.

- Cook ahead and stock the freezer.

- Stock the pantry deep.

- Stock up on paper products.

- Depending on what time of year the last trimester and postpartum occur, be prepared with the children for a seasonal clothing switch.

- In the ninth month, wash the baby clothes, blankets, etc.

If it doesn't get done, don't fret. These things will simply make life easier for you and your family. Remember, Mary gave birth in a barn and laid Jesus in a manger.

CHAPTER 47
The Buddy System

The mom of a large family quickly gets outnumbered. An extra arm for each child would be useful, but that's not what God gave us. He gave us children that grow and, as they grow in stature, they also grow in wisdom, if we train them right. As they grow in wisdom, they are more able to help Mom.

I have often said that three children was the hardest stage of parenting. After three, it got much easier. The stage of three for me was a four-year-old, a two-year-old, and a newborn. And a husband with a traveling job.

A newborn is helpless, of course, completely dependent on Mom for every minutia. A two-year-old can feed himself. That particular two-year-old was potty trained, but a potty-trained two-year-old might be more work than diapers! A two-year-old can be helpful, but their help is unpredictable! And a two-year-old needs lots of training, direction, instruction, guidance, ad infinitum. God Bless the mothers of two-year-olds!

A four-year-old is more helpful compared to a two-year-old. They, at least, know what you're talking about most of the time. They can fetch things. They can actually help quite a bit, but they are four-years-old after all and they need training, direction, instruction, and guidance as well!

By the time we had number four, the rest were a step older and a whole lot more helpful. "Many make light work," as the saying goes, and our household condition improved.

It wasn't until baby number five that I learned about The Buddy System. I don't know who to give credit for this idea, but it was someone on the Momys (Mothers of Many Young Siblings) e-mail list who related it to fellow readers. It was transforming. I assigned the oldest to the baby. Of course he didn't do all the work, but when I needed to take care of a meal or another child, he could keep an eye on the baby.

As our family grew, we assigned the children appropriately. Rarely, we changed buddies for the children, depending on the current needs. An added benefit to the help I received from the buddy system was the sweet relationships that developed between buddies.

The following is how we work our personal buddy system. I encourage the reader to use it as a guide. Each family is unique and should adapt the lists to what works best for their specific situation.

Duties of the Big Buddy

- Teach your Little Buddy to do chores by having them help you with yours.

- Put your Little Buddy's laundry away.

- Play with your Little Buddy.

- Help your Little Buddy with anything they need help with.

- Read to your Little Buddy.

Get your Little Buddy up in the morning and:

- Help your Little Buddy get dressed for the day.

- Take Little Buddy to toilet .

- Brush your teeth together.

- Get your Little Buddy a drink of water.

When we leave the house:

- Help your Little Buddy with socks and shoes, jacket, and get buckled in.

- Keep an eye on your Little Buddy and/or hold hands (whatever Mom deems appropriate).

- Help your Little Buddy get food at potluck gatherings.

Get your Little Buddy ready for bed:

- Diaper.

- Pajamas.

- Brush teeth.

Bonuses for the Big Buddy:

- The Big Buddy gets to finish the food of the Little Buddy when the Little Buddy gets full (desserts, ice cream, treats, etc.).

- The Big Buddy gets to help the Little Buddy on the Little Buddy's "Special Day".

The Little Buddy

Little Buddy must obey the Big Buddy because Dad and Mom have set the Big Buddy as an authority over the Little Buddy. However, the Big Buddy must be kind and gentle, not exasperating, in helping the Little Buddy with his needs. If the Little Buddy is throwing a fit or otherwise not cooperating, the Big Buddy must get Mom or Dad to discipline the Little Buddy.

Special Day Privileges and Tasks

Another thing that really helps things go smoothly is to assign each child a Special Day in the week. We did it in birth order, starting with Monday. Child number eight shares a Special Day with child number one, and we start over again. Assigning a Special Day eliminates squabbles and bickering over the seemingly silly things that kids like to do that make them feel special, such as: getting the mail out of the mailbox and being the first to see what arrived. Don't laugh—we have had more fights about that than anything else. It might be a completely different issue at your house to battle over. Taking turns by the calendar day might help the amount of spats in your house too.

Special Day privileges and tasks help the family by accomplishing tasks, providing learning experiences, and quality time with Mom and Dad, along with keeping the peace between siblings.

Here are some ideas to get your family started on Special Day Privileges and Tasks:

- Help Mom in the kitchen with meals and salad prep.

- This the day you get to make any special recipes you want to try. Make sure and add special ingredients to the grocery list before Town Day.

- Sit by Mom during Read Aloud Time.

- Go for a walk with Mom on nice days.

- Help Mom with laundry: Sort, switch loads, hang out, fold.

- Help Mom with library/office management: straighten books, pick up floor, sort and file papers, put on stamps, mail letters.

- Your day for computer games.

- Get the mail and be the first to look at the papers and magazines.

- Be the kid to ride along with Dad or Mom to do an errand.

Be creative and use the children God has given you to help solve the needs of others in the family. This is a great way to help knit the hearts of your children one to another.

APPENDIX A
Coping While Exhausted and Overwhelmed

We do not know what to do, but our eyes are on you. —2 Chronicles 20:12

There are many things that drag us down. Pregnancy is one of them. Illness of some sort is another. And an unexpected trial can put us in a funk that is hard to pull out of.

Attitude is Key

My first point of advice is this: Don't get resentful about your situation. This is the lot God has given you at this time, and it is for His glory, even though you might not see it presently.

Scripture promises that we "can do all things through Christ who strengthens" us.

Are you going to Him for strength and wisdom in how to cope through your situation? Pray to God without ceasing, and trust Him to give you strength.

Also, I can't say this enough: Read the Bible every single day. Read it aloud to your children. Read one Psalm and one Proverbs to them daily. Memorize verses from both together. It's not hard; just sit down with the Bible on one of your 15-minute breaks and say, "Now we are going to memorize Psalm 100."

Don't stress about it; make it a fun activity. Little children are usually amazing at memorization!

Don't stop at reading Psalms and Proverbs; read from all over the Bible. Ask your children what their favorite Bible stories are and read them from the Bible. Then do the same at another 15-minute break.

Watch What You Eat

When you're exhausted is not the time to try new and elaborate dishes, no matter how yummy and fun it looked on that FoodTV show. You will get started, maybe even complete it, but then have no energy left to clean up the mess.

Focus on whole foods and eating simply. It's easier and better for you. Packaged and processed foods are not worth the ease, and they are too hard on your health. Don't rely on them. Shop from the produce aisle instead. All that you have to do is wash and cut fruit and vegetables, and you can do that 15 minutes at a time. If that is too much effort, get frozen produce.

Your diet is critical to you and your family's well-being. When I look back on my pregnancies, the worst of them happened when my diet pre-pregnancy and during pregnancy were poor. This occurred when I didn't have enough fresh food, had way too much sugar and too much "bad" comfort food, had insufficient exercise, and wasn't drinking enough water, etc. These poor lifestyle habits typically lead to a myriad of ill feelings, including the lack of ability to cope emotionally.

I really encourage an exhausted woman to look at her diet and cut out the junk. I have found that I need a lot more nutrients than what are in prenatal or multi-vitamins. I believe we especially need more B vitamins. Our modern diets are dreadfully short on the B vitamins, and when we eat deficient foods such as white flour, white rice, white sugar, our bodies actually take what is needed to digest the whites from our bodies. Add a growing baby to nutritional deficiencies, and we become further drained. It takes huge effort to lift an arm or move a leg forward. I know; I've been there!

The other thing I have found to be a huge help in my diet, especially when pregnant and nursing, is to eat plenty of protein. Especially for breakfast! It provides long stable energy for the day. Find a protein you like, and eat plenty of it: Cottage cheese, cheese, eggs, leftover meat from supper, etc.

We need to be so careful of what we put into our bodies. It affects how we live, how we feel, and that in turn affects everyone that we live with, be it for their good or detriment.

Laundry Tips

Here's a tried-and-true trick that moms with many children use. I practice it in our family, and I know that many other moms do the same. The rule is this: If it's not dirty, don't wash it, and wear it again. Some children are messier and will go through more than one outfit in a day. Others, especially in the winter months, can wear the same outfit three days before it looks like it is dirty. Don't make life harder for yourself by washing things that aren't really dirty. Little children don't sweat like adults, and their clothes can be worn until they spill food, drink, or arts and crafts gunk on them.

When you fold laundry, do it with your children. Sit on the floor and go slow. Listen to an audio message, watch a decent show or video, and just keep moving forward, one thing at time. Make it fun for them by sending them on little missions to put things away and timing their missions. Have races. Give your children lots of praise for each thing they do. Teach them these verses while you work on folding.

> *Whatever you do, work heartily, as for the Lord and not for men, knowing that from the Lord you will receive the inheritance as your reward. You are serving the Lord Christ.*
> —*Colossians 3:23-24*

Exemplify Kindness and Love

Children can be a great help with encouragement, love, and praise. Children that are not getting these things, but have to deal with an upset Mama, will be cantankerous in return. Do not wound them.

Yes, children should be obedient, but little children in particular need so much love. They thrive on praise, they crave physical touch, and they love to do things with Mama. Make sure that your children have plenty of love to balance any chastisement they receive.

One thing that you can do in your communication with children is to memorize this verse from Proverbs 31:26:

> *She opens her mouth with wisdom, and the teaching of kindness is on her tongue.*

The King James says it like this:

> *She openeth her mouth with wisdom; and in her tongue is the law of kindness.*

This is a verse I use with my girls when I hear their tongue get sharp, which always reminds me of my own tongue. How is my example to them?

Another thing that will help in communicating with children is this simple practice: Every single time you talk to them, force yourself to smile. "Fake it 'til you make it." When you speak while you're smiling, your tone of voice changes, and you will find that the words that come out of your mouth are more gracious.

Talk to your children about this, and help them to do the same thing. Teach them to smile when they speak. It is hard to complain and whine while smiling. Have them memorize Proverbs 31:26 also. Focus on that together for a week, and I expect that you will see a dramatic improvement in speech and attitude.

Simplify and Streamline

When you are exhausted and/or big and pregnant, and you see a million things that you want to do, but lack the energy to do, here are some practical steps you can take.

First, stick with simplified routines.

Call your children, sweetly, and tell them, "We are going to work on _____ chore for 15 minutes, and then we are going to sit on the couch and read a book."

Now work on that thing as hard and fast as you can, using a timer, if you want. You are doing work together and preschoolers love this.

Then, sit down with your children and read to them, and don't hesitate to snuggle. Preschoolers love this! If you need 15 minutes more for a rest, take it. Make sure that every time you sit down, you have a glass of water in hand and drink it!

Use your timer, and after you have had 15-30 minutes of rest, do 15 minutes of work. Make sure that the work you are doing is important work; don't clean what doesn't need to be cleaned.

If you are regularly cleaning, it can't be that dirty—not compared to the dirt that eight farm children drag in on a regular basis. Just think about what my mudroom looks like, and it might make you feel better about yours!

One very cold hard winter day, in my mudroom, I had a small water tank covered with dried manure, full of straw, and a newborn calf that had nearly froze to death. After twenty-four hours of this, the whole house smelled like a barn. That same winter we had a goat penned in the garage. Every time the door opened, barn smell came in. How's that for perspective? Barn smell is nice—when it stays in the barn.

Now, look into the past and think for a minute how your great-great-grandmothers lived. Or catch up on current events, and think about how most of the world lives today.

I love clean, believe me: I think it is a natural God-given womanly attribute to clean. But sometimes we have to let go a bit. Some things in life are more important than clean. Some things in life are more important than organization.

For your 15-minute work-periods, focus on floors, bathrooms, and the kitchen. Those are the dirtiest parts of our homes. Make it as easy as possible. Use paper towels for cleaning instead of rags to save on your laundry. Use paper plates, plastic cups, spoons, and forks instead of washing your regular dishes. It will save on clean up. Paper and plastic are less expensive than household help.

On the last 15-minute work period before you put your children to bed, have a 15-minute tidy. Get a basket and go around with your children to pick up and put away. Make it a game to see how fast they are, or count how many things they can find.

Cheer when you are done! Say encouraging words, "Look at how nice this room looks now!" Don't say it in a snarky voice; that is discouraging. Don't destroy your relationships with your children with sarcasm.

Another way to keep your home tidy is to "shut off" certain rooms or cupboards for a time. If you're too tired to keep a certain room tidy, work on that room, fifteen minutes at a time, until it is the way you want it to look and then "close" it. Shut the door, ban its use, whatever works, and just try to close it down for a period. We do this with our Sewing Room on occasion. It is a place that can quickly turn into a crafting explosion. I love to see my children being creative, but when I don't have the time or energy to oversee its use or cleaning, then I "close the door".

APPENDIX B
Moving Beyond Survival Mode

I frequently get e-mails from ladies who look around and don't know where to start in managing their homes. "Do the Next Thing" is a fine saying, but if everywhere you look you see things to do, you wonder which thing is next.

It's an experience that we all have now and then. Often I spread myself too thin, and that is a recipe for chaos. Friends and family have seen my chaos and will confirm the truth that I am not perfect! This series of steps is not only for those who don't know where to start, but it will help you recover from a chaotic season.

If your home life needs a recovery session, then do each of the following steps a day. Each day check that you have the previous steps under control before moving forward.

Step One

SUPPER AND WASH THE DISHES

Pick a one-dish meal that's easy and that you have the ingredients for. If it's not too late, put it in the crockpot. Crockpot meals are what I love to specialize in when I have projects to do. Moving beyond survival mode is a project! Once supper is made, wash every single last dirty dish in the kitchen. Commit to keeping the counters clean and the dishes washed from this day forward.

Step Two

FIND YOUR CLOTHES

Sort through your clothes and find seven outfits that fit you–one for each of the following seven days. Now your clothes are ready for you to step into each morning. Commit to putting on clothes as soon as you get out of bed in the morning. This will help your work attitude and demonstrate to your children that things are changing. Locate Sunday clothes for everyone in the family so you can all get to church without a Sunday morning family breakdown.

Step Three

MORNING ROUTINE

Write your morning routine down and tape it to your bathroom mirror. The times beside these things are how long it should take when you are in Maintenance Mode (Maintenance Mode is when your home management systems are working, your house is regularly cleaned and your daily "to do" list is maintenance tasks).

- Make bed (30 seconds).
- Straighten bedside tables (30 seconds).
- Dress for the day. You do not need to stare at your clothes in a fog because you laid them out the night before (2 minutes).
- Fix hair and face.
- Straighten/wipe bathroom (1 minute).
- Read the Bible with your husband. Make breakfast for your husband. Kiss your husband good bye.
- Take supplements; drink 2 glasses of water.
- Check calendar. (30 seconds).
- Start laundry (3 minutes) and set your timer to remind you to switch loads.
- Check e-mail, set timer. Don't sit there all day!
- Make breakfast for children. Read a Psalm to them.
- What's for supper? What's for lunch?

If your bathroom is a disaster, then "straighten and wipe" will need to take longer than a minute. Don't take longer than a minute, though. Save deep cleaning the bathroom for later. Do take one minute, however, to quickly put things away and wipe out the sink.

Stop when the minute is complete and move on. If your children are awake and have not eaten breakfast yet, then do not check your e-mail! Checking e-mail before breakfast is for the early birds.

Tweak the Morning Routine to fit your life and keep your priorities straight.

Have you done all of your Morning Routine? If not, identify why not and then change things so that you can do it all.

Step Four

EVENING ROUTINE

An Evening Routine gets you to bed at a decent time so that you get adequate sleep. Adequate sleep makes for a happy and productive mom in the morning.

Part of what makes for a successful Morning Routine is a strong Evening Routine. How is your Evening Routine? Write it down and tape it on your bathroom mirror beside the Morning Routine. Also post it in your kitchen, beside your Morning Routine. Make both of these routines a priority.

Think about what is working well with your Morning and Evening Routines and keep those parts. What is going poorly? Replace a bad habit with a good one. This is why you should write it down and refer to it as you establish routines. Refer to your routines every single day for a whole month. It takes 21 days to establish new habits. A habit is something that you do automatically without hesitation.

Work on making your Morning and Evening Routines habits that you can do without deliberation:

- Check the calendar, make To Do list (3 minutes).
- Get out a big pitcher for your daily quota of water, 2 1/2 quarts. Either fill and put in the fridge or fill in the AM (1 minute).
- Lay out clothes for tomorrow (2 minutes).
- Bathe, wipe one shower/bath wall (15 minutes).
- Read (use wisdom in time allotment).
- Bible and prayers (10 minutes).
- Lights Out (set your bedside lamp on a timer for evening lights-out and morning wake-up light).

Step Five

"YES, MOM"

After breakfast, spend ten minutes reviewing "How to obey" with your children. Read the Scriptures with them. Tell the children you are sorry for your sins, and ask them to forgive you. Pray with them and ask God to help you parent better and for the children to be more obedient. Next, role-play obedience. This looks like Simon Says. Teach the children to reply with "Yes, Mom" cheerfully. Make this fun, and reward the children with lots of hugs and kisses. Explain to them that disobedience will result in discipline. Commit to this training time every day until your children respond with obedience. This is teaching outside of the moment of conflict when everyone's emotions can run crazy. It is very profitable.

Step Six

AFTERNOON CHORE TIME

Afternoon Chore Time (see below) is a very important routine that often gets pushed by the wayside at our house. That is when things start to slide towards ugly. An ugly house makes for ugly attitudes from everyone who lives here. Ugly attitudes rub off on others and bring them down.

Afternoon Chore Time needs to be elevated to one of the most important things that happen in the day. Maybe afternoon doesn't work at all for your family and your husband's work schedule, and you call it Morning Chore Time. The important thing is to do these regular chores. For my family, it is a signal that the workday is drawing to a close, and it is time to get ready to have a family meal and evening together.

For dads who work away from home and walk in on Afternoon Chore Time, it is a welcoming atmosphere. It says, "We're getting ready for you and we're glad you're home!"

Personalize it a bit to suit your individual circumstances, but don't make it weaker, make it stronger. The most important thing on the following list is to tidy the house, so whatever you do, don't drop that.

- Put on some relaxing music and light a candle (1 minute).

- Set little ones at the table or in play pen with an activity so they don't undo the work (5 minutes).

- Children: Put away schoolwork (5 minutes) and start Daily Afternoon Chore Chart (15-30 minutes).

- 10-minute Tidy: Put every thing into its proper place, straighten cushions, clear level surfaces. Assign each child a room and post it on their Afternoon Chore Chart.

- Freshen up; fix hair; do one thing to clean your bathroom (10 minutes).

- Start supper; set the table.

There are many varieties to home scenarios: big and little children, only big children, only little children, no children, grown children, small house, big house, work from home dad, second shift work, third shift work, etc.

Our homes all look different, however, people live in homes and living makes messes. No matter what, there are daily chores that need done, and it really helps to have them as a routine that happens at the same time every day without fail. Habits become reflexive and routine. When your daily work is so ingrained that you do it automatically, you might have to ask, "Did I do x task?" You don't even realize that you were doing it.

Good habits make life easy and beautiful. That is why I don't change my children's chores very often. I want their assigned work to become good strong habits, and I want them to become very proficient at each one of their chores.

Afternoon Chore Time is one of the pillars of a good day. Your Morning Routine and Evening Routine are two other strong pillars. When those three important routines are running like a smooth machine, the rest of the day will fall into place. Commit to focusing on those three routines until they become an integral part of your daily life. Make them life long habits in you and your children that are hard to unsettle.

Step Seven

Easy Menu Plan

Find a blank calendar page from an old or unused calendar. Try to pick a month that has 31 days. Another location for a calendar is the spreadsheet program on your computer. Look at the templates for a calendar. Alternatively, simply list down the sheet of a paper the numbers 1-31. Write an easy supper plan for each day with menus you already know to be tried-and-true.

The reason I like to use a calendar page is that you get a better sense of variety in the meal planning. For example: Italian on Mondays; ground beef on Thursdays; fish on Saturdays; roast on Sundays.

Write a corresponding grocery list for each supper plan. Make a couple of copies of the grocery list, keeping one in your purse.

Step Eight

Self

One thing that gets in the way of home management is our own self. This can happen in two ways. The first and probably most predominant for moms of lots of children is that we neglect taking care of ourselves. We do not take the time to eat the right food, drink enough water, take supplements, get daily sunshine and fresh air, or exercise.

By not taking care of these basic things, we are setting ourselves up for a health disaster. When our health and resultant energy quota are just enough to get by, we let our family down. They need a wife and mom who is alert and able, not a walking zombie.

Most importantly, we need to take care of our spiritual health so that we are not an ole grump to our families. The children do not need a short-tempered mother who berates them over every little thing. Get your attitude right by spending time in the scriptures every morning and every evening. The Psalms have so much to teach us about God, and they are comforting to our souls. Read one every day. Read a Proverbs every morning to your children at breakfast. This is for everyone's character training. Yes, moms need character training too!

When you work through your Morning and Evening Routine, be sure to include and do those things that better your overall health. If exercise and sunshine do not fit into your Morning and Evening Routine, then tack it on to Lunch or your Afternoon Routine. Have recess with your children. Find a good spot in the day, and then make it a habit.

Some important things to help:

- Squeeze a lemon into a pitcher of water for you to drink during the day.

- B vitamins help tremendously for emotional stability and feeling good overall.

- Cut out sugar, corn syrup, and chemical sugars. These fast sugars immediately enter the blood system. The highs and lows are very hard on your system and mood. They also suppress the immune system, are poison to your body, and feed cancer cells. Cut it out for one week, and see how good you feel!

- Eat protein. Eggs are especially good because they are brain food for babies during pregnancy and nursing.

- Fish oil is good for your health, your skin, and your baby's eyes.

- White flour is about as nutritious as a piece of paper. Your body robs its stores in order to process it in your intestines.

- Avoid processed food. If it comes in a box or package it will hurt you, not help. Eat whole foods.

- Eat salad every day; it makes you feel so much better! There are wonderful easy salad recipes. Make your own salad dressings to avoid the added junk in commercial dressings.

- Hanging out laundry is great for stretching, bending, and getting sunshine and fresh air.

- T-Tapp (www.t-tapp.com) is my favorite exercise. It feels great all over the body. It is not running, jumping, and gasping for air. It is great stretching in a physical therapy type way. A fit mama will be able to do things with her grandchildren and maybe even great-grandchildren!

The second way that self gets in the way of home management is when we let our own desires take precedence over what we are supposed to be doing. I do not mean that you need to be a doormat to your family or that who you are as a person should be smothered, but you need to keep things in priority.

When you make decisions moment by moment throughout the day, they need to be filtered through two questions: "Is this activity glorifying God and serving Him?" and "Are my first priorities taken care of?" Thinking through these questions is a habit that we deliberately need to foster. I would suggest writing those two questions and putting them above your kitchen sink or on a whiteboard in the common area of the house. When our priorities get unbalanced, our spiritual life gets out of balance as well. This affects our emotional life, and we get a spiral effect going that can spin into chaos.

How we take care of ourselves now and the choices we make will impact not only today, but who we and our families become in the future. Pray for wisdom, and commit to changing your small daily habits to be more God-glorifying.

Step Nine

Laundry

Some people love it, some hate it, some are ambivalent to it. Wherever you fit on this spectrum, laundry is necessary for a clean life, so do it, choose to like it, and if that's hard for you, choose to enjoy having clean clothes put away that are ready for you and your family to grab and put on.

You can make the chore more pleasant by:

- Beautifying the laundry area.

- Installing adequate lighting.

- Making the laundry area as organized and efficient as possible.

- Smiling while you work—choosing to enjoy the chore.

- Folding as a team with an audio story or music playing.

- Setting limits for each day (this will depend on your family size and the size of your laundry equipment). For example: Once 4 loads are done, you don't have to do any more until tomorrow.

- Delegate parts of the work to the children.

- Put away all clean and folded laundry every afternoon.

- Assign one day of the week to catching up on washing, mending, and ironing.

- Commit to doing a certain amount of loads every single day.

Step Ten

TAKE CONTROL OF THE CLUTTER

Once a day, take a box and a trash bag and spend fifteen minutes removing trash and clutter from one room. Set the timer and work until it rings. When the time is up, take the trash bag to the trash bin and put the box in the van to take to Goodwill. It is simple to do. What gets in the way are our thoughts and emotions about the extra things we think we need to hold onto. Consider the following questions when looking at your clutter:

- When was the last time I used this?

- Do I need this? Really.

- Is this item taking up space that could be utilized better?

Getting the unneeded stuff out of our homes frees time and space for better things. Stuff takes time to manage and care for. When it's gone, we can look around and be at peace.

Step Eleven

TEN MINUTES

Work for ten minutes and then take a ten-minute break. Use a timer and then start working through your house, one room at a time, de-cluttering and cleaning. Get your children involved, and make it a fun race. During the ten-minute work sessions, move as fast as you can. It's amazing what a couple of hours of this will do for your home!

Step Twelve
YOUR HOME MANAGEMENT BOOK

Read the part of this book about putting your Home Management Book together. Your Home Management Book is your guidebook to maintaining order in your home. By referring to it throughout the day, every day, you will be able to keep your home neat, clean, and prepared for anything. It will help you stay on track every day, every week, and every month. When a life event disrupts, your Home Management Book will help you get back on track by telling you what to do next.